COVERED
GOD & ME

Apostle Andrea Lewis

Selah Communications, Inc.

Copyright © 2016 by Apostle Andrea Lewis.

All rights reserved.

No part of this book may be reproduced or transmitted in any form or by any means whatsoever: electronic or mechanical, including photocopying, recording, or by any information storage and retrieval system, etc., without permission in writing from the copyright owner.

All Scriptures are from the KJV.

Selah Communications, Inc.
PO Box 79493
Atlanta, GA 30357

Library of Congress Control Number: 2016900618

ISBN: 978-0-9909449-6-6 (Hardcover)
ISBN: 978-0-9909449-8-0 (Paperback)
ISBN: 978-0-9909449-7-3 (E-Book)

10 9 8 7 6 5 4 3 2 1

DEDICATION

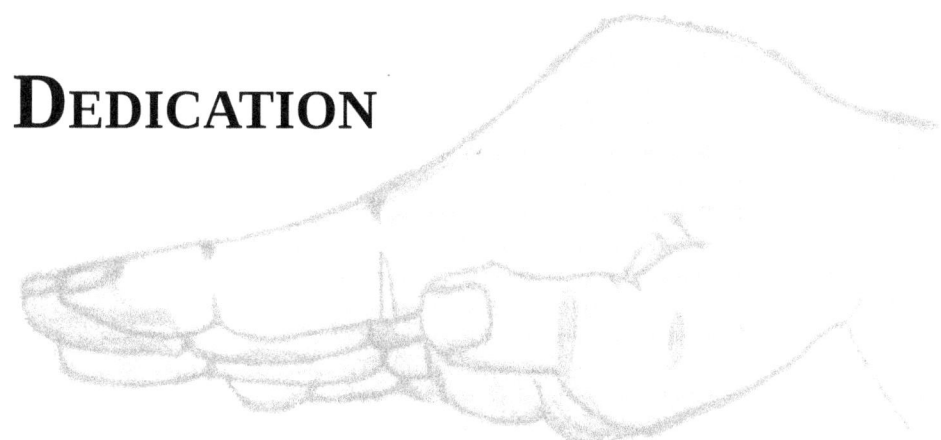

To My Friend,

Most beautiful lover of my soul. The most complete love I have and will ever know; thank You, for loving me to You. Thank You, for saving me. Thank You, for feeding me and giving me to drink. Thank You, for allowing me to love You like You love me, with the portion fit for me: for Your love is too great and excellent for my heart to contain in its fullness, and I accept that. Thank You, for revealing Your truth to me. Thank You, for teaching me, yet You are not through. Thank You, for Your kept Word. Thank You, for Your promises to me—may You be glorified. Thank You, for the way You care for me. Thank You, for all You have done, are doing, and will do.

Let me speak only what You give me to say, and go only where You send me. I want to talk, live, and walk in a manner always pleasing to You; and, in all my ways and thoughts, let me stand in faith and truth before You. Keep Your path straight before my face, and keep my eyes stayed on You. Give me strength, as You lead me, that I may ever follow You with a willing heart. Keep rebelliousness from me, keep vain thoughts from me, and keep me humble. Let it be in Your will and Your mercy, that I will love and serve You, with all my heart, and all my soul, all the days of my life, that Your presence will never be taken away from me, and that Your face will never again be hid from me. Keep me close to You, Lord. I am Your vessel; use me to Your glory. *I love You, Jesus.*

TABLE OF CONTENTS

Acknowledgments 7

Foreword 23

Section I:
Mind 27

Section II:
Body 63

Section III:
Spirit: The Call 179

Section IV:
Spirit 229

Section V:
Revelation 279

Post-word 323

Encouragement 327

ACKNOWLEDGMENTS

S ean
To: My Heart
I thank God that He blessed my life with you. Aside from Jesus, you are my greatest gift, and because I love you so much, I have laid you in the hands of God, for there is no better place. Through Him, I am to you, all that my heart desired to be when I first suspected you were here; when I went to the mall, and trusting God for my son, bought those baby boy shoes; when I first felt you move; when you first stuck out your foot, and I touched my stomach where it was, and you quickly withdrew it; when I listened to you with my stethoscope; when I got the first sonogram of you; when you came and it was confirmed that God granted my desire for you to be a boy; when I first held you in my arms and spoke my promises to you. You are a loving, kind, thoughtful, fun, and brilliant young man. Change for no one, except, to be all who God has called you to be. I have not been perfect with you, but now, God is the head of us: I see the change in us both, and God said, *"It is good."*

Sean: the name divinely given to you when I almost lost you to the apneas; it means *given by God*, and that's not just a name, that is who you are. Thank you, for being my son, I am very pleased and filled with joy that you are. With all my heart, *I love you—always*, and God loves you so much more.

Fall deeply in love with Jesus, and be in love with Him, forevermore. Stay in Him, *love Him most*, and *always* put Him first. Serve Him by doing what He teaches in His gospel. *Live* by His faith and His doctrine. Be true and faithful unto death to Him. Let Him use, lead, direct, guide, and counsel you. In everything you will say or do, think first. If deep inside, you feel God would not be pleased, don't say it and don't do it: Get away, as fast as you can. Don't give anything sinful a second thought. Just remember what I have taught you. Keep reading your Bible daily, let Him teach you, hold on to the truth, trust Him, and don't allow anyone or anything to deceive you. Stay in prayer always.

I intend to make it into the Kingdom and reign with Jesus in eternity, and I want to see you there, so hold on strong—*immovable* to Jesus, and never let go. Things of this world will feel good or seem to feel good, but be strong. It is ***all*** only a deception, and when you hold on and gain victory over it, one day, you will see the thing for the lie and deception it was.

You *know* Jesus is real, by our experiences, and what He has done for us, and brought us through. Always remember, how He loved, and cared for, and provided for, and protected us. *Know*, that His love, care, protection, and provision to us continues as long as we live. See Him, feel Him, hear Him, and acknowledge Him in all that He does, moment by moment, and day by day, and give Him thanks, praise, and glory. Never allow the enemy to cause you to doubt Him. The devil desired me, and you also. He has since your birth, when he tried to steal you from me, but God rescued and delivered you, and you were saved and covered since then. You belong to God; this is why I gave you to God in baptism at eight years old. You knew the need of God in your life, even then, and agreed to give your life to Him. Stay in God, that He may continue to cover you.

As long as I have breath in me, the devil cannot touch you because my prayers also cover you, and if I have to leave you, your prayers are enough. The blessing and anointing God placed on me, also covers you, and will remain with you. Jesus will continue to walk with you. You will *never* be alone, so pray, trust Him, and never fear. If you fall into *any* sin, don't stay there: *Get up,* and grab hold of God; if it seems like you can't reach Him, or can't get up, or can't shake that thing or thought loose, cry out to Him and He will pick you up. *Hold on! Hold on! Hold on!* No mat-

ACKNOWLEDGMENTS

ter what you feel like at any moment, and no matter what you have done, you can *always* turn to Jesus; He is also your friend, your best friend—talk to Him. I have experienced and proven Him: I have met Him in an intimate way; and, now, you have too. You are purposed and intended to be in paradise with Him. *You are His. He loves you.* Mommy loves you, too.

Thank Yous (Family)

Paul – With all that is within me, thank you for our son. Aside from Jesus, he is my all, and I know you know this. He is the best of both of us. Again, thank you for him. I love you always, you are family. Everything that is written is not to your shame, for it was me who mistreated you, while you were good to me. You were not perfect, but the blame was not yours. Fall in love with Jesus, and let Him be head of you and your family, He loves you.

Mommy (in memory of you) – I couldn't get you to stop worrying over me because we were apart for so long, but I was in God's hands, and I had never been better cared for and loved. You knew the ways He could make because He made quite some ways for you. I don't remember much of my childhood with you, and as a teenager, I hardly appreciated you as I should have, but I always respected and admired who you were in God, and always loved you deeply. I couldn't then, and cannot now, envision life without you—though I am now forced to do so. I treasure the relationship we had. I love you so much. I admired the way God used you, and the strength you had in Him. Now, that I have truly experienced Him for myself, I now understand the deep abiding love and commitment for and to Him that you held. I respect the strength you had gained from your past sufferings.

Thank you, for being the mother you were then and all my life. I thank God for you. You did whatever had to be done, so you could, in the end, give me a good life, and this was very well accomplished. Whatever happened to me was necessary for God's purpose, and He protected me very well from the things that were not. You kept saying we are alike, and you didn't know how right you were. I sure got my pride from you, and the way I kept things in until now, I got that from you. I also got my integrity, and the fact that I can be confided in from you, thank you. You and Dad equipped me with an intelligence—though I didn't always use it, thank you. As all your children are, so am I, the best of both of you, thank you.

There is another thing handed down—Satan tried to devour you and failed; he tried to stop me from being born and failed. He also tried to take you from me at my birth and failed. Surely, he was and is afraid of me/my purpose for some reason. He tried to devour me and failed, he came at me viciously and repeatedly, but is now eternally defeated, in everything concerning me; and, I will, through God, stop him from devouring Sean and anyone else I care about. If he presents himself, he will be stomped and crushed in the name of Jesus. Thank you, for your many prayers. I know they covered me, and still does. Thank you, so very much, for *all* your prayers concerning me and Sean; thank you, for watching over us now, and for all else you are doing concerning us, my Elite Angel. I love you, so *very* much, Mom.

Daddy (in memory of you) – First, let me say, I don't judge you by that incident or anything you have done, and I know I don't have and was not told the whole truth about you and the past. I had to record certain things because it was a part of my life, but it is long forgiven and forgotten, even the moment after it occurred. We both moved pass those things and times. I had not personally kept in touch with you because both of us were the same when it came to that, and because of your great concern for my finances: I didn't feel good to personally speak to you until I had something good to report. I was also disappointed with myself and where I was living, and knew you would be too, and I couldn't lie to you, so I stayed away, but God is making ways for me now. Thank you, for being the father you were to me. I know you loved me deeply, and that

Acknowledgments

love was mutual. I appreciated you, I miss you, and I love you so much. I thought of you often, and kept you always in my prayers, for health and strength—for God to heal and keep you well and that you would reign with Him in eternity. You now dwell with Him and my soul is satisfied.

Mommy Walker (in memory of you) – As my mom's best friend, you were a mother to me when I needed it, and even after I didn't. I didn't express it, but I loved you deeply. You knew I loved you, but I don't believe you knew how much. You were a true mother to me, in every sense and meaning of the word. Your memory will be honored within me. You played with us, and cared for us like one of your own. I kept your letters to me, and the one concerning my soul. I didn't appreciate the Word when God sent it through you because I didn't see my faults. I thought everything was fine with me and God, but now, since God has dealt with me, I see it differently, and now treasure it. I realized, through your words, that God was calling to me, even then, but I guess God had to work out His purpose this way. I hope, now that I am being obedient, you are smiling down at me. I appreciate your memory, who you were, and I will love you forever. You have not been, nor will you ever be forgotten. Embrace Jesus for me, till I can see Him for myself and not another.

Daddy Walker – Thank you, for standing in the place of my need when I was a child. I don't personally keep in touch, but I appreciate you and love you so much. You are my second father. May God keep you.

Big Sis. (Angela) – Shocked? I was too. God has a way about Him—gotta love Him. We have been *all* to each other: in times past almost enemies, now best friends, best sisters, partners in crime, confidants, chat buddies, and you name it. I enjoy you, I appreciate you, and I love you. You deserve the best, and God will and is giving it to you. Don't let anyone rob you of it or make you feel like you don't deserve these good things. Don't rob yourself of it, just love Him. *Just believe*. Everything is already yours because God says so and *all* His words are true. What He says, *will* be, never doubt. Have faith, and be obedient, and do what is necessary in God to receive your gifts. Pray daily, rid yourself of what doesn't belong within you (you will be sensitive to what they are), and He will lead you, opening and closing doors as is necessary for the path He wants you to walk and the things He wants you to have—which is much; as He allowed me a glimpse of what He has done for you. Receive them. It's time for you to build again and receive this first blessing. I know you feel strange when I speak concerning God to you because all we have ever done is have fun, but He has allowed me to experience Him in a different way, and it would be such a violation to my soul if I didn't speak of His goodness and that He is able. He loves you so. I'm glad you love Him and see Him daily in your life. My soul will rejoice when I see how greatly He will use you because, *this*, will be your greatest of many blessings. I love you.

Bre-Bre & TT – Beautiful young ladies. Your auntie loves you so much. I love you both; Jesus loves you both, too. I'm glad you are growing in God, and learning more about Him, and seeking to live your lives true to Him; love Him with all your hearts. I am also filled with joy in who you both are becoming, stay true to yourselves and true to God (this should be one in the same), and He will take you to heights unimaginable.

Shelley – What a beautiful young lady you are. There are a lot of temptations out there, but Auntie believes in you. Keep loving and seeking after God, Shelley, He will care for you, and help you to keep doing right, and will guide you in your purpose. Don't be deceived by anyone or anything, by letting them change the good that you are. Stay beautiful and successful in everything you do, by loving and serving God, and staying in Him. Pray and read your Bible every day; Jesus will take it from there, and teach you what to do and how to be. Jesus loves you, and you are blessed. You are forever in my heart. I love you.

Fritz (Fitzie) – Thank you, for being my big brother. I think of you

Acknowledgments

often—I understand. I love you, and will always. I admire you, and am very pleased and joyful that you are my brother. God has not forgotten you. Love Him; He loves you. He is with you—He will make you not ashamed. He will make all things well, and make you all He called you forth to be. Receive it. I love you because you are my brother and *nothing* can change that love. I loved the talks we had recently and await the time we will again.

Win. – My big brother, I love you much, and God loves you more; He *will* prove Himself to you, in fact I am believing it is already done.

Mike – My oldest brother, the beginning of the family, I love you. God has been on your side in many things, and He still is. You belong to Him. He will work out all His desires for you.

Juliet – I love you. God will work out His desires for you.

Tasha & Tony – Auntie loves you, Jesus loves you.

Junior – You are special. You were my first baby and I was your favorite auntie. I loved you like a son, and though I was so young, your mom trusted me more than any other with you because she knew you were a part of my heart. You are a man now, but you will always have that part of my heart. I see that you love God, and I am so joyful that you are living for Him. Take it from Auntie, this world may seem sweet and interesting, but it has nothing good to offer concerning your spirit. It will only wreck your soul. Wrap yourself in Jesus and hold on to the truth. He is worthy. He loves you. I love you.

I am praying that God will be the head of you all (the family), in every way.

Sis (Del) – Late to join the family, but the love is like you were always here. Thank you, for being a part of us and for loving us and being there for mom. God will work out the desires of His heart concerning you. He loves you. I love you, sis.

Sebastian, Nonna, and Sammy – Auntie loves you all. You all belong to God. Love Him and let Him use you.

Cleave – I have prayed concerning you. You are in God's hands, and that's the best place to be. You have become family through Sis, and I love you as such.

I have prayed for you all, that God will be the head of you and the family, and will work out His desires concerning all things.

Carla – I am glad you are my sister. We don't keep in touch as we should, but my love for you never changes. Stay in God: submit, and let Him use you; help the kids stay in Him, too. I love you.

Nikki and Spence – Auntie loves you both. I am joyful at the beautiful young people you are. Love God with all that's within you.

Denise – I love you, little sis. Far apart but not forgotten. I believe you are a good mom, and I look forward to meeting your little ones one day. I'm glad you are home safe from the service, especially in these times. We both got saved in God at the same time. I became rebellious. As for you, you drank of that precious living water, even then, so stay with God. You are chosen; He is calling to you: please answer yes. Let your kids grow in Him, that they won't depart. *He is worthy*.

Labon, and son – Big cuz and little cuz, I love you both. I am praying for you, that all things will be the way you desire. I believe God; your enemies *are* defeated.

Acknowledgments

Terri-Ann (yes, you too), **Latoyo, Dennis Jr.**, and **Trenyce**; **Imani**; **Munchkin (Arianna) & Tati** – All my wonderful, beautiful, godchildren, I truly love you, and I will do better concerning you all. God will continue to bless you all, and your families. Love Him, let Him work in you. I know your parents have already laid you in God's hands—and so have I—that He will use you mightily to and for His glory; to shield you from your enemies in all forms that they come; to guide your every step, and keep you wrapped in Him and the things of Him. You *are* blessed, you *are* covered. I love you all.

Dianne – "Mi fren" ("My friend"), my best friend, I love you always. God has a good plan and blessings for you: you are a child of promise. God and Heaven watches over you.

Benji; Pem (Peter); Noel [(Noey)(Christopher)]; Linky (Lincoln); Carol; Robin; Jannet, and the rest of the Walker children – Thank you, for making us a part of your family. I don't consider us just friends: we were already family before we moved in, and are still family after we left. I consider us sisters and sister, & brothers and sister; I will never forget you. I love you all. You are all a saved family, so I only pray God abides with you all.

All Other Family and Friends — Thank you all, for loving me and for being a part of my life. I appreciate you. I truly love you all. May God be with you all.

Figero - We thank God for your life, and wholeness. And, that He loves, and cares for, and provides for you the way He does. You are truly blessed among animals. We love you.

Max, Misty, Tai, King, Ray, Matt, & Precious (in memory of you) - You were more than animals, you were family. We miss you, sleep in the arms of Jesus.

Thank Yous (Special People)

Susan – We met camping at McFarland Park. I was the one with the New Jersey license plates, playing my gospel music through the night, that you said you liked and enjoyed. God touched your heart to come back to the park to see about me. You gave me your name and number, along with other places of help, and wrote me a nice little note. I just want you to know that I remember you and I appreciate you. Thank you. God bless and keep you.

Katy (DHR Supervisor) – I thank you, for your kindness to me and my son. I know God truly touched your heart concerning us. Thank you, for the really good Christmas Paul (Sean) had. I pray blessings on your life in Jesus' name.

April (DHR) – A beautiful name and a beautiful person, whom God provided for my path. Thank you, for how God allowed you to care for us. You went beyond your duty, and I greatly appreciate you. Thank you, for the hotel; thank you, for our home; thank you, for clothing us; thank you, for feeding us; thank you, for the tank full of gas—repeatedly; thank you, for your care and concern of us; thank you, for giving Paul (Sean) a good Christmas, which made my Christmas joyful; thank you, for all the help concerning my nursing license; thank you, for paying the bills; and thank you, for putting things together for me before you left—it was a tremendous help. Thank you, for *all*. You are a believer, and I pray God's blessing in all areas of your life that is good, and that all the bad areas flee from you. I pray that He brings you successfully through school, and in your career. I love you with the love of God. *We thank you.*

Pastor Neloms – I appreciate you. May God abide with you and feed you that you may feed His sheep. Thank you, for the crucial times God used you to speak into me. Thank you, for being obedient to God in car-

Acknowledgments

ing for me. Thank you, for the encouragement you gave, and for the love you showed me. I love you with the love of God.

Donna (Sis. Neloms) – You were the second person positioned by God to my aid. Thank you, for all your worrying and your prayers. Thank you, for putting up with my pride. There is something of comfort about you: because, you remind me of my sister. I appreciate you, and love you. I thank God for you because God placed you to guide me on my path to help, and to care for me. Wherever God may take me, you will never be forgotten, neither left behind. Thank you, for being obedient to Him concerning me. May God be with you and your family and bless you all abundantly. I do consider you a friend. Eyes have not seen, neither ears heard, *all* the things which God has in store for you.

Sis. Roach – Thank you, for the talks and for showing care to me. We have had some misunderstandings because the enemy tried to sever us, but I left them all in the hands of God. The closeness I felt to you is gone and that's OK, we are OK. I still love you with the love of God and always will. You are in my prayers. May God bless you and your family.

Bro. Mullins – Thank you, for fixing my car. It was good to drive again. May God bless you.

Bro. Lacey – Thank you, for changing my tire on Christmas Eve. May God touch and heal your back, and all your ailments, in the mighty name Jesus.

Church Ladies – I will never forget the way you came to my aid that day you all came over, bringing to me all the provisions I needed, and *much* more: clothes and shoes, mostly new, for me; microwave, kitchen supplies and utensils, bathroom supplies and luxuries . . . just everything, like a housewarming party. The love, laughter, and conversation—I appreciated it all and am very grateful. You cared well for me with the love of

God. I love you all with the love of God. Thank you. God bless you.

Church Children – Thank you, for all the love you showed us. We love you. Grow in God; you are blessed.

Unknown Angels:
1) The couple who gave me and my son a ride home from the train tracks. I saw you in Wal-Mart at Christmas, and was glad to see you both again, and you remembered me. I will never forget your kindness. May God bless you both.
2) The gas station attendant: You gave me money, "Just as a blessing," you said. Thank you. It was. May God keep you.
3) All the other kind wonderful people that met me, may God bless you.

I never knew people like you existed, but, through God you do, and I thank you.

Police Officer (Florence, Al.) – I forgot your name, but will never forget your deed. It all began with you. Thank you, for being in the place God appointed to receive me. This was an unstoppable plan and act of God, that neither of us understood at the time. I thank you from the bottom of my heart. I love you with the love of God, for He delivered me into your hands for safekeeping and care, which you delivered in a phone call on my behalf, to get me that room and bed at the Salvation Army. God truly set something powerful in motion concerning me, beginning with you. You will never be forgotten. May the Holy Ghost quench the thirst in your soul, and may He come to your every rescue and deliverance— on the job and daily in your life. May God be the head of you and your house, bringing you and your family blessings and great prosperity.

Police Officer (Muscle Shoals, Al.) – Thank you, for calling the warden to my help. It would have been a very long hard walk back home. May God cover you on your job.

Acknowledgments

Warden (Muscle Shoals, Al.) – Thank you, for trying to jump my car that night. When it didn't work, thank you, for bringing me to the border line and arranging for that other officer to meet us to take my son and me home. I appreciate you. May God cover you on your job.

Police Officer (Tuscumbia, Al.) – Thank you, for meeting the warden at the city/border line and taking my son and me home. You are greatly appreciated. May God cover you on your job.

Salvation Army – Thank you, for accepting me that Memorial Day weekend. Then later, thank you, for the bags of food and for the voucher for your thrift store: my son and I received greatly, and very good things. Thank you, also, for my first furniture there, as mine was locked away in another state. You were a light unto my darkness. May God replenish you to help others.

Salvation Army Thrift Store (Sheffield, AL.) – Thank you, for all the provisions I received from you. You were a gift from God. May He replenish your store so others in need will benefit as I did.

Ester (AFDC) – Thank you, for calling me into your office. It changed my life for the better. You were the third person (first of the third group) positioned by God to bring me to deliverance, and for that you will never be forgotten. You are appreciated. God will bless you, for you were obedient to Him in your guidance and your kindness to me.

Good Samaritan – Thank you: to the man who went through great lengths to give me that jump, by going to the store to purchase a battery starter pack to see if that would work on my car because the battery on your truck wouldn't hook up properly to work. Also, thank you, for the other help you offered. You are appreciated. May God bless you greatly.

Debbie – Thank you, for trying to give me that jump at Avalon drug store, and for dropping my son and me home so far out of your way when it didn't work. You gave me your number to call you if I needed anything, and though I never used it, I thank you. Thank you, for that money when you dropped me home. You didn't know my situation, but it was well needed: I realized the car had run out of gas, and that's why it still wouldn't start with your help. You didn't even know me, but God truly touched you to bless me. My son did an extremely dangerous thing when you agreed to help, by getting into your car, for which he was strongly reproved; still, it gives me chills. I am surprised and disappointed in him, but am very grateful that you were an angel meant for our good. You took a chance on us also, having your little daughter in the car with you, but God directed us well. I pray blessings into your life, and that God be the head of you and your family. I pray He strengthened you to endure nursing school, and that you are now successful, having a prosperous career. You are appreciated and will never be forgotten.

Nick (Blythe House) – Thank you, for your help and for *creating* that extra time for me when I needed it. May God bless you.

Angel (Social Worker, Neptune, N.J.) – Thank you. You were the *only* one who was **genuinely** and **consistently** caring of me and my son. While here in Alabama, I did receive your phone call, seeking to know if we were OK. I wanted to, but did not respond because we did not yet have a place to call home, but I treasured your call because you cared. Remain the person you are, and never become hardened or indifferent. Your name suits you. May Jesus be your God and bless you with blessings.

Ms. Konow (M.V.S. Nsg. Prog.) – You were an excellent teacher. Thank you, for the extra quizzes; thank you, for believing in me. May God bless you.

Acknowledgments

The Mechanics:
1) Thank you, for fixing my mom's car going to New Jersey.
2) To the other: thank you, for fixing my car and tire when I had to go over that deer. You and your children were appreciated.

To you both: thank you, for putting us back on the road in very little time and for very little money. Your work was awesome, and it got us home and then some. May God bless and prosper your businesses; may God reveal Himself to you, and abide in you and with you and your families, that all your needs be met.

Thank you to everyone whom God brought to the path He led me through. I was too prideful to ask, so God brought you. You offered, and I accepted. I deeply appreciate you more than you will ever know or I could ever say. I love you all with the love of God, and am grateful for how you all made yourselves available, and genuinely gave care to someone you didn't know. God will surely bless you with blessings, for you were obedient to Him in your kindness to me and care of me. For all you have done, we (the family) thank you!

Jeho'vah Ji'reh – Seer of all my needs Who continually provides.
Jeho'vah Nis'si – Deliverer, Victor
Jeho'vah Sha'lom – Peace

Thank You, Lord God, for being each of these to me. Not one of Your purposes in these things fell void. You were, and are, all these and abundantly more to me. I have received well, and pray I continue to receive all of who You are and want to be to me, and all of who I am in You. I appreciate You; I honor You; I adore You. You are worthy of all glory and all praise. Thank You, for being my God. My life from beginning to end is Your testimony, and I thank You for my experience in each day You lend me breath. Thank You, for calling me. Thank You, for opening my heart and mind to receive You and the things of You. Thank You, for this agape love You planted deep in my soul, so deep and so full. Thank You, for molding me. Thank You, for cutting away all that was not of You from me, and giving me a mind against them—as is Yours. Thank You, for reproving and scolding me in my errors. Thank You, for all the times You brought or allowed me back to You. Thank You, for Your mercy and Your grace, and for Your unconditional love. Thank You, for Your faithfulness concerning me. Thank You, for Your truth. Thank You, for Your light. Thank You, for Your compassion. Thank You, for being my Father, my God, and my Shepherd. Thank You, for Christ, this part (person) of Yourself without Whom I would be lost. Thank You, for the part (person) of Yourself Who is the Holy Ghost. Thank You, for speaking to me. Thank You, for allowing me to hear Your voice and not be afraid. Thank You, for when You held me, and again. Thank You, for every blessed touch.

Please continue to teach me the sound of Your voice until my knowledge is perfected. Please keep me attentive to You, and sensitive to *Your* will and *Your* desires, that I will not fall. I love You, Jesus, my Jehovah. Forbid me to *ever* leave You. Keep me this in love with You, all my days, forevermore. Keep me fully submitted, committed, surrendered, yielded, and obedient to You in every way. I pray I have been obedient in all You had need of me concerning this book. Thank You, for choosing me and not another. Thank You, for using me in **this thing** You had need of. Thank You, for all the ways You spoke, and for how You brought this to be through me. Thank You, for cleaning me out to the core of my filth and secrets. Thank You, for how You have opened me to receive all Your words, which You have spoken through me, back into myself—healing and building me in You. Help me to hold fast to them and all else You give me, till I am with You in paradise. May all Your people hear. May You be glorified. *Hallelujah!*

Foreword

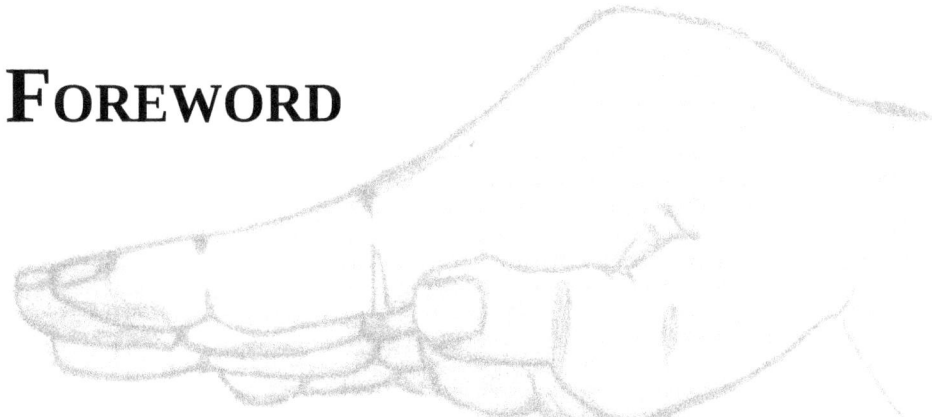

To those who may read this book, and say, I shared too much information; I have to say, this is the way God dealt with me. He needed me to completely empty myself, so He could heal me, mold me, and restore me to what He needed me to be. This was in no way easy for me, and that I would write this book, is shocking to all who know me; because, I am an extremely private person, who held everything in, and presented an iron-strong existence. I let no one inside my past, present, or my heart and mind. The only one who knew any depth to me, was God—not even family.

I fought, and hesitated, and doubted, and procrastinated, but God pressed me to do this; at times, I would say, "I can't write that," but God just made it flow out of me. This book was ordered of me by God: a book to heal me, and for His purpose. I pray, that as it has healed me, so may it touch and heal another. If through it, God brings at least one lost soul to surrender their all to Him, and be in love with Him, and serve Him, knowing and feeling the magnificent love He has for them, knowing that He is able to handle *all* they turn over to Him, and that He is limitless to give them all they will ever or could ever need in *all* areas of their life—if just one person comes to this place of peace—then my soul will be satisfied, and the way I have laid myself open will have been worth it.

"When all else fails, the Word abounds."

These words were spoken to me by God, on December 27, 2003 at 11:30 p.m.; then, immediately afterwards, a chorus was placed in my heart. It is the chorus to a beautiful song, "Living by Faith." I was reassured. God was telling me to fear nothing, that I should only rest in His Word and trust Him because He loves me greatly.

COVERED
God & Me

Covered/Cover: To shelter, to protect, to defend, to clothe, to pardon.

Section I: Mind

I was born at University College Hospital (UC) in Kingston, Jamaica, West Indies, on a rainy Sunday evening at 3:00 or 3:30 p.m. on May 25, 1969.

At my birth, my mom was thirty years old, and my dad was thirty-seven years old. During her pregnancy with me, she had a very difficult time, and did remain permanently affected by that pregnancy, wherein she could not lie down normally; she had to prop herself up to a reclining position or she felt like she was suffocating. She almost died twice while carrying me. Once because someone worked witchcraft against her trying to kill her. It brought her to death's door, not being able to get out of bed for days, but she was an Evangelist who was mightily used of God with Spiritual gifts of God. So, with that and an army of church saints forming a prayer band around her in shifts, never leaving her alone, rebuking and discharging the enemy, being in constant prayer—also the whole church holding her up before God—He responded and delivered us from the clutches of Satan and his workers of iniquity.

I'm not sure of the second cause, but because of complications from that, she said the doctor told her that she should not have any more kids, and she refused to discuss it or my childhood with me. I always thought they were good memories, and the bits and pieces I remember are, but even though we spoke a lot about many things, when I asked her to fill me in on my childhood during a pleasant conversation years ago, which they almost always are, she wouldn't, and the tone of her voice dropped to a low, sad, depressed tone. I could tell she really wanted to go, so I told her I loved her, she told me she loved me too, then we said good-bye and hung up. I was expecting heartwarming stories, but instead I got disappointment and pain. It seems there were a lot more secrets and lies that she did take to her grave, and though I wanted to know, I didn't press her or even asked again since it was distressing for her, and if there is anything, maybe it's best not to know. Whatever I should know, God will reveal no matter what, so I released her.

I have been told by my mom almost all my life that she really wanted a girl as companion for my sister and that she prayed for me to look like my third brother, and I did. Only, my color caused gossip among the people of the church, saying that a close family friend was my father and not my dad who was a dark man—never mind the fact that my features are as my dad's.

As stated by Big Sis, my mom first left the family to visit Canada when Big Sis was four years old, which would make me one year old. We always had a housekeeper/caregiver as far back as I can remember, so no doubt we had one then, too.

I must say I don't recall any abuse from my parents. Growing up in Jamaica, they and my siblings loved me much, and at times spoiled me. I recall being physically disciplined only once by my father in my forty-six years, and that was at about six years old, when my mom was due to return from the States. The housekeeper, Puncie (my dad's rape victim turned lover), told me to go borrow a cup of sugar from the Walkers, a neighbor we were very close to, and for whatever reason, I didn't want to go, so I didn't. When my dad got home, she told him, and he whipped me with his belt, which made me dislike her for a while. I believe I told my mom about it when she came.

I also recall only once with my mom in the States, when I was about fourteen years old. One day, my mom was being just miserable, speaking very loudly at Big Sis and me about something somebody had done, and as she left our door and walked down the hall, Big Sis told me to shut our room door so we wouldn't have to hear her, and I closed it a little too hard, and she heard it (I should have known better). My mom was already angry, and this made her steam. She came back into the room (she must have asked who did it, and I said me) and she gave me one hard strike with the palm of her hand across my left cheek but it also caught my ear, and it made me hate her for a while. Even many years later whenever I thought of it, hate was in me for as long as the thought remained, so I just didn't think about it. I long forgave her and recognized that I did need to be punished in some way, because that was a very disrespectful thing to do. Other than these I was well behaved and, at times, sneaky about things.

Anyway, I started school early, at three years old instead of at five or six years old, because my mom saw that I could handle it, and she knew the headmistress. I liked it a lot, maybe because all my other siblings were there, I don't quite recall. When I was sick with the mumps and chicken pox, I remember being so sad at missing school, even crying and begging to go. My mom said she wanted to send me to Vaz Prep. School, which was a school held in high regard/prestigious to many people, but my school was St. Benedict's All Aged Catholic School, and I was proud.

I remember one day, it must have been the first, I was supposed to meet my siblings, at the bus stop, I thought; it was a public bus—there were no school buses like here in the States. The bus stop was right in front of the school, on or right off the property. I walked across from my classroom to the bus stop and waited and waited and waited, till I was almost by myself. Some of the kids and also the higglers (vendors) that sold there to the school kids were asking questions, I guess to see if I was OK. I don't recall the exact questions. I didn't see my brothers or Big Sis and got a little scared thinking they had left me, so when the number bus came that would pass my stop for home (somehow I knew which one), I took it, maybe the higglers put me on it. When it got to my stop, at "nine miles" (again, somehow I knew), I got off and started walking up my street (Green Vale Road) to my home, which I believe was two or more miles away. The walking did not affect me because it was something people of that area were used to. Some even walked much, much farther maybe five to ten miles or more up that street to Cane River, which we kids walked on Sundays to attend church in that area.

Anyway, while walking I saw a young male running, then he fainted away at a gate—his or someone else's. I was frightened and ran a while, then a man saw me and knew me. He spoke to me and said he was my godfather. I believe his name was Mr. Dudley. My mom later said he wasn't my godfather, that he just knew the family. He probably told me that so I would let him help me. There were questions along the way, like, "weh yah duh wid Lewis pickney" ("What are you doing with Lewis' kid?") And responses, like, "mi si har an mi a carry har home" ("I saw her and I'm taking her home.") He walked with me and I have a memory of being on his shoulders. I guess my three year old legs would have turned a twenty minute walk into a forty minute walk. I think he carried me most of the way, and he made sure I got through my gate.

Meanwhile, unknown to me, my brothers and Big Sis were still at school. I had gotten out earlier than they did, and when they got out and did not see me, they were worried to death. I think someone (maybe the higglers) told them I left on the bus. In my thirties the subject came up, and Big Sis told me I was supposed to meet them at their classroom, not the bus stop. Well, that was an unnecessary and scary experience in which God covered me, because I could have been stolen, abused, and murdered, but God was with me, though I didn't know it.

I remember only one birthday party (with family) when I turned four years old. I remember ice cream and songs in my honor. I was happy, I was loved. I have a part of that party on cassette tape, with me, my brothers, and Big Sis (maybe that's why I remember it). I remember a green bicycle with training wheels I got for my birthday. I'm not sure which birthday though, and I think I'm the only one of the family that got one.

I don't have a clear ongoing memory of my childhood, only bits and pieces, and the order is not clear. Big Sis is the rock of my memories; though she has the same problem with memory, she recalls more than I do. I do remember my dad coming home and me running to meet him; he would always pick me up into his arms and almost always put money in my pocket (Big Sis and I tried to make sure we wore clothes with pockets). I also remember waking up in my parent's bed on sunny mornings (though my sister and I shared a room of our own), hearing my mom outside the bedroom window working in the garden or watering it—that was pleasant to me. I also remember my mom sitting in a chair by the cherry tree or by the pomegranate tree, and my sister and me playing in her hair. We would "platt" (plait/braid) it as best we could, then, being silly, we would tie it under her chin. Her hair was long and beautiful and permed; we wanted ours just like it, but she said we were too young.

I remember my second brother Clinton taking me to see Santa at a mall there, my third brother Win giving me a huge teddy bear, my first and eldest brother Mike giving me a single knife/fork/spoon set in a case (small for a child, I think)—I loved it and ate every meal with it for a long while.

I remember my mom and dad taking the family to Parade (the town square) every Christmas morning. They bought us presents and starlights. The starlights looked like incense on long slivers of wood that you hold in your hand; when lit, they would burn with bright sparkles and a sizzling sound till they got to the bottom and went out. I loved starlights. They would also have costume masquerades at Parade (the town square), with men on stilts (Big Sis said, that was in celebration of independence day). I also remember my dad bringing home many crates with bottles of Jamaican soda—I loved the grape ones most; I'm not sure if those occasions were at Easter, or Christmas times, or just done randomly. Those were some of the many good times that were had by my family and me.

I went straight from second grade to fourth grade because I was handling school well. This would be my last year at St. Benedict's. I remember my mom used to pack our lunches, and a couple times for a treat, she would put Jamaican syrup with a "likkle tups" (a "little bit") of Red Label wine into Big Sis and my thermoses. When it was lunch time, we were supposed to put water in them and mix it to make a drink, but we used to drink most of it without water because it was so good; our friends wanted some, but we hardly shared that. A few of years ago, Big Sis and I reminded my mom of it, and she fully denied it—out loud. I guess she denied it because that was not something she should have done, but we loved her for it and thought we had the coolest mom; we felt very special that she did it.

Another memory is, my mom used to travel a few times (through the church I guess), and our neighbors, the Adlams, always spied on us and knew our business. Their kids would go to school and tell all, then make up what they didn't know, so Big Sis and I used to be teased at times by the Adlams while their friends and others stood around. Though we were well liked and had our own large group of friends it still affected us. They used to say things like we "are rich," and how our "mother had gone away to foreign (the States) and left (abandoned) us," and other things. It seems like nothing now, but kids know how to use anything and make it hurt your feelings. I remember feeling very embarrassed and hating them. I don't recall if we answered back, because that's not the way we were raised.

I don't know if I remember it on my own or because it was said—that my dad used to be drunk a lot. I do remember a particular fight between my mom and dad (he was drunk) where the large picture window in the living room got smashed by the vase that was sitting on the center table (coffee table). I think my mom threw it at my dad. I now know what the fight was about, and it was for something wicked my dad had done to one of us kids. There was broken glass everywhere (in the living room and on the veranda), also, yelling and fighting. My dad didn't want *any* of us in the house that night after the fight, he told my mom to take "her" kids and get out of "his" house. I remember my mom and us kids sleeping in the car porch that night. My mom took the cushions off the chairs on the veranda, laid them on the ground in the car porch, and made us kids lay on them. It's the only fight between them that stuck with me: I was maybe between three and five years old; I don't recall any other.

I came home to that house at birth and grew up there until I was eight years old. During that time, my mom went back and forth to the States, while my dad had affairs with the housekeepers, some whom he had held down and raped, and other women. None reported him because he was giving them lots of money and some were also stealing money from him. I want to remain here in this age range a while—this was a time most pleasurable to me and the most innocent my life would ever be.

As I write, memories flood my mind—*thank You*, God. I remember playing with Big Sis with a tiny set of Dutch pots my mom had gotten her (doll-sized but real). Every time Mom would cook, as we played, we asked and she would take bits of what she was cooking and give to us to put into ours. When my mom wasn't cooking, we would make pretend dumplings molded from clay like dirt and take some of the tiny banana flowers off the banana trees. We did many fun things. We would play hopscotch, hand games, dandy-shandy (like dodge-ball but **much** more fun), Jamaican jump rope (jump rope spiced-up), Chinese jump rope (a stretchable rope, made out of the rubbery lining of Jamaican soda bottle caps, linked together, was what most kids made and used for this game), and *many* more games. We and the neighbors that were like family (the Walkers) made and walked on stilts. All the fun childhood Island games; they are just flooding my mind, making me smile from ear to ear. I was great at many of these games and very competitive, always aiming for the most points and was successful most times.

I was also a climber, a really good one. There wasn't a strong tree, pole, fence, or wall I couldn't climb—truly. We had a great number of fruit trees in our yard; you name it, we probably had it, and I climbed them all. We had an ackee tree, which my mom warned me on occasion not to climb, but I climbed that tree at every opportunity because it was the tallest of all the trees (it towered), and I would climb to the very pinnacle and look out over everything. It was amazing (Funny, now I have developed a fear of heights since my mid twenties.) I would climb the other fruit trees and sit and eat fruits till I was full or I would just climb them and sit. There was a mango tree beside the house which I would climb and cross over to the roof of the house and just hang out there.

I remember when my dad was adding on to the car porch, there was a pile of sand on the ground in front of it, and my forth an fifth brothers

Alli and Fitzie would take the pillows/cushions from the lounge chairs on the veranda and put them on the sand heap; then, they along with Big Sis and me would climb onto the roof from the mango tree and take turns jumping onto the pillows and sand below (I cannot recall if my third brother was also with us). Dangerous but mega fun for us—no fear.

Also, we had real tile floors throughout the house, so Big Sis and I found a way to have fun. On Saturdays my mom and dad would go to the market and the supermarket to shop and would leave us kids home to clean and do our chores. After the cleaning was done, Big Sis and I took the dining or veranda chairs, made with cast iron frames, flipped them over, put its cushion on top, and each of us would get on while the other one pushed as fast as she could from the living room down the shiny hallway and back. Until one day, while I was on, we hit a rut in the tile and I went flying forward; I fell on my face, and broke both front teeth: we searched for the pieces that broke off but never found them. Our mom was not pleased when she returned home. I don't remember us playing that game again.

I don't remember how old I was, but even then, Satan sought opportunity to eliminate me: I was walking home from my neighbor's house around the corner when it happened. [Now, Big Sis says that they told me not to go, and I went anyway, so I was by myself.] I was walking on the bank around this corner, but this bike took a sharp corner, lost control, and rode up to where I was, and ran over me, but God was once again with me. I was injured about the head. I remember a bandage wrapping around my head and a laceration by my eye and ear, but I was alive. Everyone in the area knew us, so a witness ran to my house and got my family. Another incident: a bicycle ran me over, but I don't quite recall that.

Again: I was visiting my aunt, Loretta, with my family. She was strict/serious, and I was afraid of her, so I didn't say hello, and she threatened to beat me. Someone said that my aunt Marva (not much older than me) had just gotten a whooping for the same thing; I think my cousins were just teasing me but I believed it. So, I ran away from her house and stayed away till my family came out and found me. Then, we drove to a huge water pump that pumped water either to their house or to the area. They were showing it to my dad who supervised construction. To me, it was big and open with rushing water, and somehow I fell in and was almost washed away/drowned, but they quickly grabbed hold of me and pulled me out. I still remember the yelling and commotion as they attended to me.

Another incident: Big Sis and I were outside eating ice that we snuck when my mom's back was turned. (We had a refrigerator but an ice truck would drive by our gate every-so-often and bring huge blocks of ice that you had to use an icepick to break.) I had a large piece, and it slipped down my throat and got stuck, I could barely breathe. Big Sis took me over to the pipe, and as I tolerated it, she helped me drink the tap water till the ice melted enough and passed through.

Again: I believe was seven years old, either I missed the bus or I was trying to save money, but I was walking home from school, I was almost at *Nine Miles*, walking by *alligator pond*, and this car zoomed by and tapped me on my left hip. I always thought that man to be cruel and how he could have killed me and didn't even stop, but one day recently I thought how scared he must have been when he felt it and that he must have seen that I was OK in his rear-view mirror (because God kept me on my feet), and I forgave him. It felt a little uncomfortable for a short while, but God healed me. There was no real pain that I remember, and I never told a soul until November 2003 when I told one person to whom I was baring my soul. It was just me and God. Though I didn't feel the closeness I feel to Him now, He was always there, and through every incident and attempt of the enemy on my life, He felt close to me.

Now, I was eight years old, and this year my mom left permanently to make a life in the States because she left my dad. Right before she left, she made arrangements with one of her best friends, Mrs. Bailey (now deceased), to care for us kids till she could be with us again, so the day my mom left to the States, so did we three kids leave to live with the Baileys. It must have been overwhelming, but she loved our mom, and us, too. We missed home but they cared for us well. Those of us who went to the

Baileys were the three last ones me, Big Sis, and my fifth brother Fitzie. My fourth brother, Alli (Albert), was taken in by the Walker family (really close family friends/neighbors/extended family). The Walkers were *just* making it, but they said they could better care for my brother, and there was no way they would allow him to live with anyone else. Alli had a heart condition from the time he was a small child, and they could rush him to the hospital if need be, besides, they had a special love for him.

My other three brothers were already out of the house. My second brother, Peppem (Clinton), was in the army. Some mental trauma was suffered by us four kids at this time because the family broke apart as it did. Though we did get to see each other regularly and spend time together, the family was split up in three different houses along the same street. The Walkers, with whom my brother Alli lived, was an equivalent of two blocks around the corner from my dad's house. My dad's house was in the middle, and on the opposite end, about half mile to a mile away from my dad's house, at the Baileys, were us last three kids: Fitzie, Big Sis, and me. We passed our dad's gates back and forth but were not allowed to go through them. I don't think it was said by anyone; it was just something we knew or thought not to do—something we felt/sensed, and we were also afraid to.

We were at the Baileys only a couple of weeks maybe, but to me it seems like days. Then, our lives took a turn for the worst, though we didn't know it then. My uncle, Mancile, my mom's brother (now deceased), sent our aunt, Becca (my mom's sister), and took us three kids from the Baileys because he said, his baby sister's kids should not be with other people. In the beginning it was OK, because a female cousin we were used to was sent by her mom (the aunt who took us from the Baileys) to live with and care for us. This cousin was still in secondary school herself (in her late teens) but this was done because there were no other females in the house to care for us. This uncle was wealthy, he had a huge property with a main house containing at least eight bedrooms on the front of the property, then a row of efficiencies/rooms made of bricks like the main house, then a two-room board shack (which had holes in and between the boards; you could see through to the outside or from the outside to the inside). These were on the back of the property which he rented to tenants (*only* people from his church: Andrews Memorial Church in Halfway Tree), and there was a bathroom/shower separate by itself for all the tenants' use across from the rooms out back. Then, on the other part of the front property, he had one of his welding businesses. We all stayed in the main house.

Three of my uncle's kids, two boys and a girl, lived there off and on. I'm sure the youngest boy went away to school, because I remember him in his uniform, but I'm not sure where the girl and the older boy went when they weren't there. They were probably at boarding-school also. My uncle's wife (their mom, now deceased) was living in Florida. My uncle was a Seventh-Day Adventist and kept devotion faithfully every single morning, but I have no memory of his kids ever attending. Devotion is a good thing, but he would make us three late for school every morning.

Living there, we now had to take two or three public buses across town instead of one, and we would always miss the first which would make us even later for the others. To make life worse, he never gave us enough money to get to school and back; we always had to skip lunch or compromise somehow to have bus fare home. It was the little pocket money (literally, one or two American dollars to me, and maybe five dollars to the older ones) that our mom sent in her letters to us that helped to maintain us at times (even in the end when we had to buy our own little food).

I transferred to a different school because my sister graduated sixth grade, at St. Benedict's, and would be going to a different school, and my uncle didn't want me taking the buses across town by myself. My new school was Tarrant Primary, and I was in the fifth grade. One good thing about that school was it was now within walking distance, so no more buses for me, but the devotions still made me late almost every morning, and if I was late, my sister and brother were extremely late.

It was so embarrassing, attention would be drawn to me, and at times, I would be punished. The whole school saw; there was no escaping, because most times I would arrive when all the classes were gathered together in rows by rooms of our classes/grades out in the courtyard to pledge allegiance to the flag and sing the national anthem. There I would be, all eyes on me. After I made friends we would cover for each other (though they covered a lot more for me) with distractions and other things and let each other cut lines, and so I would manage not to be noticed by the teachers, though once in a while we did get caught.

It wasn't all hell with my uncle; there were some really good memories and fun times mixed in. After devotion every Sunday morning, he used to pile everyone in his truck and take us to the beach, and we had fun. He had a way about him though; he would swim what seemed like a mile or two out into the ocean by himself and stay there. All we could see was one tiny head way out on the water, I still wonder why he did that; maybe he was meditating. After a long while, when you saw him floating back in, you knew it was time to go.

We went to Bible class and went on hikes and outings and saw films and had dress up nights (dressing like a clown, bum, or whatever you felt like) and did lots of different activities through the church. It was all a very good time, which we needed.

We were also members of the Pathfinders. Big Sis and I were in different squads because of our ages, I don't recall if my brother Fitzie was also a member or if it was only for girls. I loved my little khaki uniform, with my little yellow scarf around my neck, and the pin, and the drills, and marches, and practices we use to have. In thinking of the name of my group, the name Bumble Bee comes to mind, also, the theme song we sang. The first line of words and the tune would come to me and the rest would escape me, but now I remember it all. What beautiful memories.

While living there, was when all us cousins first tried smoking. First we picked dry leaves from a breadfruit tree, crumpled and rolled it in paper, then lit it. We all tried it, and it was nasty; it was probably poisonous too. I had some money, so two of us ran to the shop across the street and I bought one cigarette for each of us. (People could buy less than a pack—the shopkeeper would open things and sell only what was needed, one-quarter, one-half, three-quarters of a loaf of bread and such, or parcels of sugar/rice/flour and such, or a few cigarettes and such.) So, we all took puffs of the cigarettes, and that was nasty too. It made me realize I had no use for such things, thank God! As far as I know, my brother and sister or my two cousins never picked up another cigarette since that day.

I think we lived with my uncle almost two years. During the latter half of our time there, we were outright neglected and put to live in the board shack in back of the main house as soon as the little old lady (Sis. Pitter) who lived there moved. Years ago, one day, while at Big Sis' house, Julie Parker and I were in touch with each other; we reminisced about the past and caught up on each other's lives. In our reminiscing she told me that my brother, who was about 14 years old, had put leaves in an envelope and left it on my uncle's bed and that was why my uncle had put us out of the main house. I guess they were dried-leaves/trash which was telling my uncle that he was trash for his treatment of us. If what Julie said was indeed the reason, that still doesn't sit well with me. Understandably, my uncle demanded respect, but how could he feel justified to put three children in a wooden shack and not be concerned with feeding them because he felt disrespected by one of them, who was only reacting and fighting back against the severe neglect of him and his little sisters. My uncle's elder son was also very abusive: forcing himself on the innocent.

At that time, either they provided us only with dinner, or they didn't give us anything at all; because, I remember us using the dollars our mom sent us (at that time it was one U.S. dollar to three or five Jamaican dollars). We would buy a parcel of brown sugar (a large scoop or two weighed/measured out and wrapped in paper) which we mixed with tap water and drank with Bulla (these individual portioned ginger spiced cakes) or Jackass Corn (these really hard kind-of sweet cracker/flat-bread things) that we loved. I remember us three gathering at times, and Big Sis or my brother Fitzie would ration it out, then we would eat and drink; I remember us going to bed having eaten only this.

There were these tenants, the Parkers, we all (everyone in the yard) called the mom nosey-Parker because she was always minding other people's business; ironically, she also had some sort of sinus issue and was always blowing her nose. Her son was Peter Parker, her younger daughter Julie Parker, and I don't recall the eldest daughter's name. Their mom was hateful, but they were nice and seemed to really like me. I remember my brother and sister being upset with me because when these teen-aged kids cooked, they would find me and offer me to eat [they would cook these really large wheat flour dumplings with whatever meat-kind —makes me smile thinking about all that]. At times I would take and eat what they offered, but my brother Fitzie and Big Sis didn't want me to eat from them no matter how hungry I was because they were in malice with each other. Till we were separated, we were raised by our parents to keep to ourselves, our friends were basically chosen for us, any friends we would make on our own were hardly, if ever, allowed in our yard or in our house. If we had them over, they had to hide and run away when our parents approached home. Our parents were proud people and we were proud kids. Anyway, those kids (the Parkers), and us didn't always get along, and we would stop speaking for long periods (which Jamaicans called "malice"), but they would always befriend me. Many times they would hide me in their room and keep watch while I ate, and so God caused them to feed me. Presently, I contemplate what my poor brother and sister did and how they made it because no one was feeding them, surely, they suffered more than me.

I don't fully understand why our uncle treated us like that, because we were good quiet kids who suffered all in silence. One reason may be because I was on occasions a bed wetter until I lived with Mommy Walker, then I stopped, but we kids are in agreement that a big part of the reason we were neglected was because he loved money and was known quite well for being a miser, except to his church, to which he was very kind and would do anything. So, when he took us he was probably expecting a good sum of money from our mom, and he got only what she had, which was little, and that displeased him.

The more I write, the more God rolls back the curtain. I remember there being talk of money, that my mom wasn't sending enough, and there was talk of my dad, and that he should be contributing. Personally, I'm not sure he wasn't.

My father was a millionaire, but I grew up poor to middle class, mostly on my mother's income. He was a very generous man, but was not thoughtful nor proactive toward his immediate family. He would give mostly only when asked of him, I choose to believe it was because he expected his children to work and think wisely and be a success as he was and be a help to each other. Also, he would not help unless it was asked of him respectfully, such as *"may I please have?"* or *"can you please?"* but most definitely not, "The teacher said **I have to have**!" or "The teacher said **you must**!" because then, you would hear some words, and receive no help until you asked properly. And, I guess he was right; he didn't **have** to do anything. When we were little, that behavior from him is something to ponder and be bewildered by, but when we were all grown, that behavior would have been just, because he was no longer obligated. But, my independent spirit would not allow me to turn to him or anyone unless extremely desperate, and at times not even then, though he would have help.

Anyway, none of this was our fault. We didn't ask, neither did our mom, to be taken from the Baileys. Yes, he was right that our dad should have been contributing (if he wasn't already), and our dad was well able, if not for his stubbornness and anger that my mom left and took us, but this uncle was also a rich man and was well able to take care of us instead of the abuse and neglect we received. You don't abuse children because of the parents' behavior. This same uncle took his **"baby sister"** (my mom) in when she was 10 years old because their mom (my grandmother/Naana) had died. She died on August 6, 1950 at the age of 49, from cervical/uterine cancer and pneumonia, which was five days before my mom's 11th birthday. He took her in and neither loved nor comforted nor spoiled her as his own, but put her to work. He had a wife present in the house, yet, he had my 10 then 11 year old mom taking care of them all: himself, his wife, and all his kids; washing (by hand), cooking, cleaning, she had to do this for years into her adulthood. He took no measure to ensure my mom's schooling/education; she found her own way to do so. His kids love their *aunt Girlie* (my mom) to no end (because she raised them), but it's what her very own blood brother did with his very little sister that is despicable. Still, I supposed he loved her and no doubt trusted her, because on his death bed he asked for her only, and would eat for no one but her as she fed him. [I ponder over the treatment of children when taken in by others, whether family or not. Why can't they be treated with love and respect as your very own? Why must they be treated like work-horses or some other abusive form? What is it in the care-taker that makes them feel okay with giving such treatment to that little one who depends on them? I find this to be so across all nations, in all countries, in all races, in olden times, in present days, and even in shows and media (art represents life). Why? Just why? Nothing inside me can think of *any* just cause to do anything but love and spoil a child with the best I have to give.]

While away, our mom would send barrels of things for us kids, and while with our uncle, a shipment of no fewer than two barrels of clothes, shoes, and things came for us, and I know food was in them also; no one ever sent barrels without food, especially not *my* mom. Uncle Mancile kept the barrels locked away, maybe from us. But, our cousins (Uncle Mancile's kids) stole them and sold them, and we got nothing. (Our other cousins—our aunt's daughters who lived in the main house—told us that they saw other people in our clothes). While we were being neglected, my uncle had the cousin who had been sent there to care for us, taking care of the main house and himself.

Sometimes things are best forgotten, but I'm not alone, so as God rolls back the curtains of my mind to reveal certain memories, He is here healing me. *Thank You Lord, I love You.*

My uncle wanted to go away to Florida on an extended visit to his wife—also a good time to get rid of us—so he said we had to go, while our female cousins remained (the one sent to care for us and also the one who was my age). The Walkers took Big Sis, because now she was a young woman, and they wanted to keep her out of trouble. I was taken by my aunt, the same one who took us from the Baileys and whose daughter was supposed to be caring for us.

I remember being alone, but Big Sis said that my brother Fitzie was taken to live there with me, so we both suffered the abuse and further neglect under my aunt's care, but he couldn't take it so he ran. He couldn't do any better; he had to leave me, he was just a kid himself. I now wonder if the reason I don't remember him being there with me was because, maybe, I was mad at him for leaving me, so I blocked him out; I don't know.

Presently, I am having flashes of him, but I'm not sure if they are real memories or because Big Sis said it. No, I do remember him being there. Not many memories though. He went to live with the aunt I ran away from as a small child, because he saw her kids (our cousins) daily at the bus stop at Parade (the town square), and they talked; he told them everything, and they told him to come live with them. I pray his time with them was even an ounce better than it had been because he never spoke of it that I know of.

So, now I bore it all. God truly walked with me then, though I knew it not. That whole experience changed me and made me strong, independent. I endured her (my aunt) and her bad treatment and neglect and favoritism and invasion of my privacy: telling me to give her the letters my mom wrote to me and reading them; then making comments such as, did I think she wanted the money that was in the letters? Also, opening and reading my letters to be sent to my mom to see if I was telling my mom of her abuses, but I wasn't, because my mom had enough stress. When it all got to be more than I could take, I became self reliant.

We had grown up in close relationship with this aunt and she was wonderful, we loved her so much, but she was wonderful because we were babies or because my mom was around, but now she (my mom) wasn't. It was clear to me then that I was on my own, so I came and went as I pleased, never rude or out of order or fresh, only self reliant. I tried to stay away from there as much as possible by staying out on the street with a school friend or by myself and not go there to them till dusk or night. I would also go visit Big Sis a lot and stay till night or stay a couple days.

During that time period was when I first experienced a dying person.

I was at Parade (the town square) looking to change buses to go to them in the country, when this man was gunned down in the crowd by the police, and I watched along with everyone else as this man lay across the gutter and sidewalk with blood bubbling from his ear. I don't know what happened to him, because I had to get on my bus, and it drove away as I looked out the window till he was out of sight.

Occasionally, my aunt would come crying to the Walkers that I ran away, but that's not true. I walked away only from abuse. No, I never told her where I was going, but deep down she knew why I left and knew where to find me—where she came crying those fake tears. I don't mean to sound angry still, because I'm not. It's all been given to God and forgiven her, and I love her. We now respect each other as adults and speak as such.

So, back to the mess. Eventually, one day, while visiting Big Sis, I decided, no matter where I ended up, I was never going back there to my aunt. Big Sis got scared and talked with the Walkers, and I moved in with them.

We did a lot of walking, God and me. I was just a child of ten years old, wandering the streets in an act of self-preservation; I must have talked to God a lot. Walking for miles and miles, literally from the center of town to the deep country, I must have talked to Him, I must have cried, but I remember none of it—all covered memories, covered pain, covered agony—all covered and sealed by God to preserve my sanity. Walking from my school (Tarrant Primary), to Halfway Tree, then to Constant Springs, then to New River—that's a long way with God. Sometimes I would walk only part of the journey, but other times I would walk the whole way to pass the time till it was dusk. Most of the journey from Constant Springs to New River was a narrow road with a wall of rocks on one side and the other side was a precipice with a *very* short wall and other parts had none. I remember hugging/clinging to the rock wall numerous times, as country-buses passed me by, so as not to get run-over. Many times they would pass by so fast they would create a wind that had my dress or uniform blowing in the breeze. I also remember talk of "the black-heart-man" (there were children who were missing and children who were abused and killed), so all those criminals were just "the black-heart-man." I believe God naturally walked with me in those days and times to keep me from being found a body in the bushes, if found at all. There's no other way that I'm still here, but God. ***Again, I thank You, Lord.***

So, now I was in the sixth grade, back on the street I grew up on (Greenvale Road), living with the Walkers. Soon after I moved in with the Walkers, I betrayed them: One evening, I walked through the dining room/kitchen area, there was money on the table and I took it. For the first time in my little life, I was a thief. My uniform was pressed and hanging on the wall for the next school day: I placed it in my uniform pocket and went on. Soon after, the money was noted missing by Mommy Walker, and she called everyone and asked if anyone had seen it, and everyone said they had not, including me. Now, for the first time in my little life, I was also a liar. It was told that the missing money was for the payment of a bill or bills, so everyone began to search for it, and I also helped search because I felt sorry that I had taken it and wanted to give it back and had thought of a great idea to return it. I would place it under the table in a hidden spot and pretend to find it. So, I went and got it out of the pocket of my uniform and began to search, then went under the table, but I could not find the opportunity to carry out my plan because, immediately, someone joined me under the table to look, and I feared greatly that I would be seen putting it there, and to put it elsewhere would have been very obvious that I was the thief and not the heroine that found it. So, I kept it and put it back into my uniform pocket.

I hated that I had stolen but I hated even more that I might be found out, because I hate to feel ashamed in anything—even now in my life—so I seek to live honestly and speak the truth.

Later that night, as I was going outside, when I got to the kitchen door before I stepped outside, I saw Mommy Walker and her eldest daughter. They sat outside talking and stopped talking when they saw me, but it was too late. I had already heard the conversation. Mommy Walker told her daughter Joan that she knew I was the one who took the money.

I felt such guilt, but I could not reveal myself that she was right for the even greater shame I would feel. Somewhere in me there must have been the thought that it was better to only be suspected than to be a known thief.

I seek always now to have innocent hands, mind, and heart before God in *all* things, so now, even being suspected of wrong brings a small level of anxiety within me for the guilt being cast upon me. This brings, at times, anger that I have to turn over to God, because I hate *all* acts against God, which are all wrong, but I have come to hate lies and thievery with a passion and hate them near me or against me. Of all the things I have done in my life, this is the part I left out and had no intention of revealing for the shame of it. Even now in my adulthood, I tried not to think of it. I tried to bury it. It was a weapon the enemy used against me, filling me with shame and the need to cover it.

This book was almost finished, and still I covered it. I resisted God, but He said *everything* must be cleaned out. I was covering for the devil, and as long as I did, the enemy would hold that secret with me and against me, partners in a secret of an act of wickedness. So, I listened to God and received this revelation with perfect understanding and could not allow it to continue. I had to cut off the enemy's access to me by obeying God in exposing this wrong I had done. As soon as I decided to be obedient and to let it be written, I felt *such* peace, no longer tormented, so God guided me to go back and insert it here into His book where it belonged and needed to be.

Though I had betrayed the Walkers, they loved and cared for me, and there were no more betrayals because I had learned my lesson—forever. Now I didn't have to roam the streets, so I went home, and it was good; but, I was different—no longer innocent. Still, no one knew I was a victim because I hid it well.

And yet, there was even more trauma: daily in my comings and goings, as I walked pass my dad's house, hearing the laughter of children I didn't know and seeing them running and playing in the yard. That yard I knew every inch of but whose gates I could not enter for fear of the man into whose arms I had run and had been scooped up with love as a child. It didn't cut my soul; I was strong; I shook it off. I was somewhat hardened—no longer a child inside.

The Walkers were extended family to me, my second mom and dad. I was greatly loved, and I loved them. They had little but cared for us very well. Our needs were met. God provided them. There was no difference between their kids and us. If one had, all had—or nothing, and we all got along. I don't remember us kids arguing or fighting, but it wasn't safe. The devil was still out for blood and possibly still mine.

It was election time in 1980, maybe only a couple of months after I moved back there, and our street was targeted. Never before was that street anything but safe, where us kids ran carefree at all hours and where everyone along that entire street knew us: like "Oh, those are Lewis' kids" or "Oh, those are Walkers' kids (they called our dads by their last names regularly). Armed gunmen blocked off the bottom of the only two main street exits to that area; both were barricaded. Even the police could not get through or were afraid; no one could enter or leave the area, even for work. All were at their mercy. They started at the very top of the street, at Cane River, and were working their way down, house by house—or their targets—because they previously had spies in the area, so no one knew who would be hit. Whatever their real purpose, it was told that if you were not of their party, they shot you all dead and burned your house down. There were many burnings and much gunfire and screaming all day, and we were helpless. We could do nothing but wait our turn.

My independent spirit would not allow me to just wait to die. I don't remember when I packed it, but I always had for an emergency a cloth khaki backpack, packed with what I felt was essential to me then. I don't recall why I felt I needed it, but it was there, ready and waiting, always, till I came and fully settled in with the Walkers. Then, as it was assembled, so it was disassembled without specific thought. Anyway, we kids discussed it and decided we would try to escape. [I don't think we told our parents (the Walkers) and I don't know where we thought we were going without them]. So, I grabbed my backpack, and we took off into the woods behind the house in an attempt to escape that massacre, but when we got only a few yards out, we heard gunfire. It sounded as if they were right next to us, and they were, because some of them had gone up to the houses on the hill behind our house, so we ran back into the house and waited. God was with us, because when these gunmen were no more than five houses away from us, God allowed gunfire to be turned on to the leader, and he was shot dead, so the whole army of these murderers gathered up their leader's remains and pulled up out of the area.

There were a lot dead or shot that day, some we knew well—even kids—and there were funerals that week; I attended one or two of them. I was worried about my dad, but we got word that he was OK. I heard they did let him through to go to work. (My dad had no fear and he didn't play. They probably knew him; everyone did.) But we heard a lot of people got turned right back around by these men to await their fate, and if you tried to force pass them, they would shoot you.

Moving on, I took the Common Entrance Exam when I was ten years old in the sixth grade (6A), but I failed because of reasons I will discuss later, but because I was so young, instead of making me go to secondary school, they made me repeat the sixth grade (6B), and now that I had turned eleven years old, I got to take it again. By now, my life, despite the love and care that I was now receiving, was beginning to affect me. I was slacking off on my homework a lot and didn't study and wasn't great in class, so my teacher was hateful to me. She was talking about me to some other teacher and said, "All she, it will be a cold day in hell before she pass" ("You see her, it will be a cold day in hell before she passes.") I heard her and never forgot those words. She was speaking of the Common Entrance Exam. This is a national exam that determines whether a child will go to high school versus secondary school. It is a prestigious thing to pass, and a shame and a reproach if you didn't. And that's what she spoke over me, that I should suffer disgrace.

When she talked about me, I hated her even more than I had. God sure did prove her wrong, because I passed, and God used it to shut her mouth, because she said not one word when she found out. I don't remember her even pretending to be happy for me. I only remember watching her out of the corner of my eye as she stared at me when she heard.

God did send a little help though. I don't know if it made me pass, but I'm sure it gave me a higher grade. I didn't understand long division at all, probably because I wasn't paying close attention to it, because if I had, I would have seen how easy it was. Even though my friends tried to show me, it just didn't click, so all my divisions were short, no matter how great the number, which helped me later in mental math, but then, doing that at such a young age, at times I would mess up. So, during the exam, one of the examiners stood over me and looked at my work as I did a problem and said to me, "Are you sure that's the answer you want to put there?" She left, then circled around, and when she got back to me, she did it once more as I completed another problem, saying the same thing, then leaving, so I recalculated the problem each time. Now, she didn't give me the answers, but she wasn't supposed to do that, either. I don't think they are supposed to speak to us at all. God sent that examiner to let me know that He was with me. I have always remembered her and have been grateful and appreciative of her, but never really understood till recently that it was God fighting my battle for me against that nasty, wicked teacher.

That same teacher was also hated by my brother Peppem. For about a month, his base was stationed up the street from my school, so after school my friends and I would say good-bye, because they had to get home, and I would go visit him. Sometimes my friend Jennifer would go with me. I did introduce them all to him, but Jennifer was the only one who could stay with me.

Anyway, this teacher would beat me a lot, and she sought opportunity to do so. Teachers were allowed to beat kids, but she took it to extremes and pleasured in it, so I used to watch myself around her, and my friends did too. The whole class knew how she was. Most of the class didn't like her—no talking or fooling around when she was looking and no playing at recess that would cause our clothes to be wet with sweat. Yes, kids were to take pride in themselves and keep their uniforms neat and clean, but she just beat way too much. We also prayed she didn't call on us to do a problem or anything on the board, because if you got it wrong, it either was ridicule from her, stand facing the wall in punishment, or a beating.

All the previously mentioned things and more were causes for beatings from her. I got more beatings and damage from her than I did in all my years from my parents or family. I remember the boys used to play really hard because they would say they don't care, but when it was time to come in and their shirts were soaked they knew the consequences. So they would prepare, we all would, by picking certain green leaves off the trees and rubbing them on the palms of our hands and other methods. For some reason it made the pain much less. Sometimes, however we prepared didn't matter, because if you didn't or couldn't hold out your hands because the pain was too great but she wasn't finished; the beatings would go to your back or legs or wherever it fell. Don't think you could act tough like you felt nothing, because that would only be your death-sentence. She was a dangerous teacher, and we knew it, and we wanted to hurt her and made our little plans for her and how we would report her, but we didn't because we didn't believe it would get anywhere.

Anyway, while my brother was stationed by the school, one day she beat me for getting something wrong on the board, and she did a thorough job at it. I think I had made up my mind that I wouldn't give her the satisfaction of seeing me cry. For a child being punished repeatedly and unjustly this is a show of ultimate strength, that they will endure and will not allow the punisher to break them. But to the punisher this is the worst thing a child being punished can do, it speaks to the punisher that the child is most insolent. The child is called "bare-faced and dry-eyed and daring" because with that kind of punishment there should be many tears and they are expected, but there is none, not one drop. It is the ultimate form of rebellion from a child who has simply had enough and has taken back control the only way they know how and the only way they can. This made her more and more angry, and the harder and harder she hit till she gave up. When she was done, my palms were **very** swollen and red, and my wrists and up my forearms were black and blue and also very swollen. The gross welts could be seen along my arms from the thick leather strap she used. All my friends had pity and hated her for me but could do nothing. When Jennifer and I went to visit my brother, Jennifer tried to convince me to tell him but I wouldn't, so she grabbed and held up one of my arms before him; then I showed him both hands and arms, and we told him about her.

    He was so angry at the damage to me he wanted to hurt her. He said he was going to confront her and make sure she understood that she would never ever do that to me again or to put her hands on me again. Though Jennifer and I were glad to hear this, and wanted this, because something was due her for all she did to us, I begged him not to, and it took much to calm him down. But I let him know that he would not always be based there, and when he was gone, she would probably do much worse because she already hated me. So, for my sake, he let it go but said if she ever did it again he was going to see her. But that was the worst damage she ever did to me. I guess after that incident it dawned on her the inexcusable, unexplainable damage she did and was probably afraid. Or, maybe, Jennifer ran her mouth about my brother *"the soldier"* coming after her and it got back to her, because she did leave me alone after that time, except for her remarks of reproach and looks of hatred. I think if I had shown my hands and arms to the principal, Mrs. Young, she would have fired her.

    Either way, I didn't tell my brother anything else, and not long after that, he was relocated. We were not able to say good-bye, because his company left abruptly and another came. I could not tell the difference between companies, so when I went to visit where his tent was, the men now stationed at that spot told me that my brother and his company were gone, and I missed him. Jennifer missed him too, and we comforted each other, but I now think she missed him only because he used to give us money or I would share what he gave me with her. Yes, the money was good for me too because I liked having it. It gave me certain freedoms and options during my oppressive circumstances in my home-life, but the real issue for me was that my big brother was gone. I didn't know when I would see him again, and my protector was gone. I felt loneliness and a sense of loss daily as I walked by the area where he had been, and it was now empty (All the companies had now left).

Anyway, back to the exam. The way all found out if they passed or not was when the results came out in the newspaper. If you didn't see your name, you would call the paper to see if there was an error why your name wasn't printed. I looked under the school of my first choice, Holy Childhood High, and my name was not there. I looked under the school of my second choice, Immaculate Conception High, and still my name was not there. We four friends had chosen the same schools, because aside from being the best-known high schools at that time, we thought their uniforms were just hot, just awesome, and they were widely admired by kids.

My family and I looked up and down the lists under those schools a few times, but my name wasn't there. I found my friends' names under our first choice and was truly happy for them but was disappointed for myself. I didn't want to go to school that next day because I couldn't face them. We had made such plans for ourselves together as a group—together forever—and I broke my end of it. However, I dragged myself to school and I saw them standing outside waiting for me, and when they saw me, they ran to meet me with excitement.

When they got to me, they started jumping up and down shouting, "We passed! We passed!"

I said, "I didn't."

But they said, "Yes, you did!"

I told them I didn't see my name, and they showed me the paper they had in their hands. They said it was under a different school, one I never chose, Excelsior High. They showed me my name, then we all jumped up and down together and hugged each other. I was so relieved, but we were still going to be split up, and we weren't happy about that, and I hated the uniform that school wore.

The family quickly got the news that our visas to come to the States were approved. About to graduate from Tarrant Primary (still eleven or just turned twelve years old), it felt good. I didn't have a party, but

I celebrated with my school friends. I was happy at school. I had some really close friends—really tight. There was Heather Lyons; I felt closest to her. There was Jacqueline (Jackie) whom I got to know because she and Heather were friends first.

There was Jennifer; I liked her more than the others did. We all used to malice a lot (stop speaking to her a lot), but she and I couldn't stay away from each other for very long. Because of my pride, she would mostly make the first move, but we would write each other little make-up notes in class and go sit by each other and start speaking again while some in our group whispered to me that I should not speak to her, and the others in our group stared at us, being upset with me for doing this. Eventually, I would get the others to start speaking to her again. There seems to be another friend whose name escapes my memory.

This group of four or five of us was the main group, then there were others that we as a group joined and hung out with at times. My clique of friends and I would stand outside and wait for and look for each other till the last possible minute before and after school and traveled together to Parade (the town square), then we would say good-bye and split up to go home. We hung together all through school and ate lunch together, shared our food and money and treated each other. Almost every day we would save back some and at times all of our money and walk to a restaurant or to the higglers outside the school gates and buy food or treats. We bought patties (Jamaican patty - cooked seasoned ground beef with curry colored dough crust baked in an oven) and cocoa bread (a slightly sweet hard dough bread, shaped and baked for individual serving portions), meatloaf (shaped like the patties but with cocoa bread dough crust and seasoned ground beef filling), bun (a form of spiced cake) and Jamaican cheese, cornbread (a yellow, slightly sweet bread roll) and Jamaican cheese, sky juice (bag juice made to order with shaved ice), King-Kong (sealed bag juice manufactured and sold, like a very large and broad ice pop but it's juice), suck-suck (Highly sweetened juice, frozen in little plastic bags; you bite off one corner at the bottom and suck until the juice and ice is all gone.), Jamaican soda, and cooked food such as oxtail and curried goat—all the good Jamaican foods and drink. After we got our food, we walked to the bus stop.

We also used to plan to dress alike every day. We wore uniforms, but there were choices in that. There was a choice of green or orange-colored full uniforms with short sleeves and a collar, or cut out with a white blouse, or a green or orange skirt, and a blouse of the same color or white. If we decided on wearing a skirt the next day, and one of us didn't have one prepared, on that day that person would fold down and tuck in the top part of the uniform inside the waist, and no outsider knew it wasn't a skirt.

It was a blast being with them—just really tight. In the end, near graduation, we wanted to go to each other's houses, but it just never worked out. Their parents were strict, and they had to be home by a certain time, so they wanted me to come to their houses, but it never worked out for me to go, so we just hung out after school for as long as possible, which wasn't very long.

With the upcoming graduation, we all decided to dress alike, down to our shoes. The dresses all had to be white but could be any style, so we thought of and chose one style, based on the most popular style at the time, and had them made through separate dressmakers our parents chose.

We were almost a little late for graduation, because my dress wasn't finished till the last minute. My friends followed me to my dressmaker, who's house was close to my school (she was also my dad's lover). I got dressed there, and we walked back to the school together. I don't remember how we met up. I think graduation was after school, or more likely, knowing us, we planned to meet somewhere and did.

I remember an incident while living with the Walkers: mommy Walker told me to wash the dishes after breakfast one morning and the sink was full so I didn't want to and said no. She wanted to spank me for disobeying but my brother Alli felt he should do it, and mommy Walker agreed. I didn't want to be spanked so I ran off to the bushes and sat on a large rock behind the house. My brother didn't chase me; I sat there for hours. The Walker boys came back and forth talking to me and giggling when I said something they thought was funny, and they brought me lunch. Eventually, I gave up and went back down to the house where my brother was patiently waiting with the belt. He spanked me in my hands and talked to me, reminding me how lucky and grateful we were and should be that the Walkers loved us enough for us to be there with them. I stopped being stubborn and apologized to mommy Walker for disobeying and telling her no, then I went and washed all the dishes from breakfast and lunch.

A few months prior to graduation, daddy Walker felt extremely disrespected by Big Sis, so we had to leave the Walkers. Though they loved us, all of us had to leave. My brother Alli, being the head of us that were there with the Walkers, was encouraged by them to go speak to our father about us going back to live with him, so he did, and we moved back home. My brother that was with my other aunt (that I had run away from as a child because of her threat of a beating) also came home to our dad's house.

I was self reliant, independent, changed, caring for myself, and mostly coming and going as I pleased. I had toned it down out of respect for my second mom and dad and because I felt safer, cared for, and loved, but it was now in me; a pattern.

When I went back to my dad, the pattern showed itself. Mommy Walker was a stay-at-home mom with us, and at my dad's there wasn't that structure. I was supposed to be home before dark, but I would stay out all hours doing nothing, then when walking home in the dark at times, my dad would be on his way home, too, and pick me up in his car. Maybe I lied and covered my tracts before the questions could be asked or maybe I was just silent, I don't recall. He was never angry or punished me or called me on it at all—not one word. Not that he didn't care, but maybe me being the baby of the family, he could see in me the hardships I had suffered and saw how it had toughened me, that my innocence and naiveté were gone. I had matured, so he just let me be. That was his way to love me now, to just let me be. [All the years we weren't living there, he would just drive past us without stopping or saying hello and we would just hold our heads straight, pretending not to notice he just passed, even though sometimes those we were walking with would call our attention to it. At other times he would blow his horn in acknowledgment as he sped by. I don't remember him stopping. Well, I guess no man would want to stop, have their child get in, and drop them off at someone else's house which they called home. The love was still there, but I guess no one knew how to be with each other. It was a terrible time in our lives.]

Being responsible now, I was also given full charge of my little cousin, Susie, she was about 5 years old. I was to take her to school and pick her up from school and see about her. It was a job forced upon me, and she was annoying at times, but I did take good care of her, and sometimes I *was* proud to have her with me.

I was very bony, looking malnourished from previous years, and my mom had seen a picture of me and was *not* pleased; so, she talked to my dad about it and he spoiled me with lots of milk and good food to fatten me up, and it was working. It was working so well that one day at recess I overheard a girl telling her friends about me; not really teasing, but kind of in wonder because I was so skinny/bony just prior. Still, I felt self-conscious and hated that she was talking about me at all. I did love the fact that now, properly nourished, my breasts started to develop; Jennifer noticed and wanted to see it, so, though slightly embarrassed, and we were in the middle of the school grounds, I opened a button of my blouse and showed it to her, then carried on with the rest of our day.

Home. I was among my trees again. I guess if they couldn't find me, all they had to do was look up. After a little while, our American visas were approved, so in a rush we had to pack up and leave. We couldn't tell anyone, or really say good-bye to anyone, because people would try to kill or hurt you so you couldn't go, so you wouldn't succeed over them, because they thought you were going to paradise.

I was happy to go be with my mom and that I didn't have to go to a school I didn't care for with what I thought was a horrid, wretched plaid uniform. We had called to inquire why I didn't get the school of my first choice, and they said because it was out of my area, but that was ridiculous because my dad passed by the school gates every morning on his way to work. I think they had an overflow of applicants to both schools, because every kid loved those two schools, and I guess they had to pick and choose who they would allow in.

Anyway, thank God I didn't have to worry about that anymore. My school friends and I had already said good-bye, and they all had given me their addresses so I could write to them. I packed that paper in the pocket of the suitcase my sister and I were sharing, but we were told that we packed too many unnecessary things, that our mom already had many things waiting on us, so it was re-packed by someone else in another suitcase. That was the end of my beautiful friendships, because I never again saw that paper with the addresses.

When I arrived in the States and realized it was not with my things, I sent back to Jamaica to inquire about it, but it could not be found. I then regretted very much that I had not gone to their homes like we wanted to, because if I had, I would then have known how to contact them. I had asked my cousin who also attended that school with me to look out for them in case they came back to visit the school, but she never saw them. She saw Jennifer once before I asked her, but not after. I missed them so much for years, and wonder even now if they thought I threw them away as friends. I learned to just cherish the memories, because if we were to see each other today, it would probably be a very awkward experience. Our lives are probably so different and there are now blanks in my memory. I pray they are still alive and well. If not alive, then I pray they have found my sweet Savior and are now resting in the King's arms.

In America with my mom, we would walk to the boardwalk in Asbury Park; it was really nice then. We rode the rides and played the games and had fun. My eldest brother was already here for a while. He was approved first so he could help my mom.

My second brother, Peppem, had escorted us up but went back down to take care of his business, so he could come back up for good and transfer to the U.S. Army. But, he never made it back. Within a week or two after being back in Jamaica, he was murdered at twenty-three years old by army buddies he thought were his friends but were not, to whom he made the mistake of telling his plans. Even though my mom drilled it into him to keep quiet, he thought he could trust them, but they then set him up to go out with them and murdered him there. They set it up to look like a drowning, but my brother was an excellent swimmer and the water they dumped him in was shallow. I was also told the autopsy results revealed a blow to his head. In my adult years, I have seen the report, and among the closed head wound and other things, it reveals he had also aspirated some of the contents from his stomach which speaks volumes to me of his struggle to survive all their wickedness and attacks, and of the vicious blow he received. They got away with it because my mom never followed through with charges, but they will stand in judgment before God. I also believe they all lived or are living a very tormented life.

My mom went down, and together with my dad, buried him at Dovecot Cemetery. After that all the rest came except my third brother: my dad escorted them up. For **many** years my third brother refused to come to the States because he said everyone who comes here dies—speaking of his brothers.

My mom said that while here, my dad said we shouldn't be living in an apartment, so he went out and got a house and put us in it. Then shortly after that, he went back to Jamaica and left my mom with the responsibility of paying for the house, for he thought that my eldest brother would help her, but it was not so. But, God was with her: she paid all the bills and raised us the best she knew how.

Once per year, either my mom would go down or my dad would come up because they were back together in a long-distance relationship. My dad wasn't comfortable living here; he was very well established there in construction, being in charge. He did work here for a short while in the construction of a few houses. I think of him with love every time I drive by them. Let's just face facts, my dad simply wasn't a family man; he did not invest in any regard into his children or his marriage, neither did he treasure any. Yet, he kept having us kids in a timely manor and made sure to marry my mom so as not to lose her: I wish I knew his heart and his intentions in all this.

I started school. The first day was different but great. I missed my friends, but—how strange—I saw kids who looked exactly like the ones from my old school. Things were looking up. When homeroom began, the teacher introduced me to everyone, and they all liked me and wanted me to sit beside them. I had a good day and was looking forward to the next.

Then my mom doomed my social life forever. She had a brilliant idea to save herself laundry and told us we had to wear the same clothes for two days. But, did she space it out? *Nooo!* We had to wear the one set for two days in a row because once worn she didn't want it hanging back in the closet. So there I was at school the second day in the same dress, same socks, same shoes, like I had never gone home. I guess I didn't mind it, because I was new here and used to wearing uniforms. I didn't know how things were done here, but I surely found out this was not cool when I heard the kids talking and snickering behind my back. I pretended not to hear, but it did not feel good. I went from being "all that" in my old school, and the fascinating new kid everyone wanted as their friend, to being a present joke.

This second day that I was looking forward to had quickly turned me into a social outcast, not even hanging with the unpopular kids. That, along with the fact that I didn't speak their slang, kept me a loner till ninth grade.

Now I was bored, and most of the work I was getting I had already done in my old school because the work was more advanced, so I lost further interest in my work. They wouldn't move me up because of my age and, in fact, wanted to put me back into the sixth grade until, I guess, they took a good look at my records, or my mom protested.

Now things got worse. My brother Alli got sick and was in the hospital. He used to send his snacks home with mom for me. Since Jamaica, he was also always making me exercise, which I didn't much like but needed. Anyway, his doctors took him to Pennsylvania for heart surgery. They said it would be the last one he would ever need, that they would correct it all. He also had an uneven chest from badly healed bones from a previous open heart surgery. They did the surgery, but he wasn't conscious long that I remember. He went into a coma from pneumonia. It was told to my mom by other staff that this happened out of neglect. Charges should have been filed there, too, but again my mom let it go. I guess I now understand it was maybe because she already had too much stress and grief and just wanted to find a way to go on.

One day while at school, I was called to the office. When I saw my mom, I knew it wasn't good. My brother was dead. I couldn't stop crying. After a while, one day I remember my siblings teasing me and my mom telling them to leave me alone, that I missed him. I just lay on the sofa and cried and cried. I also had guilty memories from when we were here, he would try to play with me and tickle me, and I was just a spoiled brat to him, crying out to my mom in order for him to stop and leave me alone.

Now he was no more, at nineteen years old, not here to play with, not here to talk to, nothing. He had been such a talented artist in drawing, just anything at all. It seems the whole family is touched with this talent to draw, but he was the absolute best and made plans for a career in that field. I saved some of his drawings somewhere still to this day.

His spirit remained with me in my dreams until I was about twenty-five years old, then he became disappointed with something I was doing, so he left me and never returned to my dreams. I was in an adulterous affair and in much pain from it, and I dreamed of my brother. His spirit was angry at this man, and it seems he would hurt him in this dream, but I begged for him not to harm this man and in doing so, I chose this man and this pain I was in, so my brother's spirit left me and never returned even to this day.

I was able to go to this brother's funeral twice. My mom had one funeral here, then she took his body to Jamaica and took me with her. There was another funeral there, then she buried him right next to my other brother. It was exactly four months and one day between their deaths; August 22, 1981, and December 23, 1981. I don't know how my mom stood, but she did, very strong. I just cried and cried and cried. God brought us all through. [I felt the strength of my mom when she left me. Then after a few months I absolutely broke. I don't know when her grief took its toll because I never saw her cry. Indeed, it is God that keeps and gets one through such devastation.]

Section II: Body

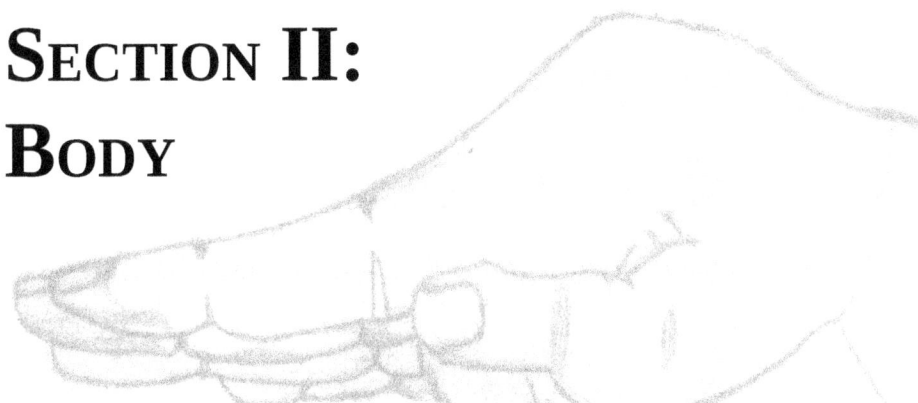

As an adult, I now have the full knowledge that us kids grew up in a nest of pedophiles, predators, incestuous practices, abusers, neglecters, and wicked-ones, with *only* our mother to defend us as she could. When she was not present with me they sought every opportunity.

Now, I must go back in time and cover some other significant things that I deliberately left out until now because I wanted to deal with it as a whole, not in bits and pieces.

As far back as I can think to my earliest memories, I don't recall thinking that sexual things were gross like kids of that age usually do. I remember playing nasty games with my boy cousin of around my age, then with two of the boys I grew up with who later became my brothers in my second family. Also, myself and the female cousin I went to school with taking turns practicing kissing with our little girlfriend that lived with her mom as a tenant in the yard with us at my uncle's house. The kiss was bitter, which grossed me out at the time and made me not want to kiss anyone else, ever. I remember my cousin helping me to write little nasty notes with explicit sexual drawings to this boy I went to school with at Tarrant Primary who liked me, I think his name was Richard. My cousin delivered them, at times with coins I had wrapped inside the notes. I do wonder where I got such thoughts from because he *never* asked me for money and he liked me regardless. Except for when he would come by my uncle's gate on his way home and flirt sexually with me, I never saw him. Though we were the same age, I was ahead, and he was in my cousin's class and also already had a girlfriend, with whom he was sexual.

I don't know where, when, or why those thoughts started, I just did them and liked it. But in all that, I don't recall any arousal in my body. They were just actions, something my mind desired to do, but no real feeling was associated with those things. No fantasies, just spur-of-the-moment things we thought of and did when together. I don't know why.

Then there were things I didn't like. I remember walking up the stairs at Tarrant Primary, and this boy touched my bottom. I never saw him or knew him, because he hid and ran away, but because he touched me, I hated him.

I also remember being at my aunt's house, the same one I lived with later. Those cousins and we kids were very close, more than any other set of cousins. We used to spend a lot of time visiting each other and sleeping over. They lived in the country, and we lived near the town at Bull Bay. We had fun, and I loved bathing in the river when I went to visit. When there were many of us, my aunt made room for all. We all piled into the bed. It was on bricks or wood I think, and the mattress was stuffed with straw. My aunt had made it, and it was huge and comfy.

Anyway, we all piled in together, boys and girls, and when we ran out of room, we turned head to foot, it was fun. Only, one night (the part I hated), while lying there beside my older male cousin Namon with my back turned to him, he got ideas. There were others in the bed with us, but the devil got hold of him, so he didn't care. He took out his penis and rested it between my thighs and left it there, I guess to see what I would do or for some sick pleasure. As soon as he did it, I realized what it was on me, so without looking at him or even making a fuss, I just shifted my position and got him off me then went to sleep. He never tried it again as far as I remember, and I kept silent.

In my twenties while on a visit to Jamaica, the subject of him and another male cousin came up with an older female cousin of mine (the daughter of my mom's eldest sister), and I told for the first time what he had done to me as a child, and she revealed other perverted things he tried with her. I wasn't alone but didn't know it then.

Again, while living with my aunt, I was still ten years old, about to turn eleven (I moved away from her during that time period). I was in the sixth grade (6A) and it was time to take the Common Entrance Exam for the first time. Since my aunt lived in the country and my uncle lived within walking distance of the school, I was told to stay there till the days of the exam were over so I would never be late by missing a bus. While there, I went to bed early so I could wake up rested and ready to beat that test. My aunt and cousins (three of her daughters) were gone out to a tent revival meeting (tent church). One of my aunt's daughters, the one I went to school with, is not quite a year younger than I am but was in the fourth grade. Another of the three daughters was the one that had cared for me and my siblings while I lived with my uncle. She still lived there, and I was staying in her room.

I was in her bed sleeping, then I was awakened by someone's footsteps walking on the bare wooden floor. It was my older male cousin Richmond who lived there off and on. He had come to my bed, picked me up, held me across his arms and was in the process of carrying me down the hallway to his room when I was awakened by his footsteps. God was with me, and when my eyes opened, He made me aware of what was about to happen to me and kept me still and motionless like I was still asleep. My cousin took me to his room and laid me on his bed; I was still motionless, pretending to still be asleep.

As I peeked at him, I watched him unbuckling his pants. He had left his room door open because we were all alone in this huge house, and my aunt and cousins weren't due back for over an hour or more. As he unbuckled his pants and started to remove them, God said, "Move now!" I didn't hear His voice, but He surely prompted me to action, and I took off running. My cousin chased me down the hall and around the dining table, but I escaped him through the back door to outside. If he had come after me through the side door that would have been it for me. He didn't follow me out because there were tenants living in the yard in rooms behind the main house. I ran around the side to the huge iron gates in front and stayed there till my aunt and her daughters came home. I don't recall how long I waited for them to get there, but when they did I told them everything right there at the gates. My aunt said she would look into it, and I trusted her to do that, but days later I heard nothing, so I asked my cousin (the youngest of her daughters, the one I went to school with). When I asked her what happened about that situation, she told me her mom (my aunt) said I "must have had a nightmare while sleeping." So, I kept my nightmare to myself and never mentioned it again till in my twenties, when I told my female cousin with whom I discussed the first incident, and not again till my thirties with Big Sis.

Needless to say I failed the exam for my school that year. I was recently thinking how very different it would have been if he had attacked me there in the bed where I lay sleeping. But I realized that God allowed that way to the enemy, allowing the perversion to work in his mind where for some sick reason or maybe even for an alibi or to hide evidence, he wanted me in his own bed.

God allowed that to make the way of escape for me, otherwise I would have awakened to a horror that had already been done—trapped. He must have raped before to be this confident and bold, but, *I thank You, Lord. I love You, Jesus!*

[True indeed. It is a very hateful situation, because had my aunt done right by me it would have stopped another nightmare that I learned of recently: he was repeatedly raping someone else and that could have been addressed and stopped if my attempted rape wasn't swept under the rug. But, when nothing was done for me that person saw every reason to stay silent and bare it. May God heal all his victims.]

The third incident, perhaps the second—my mind won't allow me to recall the time sequence—was with the female cousin in whose bed I had been staying, the same one who had cared for me while I lived with my uncle. It happened during the same time period that my male cousin tried to rape me, and I believe my telling on him deterred her from doing it again. I never told on her, because she had brought me shame. We were both lying in her bed after turning in for the night, and I was sleeping. I must have been asleep, because I don't remember how she got there. I just remember her there. She molested me. I never told a soul till in my thirties when my sister and I were on the phone, and for the first time in our lives, we started baring our souls, trading war stories, and in our conversation where we spoke for hours and hours, I told her all about my male cousins and about this female cousin Charmaine.

I greatly hesitated in telling her and thought I would take this incident in secret to the grave with me, because the incident greatly shamed and embarrassed me. I carried much guilt and other feelings I could not describe against myself over this, because the act of what she did was physically arousing to me like nothing I had ever felt. I liked it and didn't want her to stop, but she was called away. The perversion she had just infected me with led me to get up and go seek after her like a little puppy to see what was taking her so long to return to me. I wanted more of this predatory sickness, but God allowed the men to keep her busy getting them things as they fixed a truck outside, so I went back to bed and went to sleep. [Presently, I believe that when I went to seek after her, my male cousin saw a look in her or felt a vibe from her. I believe he realized what had occurred, so, he decided to take his turn at me, because predator recognizes predator and also recognizes prey/victim.] I don't recall ever giving her a second thought after that night or wanting that again, and after my male cousin tried to attack me, I walked away from that whole sickness. That's when I moved away from my aunt's house completely without telling her, she later brought my things to the Walkers.

For years, I was disgusted with myself, and I still think it was sick of me and that the incident spoiled me. It seems this sickness in her was a habit, because I have recently learned that she defiled others also. In writing just now, I had never brought that part of the molestation to light before, but I had to be honest with even myself. As I wrote I felt the contortion in my face because I was revolted. It was awful enough that the violation against me had brought me pleasure, but to know and dig up and admit that I sought after her is a hard part of me to accept and deal with.

[God just gave me a revelation that made me love and embrace this little child that did this. The revelation is this: That was not me, it was the oppression of the devil working against me, working in my flesh trying to possess my mind. From the time I was in my mom's womb until that time, Satan had been after me, and with the violation of this molestation, he had finally gotten access to me, so he used it. He found my sexuality as a way to use me and possibly destroy me. That was not me, that was not the act of a child, that was the enemy working in my flesh, no child wants to be violated. The same sickness that infected her and made her think it was OK to touch a child is the same sickness that was infecting me making me think it was OK for her to touch me. She was my caretaker and big cousin, I loved her, but that was not OK, and it was not my fault nor my shame, it was and is hers alone. Thank You God for opening the eyes of my mind to this child in me and allowing me to forgive her for giving in to the wickedness against her.]

I don't know where it came from, but a sexual interest was always in me. My sexuality (interest) didn't begin with this cousin who molested me, but she brought me to an evil place, sharing with me her demon of sexual perversion and depravity and allowing it to oppress me. Anyway, with all that sensuality in the body and mind of a child, I molested her youngest brother of my age one day by handling him. It was during this incident that a little girl child learned about the sensitivities of the male organ, something which a small child should *never* be aware of. Even though we were both children, I say molested because I am slightly older than he is, I did not ask neither received any consent but did touch him in a sexual manner. This was the same cousin I used to play nasty games with, but our games were never before like that. It was a source of shame to me, so it was another secret I kept till November 2003 when I bared my soul to someone I feel completely open to about everything I remember.

God sealed up and suppressed this demon of sexual perversion and depravity from oppressing me, but only for a while. After I came to America, I was about thirteen years old and had grown nicely. My father visited us often, but his business was in Jamaica, so he always went back. On this visit when I was thirteen, my dad came into my room as I lay on my bed, and he sat beside me and complemented me on how nice I looked and how I looked just like my mom when she was that age (referring to my breasts that were developed). Then he reached over and tried to brush his hand against my breasts. I realized what he was up to, so I shifted my position and avoided him touching me, then immediately got up and stood away from him. So, he got the message and he got up and left my room, neither of us saying a word. He never tried it again. Another secret kept and buried because I didn't want to cause my mom pain or have her end up in prison. I told Big Sis only, when I was in my thirties in the same phone conversation in which I told her everything else. My feelings toward my dad were by then indifferent. I neither loved him nor hated him, and after the incident I didn't hate him. He was to me just one more person coming at me.

[Revelation is a *mother-ship*, reading over that last sentence opened me and made me realize something very telling about myself. With all the people male and female coming at me in my childhood and youth, it has caused me to be a very controlling adult concerning love. I have never wanted *anyone* who actively wanted me when they wanted me and have usually fallen in love with people who were just slightly out of my reach. I went after who I wanted till I got them, all the while knowing somewhere inside that I wouldn't be able to keep them, and those who wanted me I had no interest in. My son's father once told me that I didn't act like I wanted him until times I thought I was losing him, and it was very true and not till this very moment did I understand why. I never truly understood why I treated him that way and blamed it on feelings I had for someone else but it was this hidden thing in me. In essence when someone wanted me and showed interest they were subconsciously to me as my molesters because they also *wanted me* and made it known. I compensated for this issue by choosing who I wanted to have me, which is someone I would make want me. All who I loved and went after, I bedded, but could not keep, and had I been able to keep them would have destroyed them. I gave my body but not my whole heart, and all who I chose to have me gave me their bodies but not their whole hearts. I thought my heart was choosing who I loved but it was my issue that was choosing and destroying lives, especially mine. I carry a hidden issue rooted in me from the past violations against me that I now give to God to pluck up because this cannot and will not remain in me. There is a whole lot that is making a whole lot of sense right now.]

OK let's get back to the past...

There was another episode with an older male family friend, Nigel. While the family was in a store shopping for clothes, he touched my bottom, and when I turned and looked at him, he was looking in a different direction like he hadn't done anything. I stepped away from him, and from that moment on, made sure he never got the opportunity to do anything else.

Anyway, my dad was forgiven and it was buried, just as the incidents involving my male cousins were buried. I didn't start to love my dad till I had my son and took his grand-baby to meet him when I was twenty-two years old. I saw him differently; he was a person, humorous, and playful in a good way. He was a decent man, and he loved his grandkids (he kept their baby pictures stuck on his dresser mirror until the very end.). He had respect for me, and it showed in the way he spoke with me, and from that time I loved him and love him so very much still, though he still may have had many issues and demons that I don't know if God dealt with. I prayed much for him that he would be healed of whatever caused him to do the hurtful things he did, and I believed God for it. [Mom told me dad said he was molested repeatedly by a woman, who was a family friend, when he was about 7 years old: the woman used to lay/position him on top of herself.]

When I was twelve, here in the U.S., I fell in love with the son of a family friend who was six years older than I. My feelings for him came about because I felt he was being mistreated by another and felt really sorry for him. Then that pity turned into a desire for him, then love. I let him know how I felt in a letter, and he let me down easy by telling me he could not be with me because he was already involved with someone, which he was, but I knew that was not the real reason. For almost two years he didn't want me, but I continued to let him know exactly how I felt about him and sometimes wrote explicitly the things I wanted to do to him—all filth.

He took them all and read them and kept them till I got caught by the adults, and his parents met with my parents, but that wasn't what stopped me; it was because just before the meeting, he returned a couple of my previous letters along with a letter he wrote me telling me not to write to him anymore, so I stopped. I got caught because whenever I couldn't get the letters to him myself, because I didn't see him, I would use his little brother to deliver them to him. He was specifically chosen from among his other siblings because I knew he wouldn't be able to read them because they were cursive letters (he was about five years old). But one morning this poor little boy, who was being so used, jumped up out of his sleep afraid that he wouldn't be able to get a letter delivered before his brother left for work. Freshly awakened from this nightmare I had caused him, he kept repeating, "I have to give him the letter. I have to give him the letter." So his dad/uncle, also our pastor, took that letter, then asked his brother about any other letters, and he gave them all to him. His dad/uncle (he was raising his brother's kids) kept them in his briefcase for months maybe even years after, which I thought at the time was very strange, and my siblings and I thought it was perhaps sick of him, but now I think he did that for evidence and protection of his son, because I was a minor.

At the time his dad did have a talk with me. He was gentle and caring, and I appreciated him for that, because my mom said vicious things to me. He let me know that if I wasn't so young it would be OK, but because of my age, what I wanted could not be, and he schooled me on the jail bait issue that I was unaware of.

I never stopped loving him for a moment, but I kept it to myself. After almost a year he started coming by the house regularly to drop off and pick up Big Sis' boyfriend, and each time I would say only hello or goodbye, then out of the clear blue he started calling me. He asked me out and we went out to a very R-rated movie, and soon after, a friend of ours (Big Sis' boyfriend) reminded us of the illegal aspect of things, so we spoke and broke it off, but only for maybe a couple of weeks.

He started calling me again, and I wasn't about to say no. I had waited for him over two years. At fourteen years old, we began a secret relationship, calling each other and talking for hours at a time, falling asleep on the phone many times because neither of us wanted to hang up, but sometimes deliberately because that was a way for us to spend the night together. Whoever woke up first in the morning would hang up because we hated to hang up in each other's ears and would count to three then both hang up, and sometimes neither of us would, and we would count again. Off and on for the first year or so, he told me he loved me, but eventually we both knew it was a lie or no longer true, so he stopped telling me.

A few months into our relationship, about a week before his twenty-first birthday, he asked me if I would be with him sexually for his birthday gift. I told him I would think about it and I did, and decided I loved him enough to do that for him and that I was ready. (In thinking about it now, I realize why it was not a heart-wrenching decision for me. Intimacy had already been introduced to me, and it was all ugly and shameful. This was beautiful, this was love, this I truly wanted, never contemplating the sin of it.)

While on the phone with him another day, I reminded him of his request and told him the answer was yes. He was very exited. I gave myself to him on March 21, 1984 at fourteen years old, and carried on with him doing sinful things right under the adults' noses, and at times in the very presence of them.

There was a time when he got sick, and I had been with him the night before. When they took him to the doctor, he was diagnosed with hepatitis and treated. The doctor asked him to name who needed to be checked, and he also named me. No one understood what was going on, but I was checked and cleared (covered, though filthy with sin). The doctor did ask me plainly about our relationship, but I denied it.

A while later he impregnated the girl he was with before me and still saw occasionally, so his family made him marry her. There was also another after me, with me, until his marriage, I believe, but we never left each other because I had lain down all of who I was for this man, receiving abuse in a different form and seeking after it again by allowing it and remaining with him, never telling him no.

We would break up a lot, at times for long periods but always went back together; me for love, him for sex. He didn't love me, but he loved sex with me, and I justified my adultery by telling myself that I was in love with him before she *made* him marry her, so the relationship went on for almost a year after.

That relationship really messed me up. I cared about nothing else but him and was suffering in silence because I was keeping yet another secret. No one knew about us or could know about us. Big Sis and her boyfriend knew a little but couldn't admit to it because they found out by reading my diaries. I found this out because my diaries weren't the way I left them.

Big Sis and I had brief words, I let her know I was aware of what she did, then I destroyed them, and to this day have never kept another because of that. I stopped caring about myself and my own life and thought of hurting myself just enough to put myself in the hospital where he worked and fantasized about him coming to see me and how sorry he would be for the way he was treating me.

After I had convinced myself that it may work to bring him closer to me, I prayed not to lose my life, then I did a half job of trying to bring this about by taking about six to twelve regular-strength Tylenol, which was all I could gather at the time. I took them with milk of all things, which I later figured may have caused my mucosa/intestinal lining to be coated and prevented much absorption (among other things, milk produces mucus).

I could have been really sick or lost my life over what I realize now to be nonsense, when all I had to do was hold on for a brighter day, which did come. I thank God now that He said, "No, I will not allow this. I have plans for you."

Because of my inner turmoil, I started skipping school a lot so I wouldn't have to be around people and be forced to smile and be pleasant when I didn't want to.

One day about two years after this, I was at work at McDonald's after school, and this boy from school, Eric, who was in one of my classes, came in and asked me if a boy I had asked him to give my number to (they hung out together) had called me (he had not, he only wanted to mess with me in class but not for anything else). He asked me a few questions about myself and why I didn't like to come to school. I told him the truth the best I could explain it, and on a couple of occasions after that while speaking to me, teasingly, he called me "the girl who didn't like people," but the fact is I just didn't like myself.

Once I was at school, I was OK most times. Sometimes I had fun and got very good grades, including A's—quite something for someone who didn't study and didn't care. The problem was just getting myself there, gearing myself up to face the world. At other times I would just sit in class and daydream of him or stare out the window at the hospital where he worked (if I could see it) and think about him; having roses delivered to him on his job because I could not send them to his home, for his wife was there, and wondering if he had yet received them; longing to get out of school so I could hear from him and be with him. I skipped so many days they were about to put me back into the ninth grade, but they had a meeting and talked with me and my mom, and they told her I was "severely depressed." In order for me to move on to the 10th grade, they told her to put me into counseling and I made up the days and work in summer school.

I saw someone for a couple of months, and she told me point blank I had to break it off with him, so every time he called, I would tell him I just wanted us to be friends, and he would say, "What's with the friends thing?" I would just repeat that, but I had a great weakness for him, and he knew it, so each time he came and got me, I would go with him. He knew I just wanted to spend time with him, so he used one of these times to blackmail me by telling me if I didn't give myself to him, he wouldn't stay with me; he would go home. So I gave in just so he would stay, but the desire for him left me right then. [Looking back, in that moment when he demanded my body by blackmail, in essence forcing himself on me, it was to me no longer my choice for him to have me. He was then, to me, as one of my molesters, so I instantly lost my desire for him.] That was the last time I ever let him have me.

I was already starting to turn from him because after we were intimate, at times he would say things such as, "Thank you so much, you don't know what you're doing for me, because of this, I feel like I can go home to her." I was in no way complimented. It was very clear by his treatment of me that he had no respect for me. I felt intensely and immensely used and was praying for God to rescue me, and that last night just pushed me over the edge away from him.

When I saw the counselor after that episode, I told her about it but was ashamed, so I left out the part where I gave in to him. I also told her I didn't love him anymore, but that was not true, and she knew it couldn't be. I believed it when I said it, because I was newly pumped full of strength and joy in escaping, but soon came to realize that it was only the desire and not the love for him that left me.

Soon after, maybe about two weeks, the counselor had to transfer, and I didn't want anyone else in my head. I was also relieved of her transfer because I had another secret I had to bury. The old demon of perversion was raising its head to oppress me toward her because of my brokenness and the attachment I felt in telling her these deep feelings, but again those attacks of the enemy were suppressed. It took me a while to be truly close to someone male or female, my age or old, without that feeling of a sexual nature rising up in me: this is the perverse demon I speak of, who didn't know nor respect boundaries with my elders or those put in charge of me. The sickness that infected me when my molester and attempted rapist attacked me and did not respect their boundaries with me.

I fought with the love of this man for almost another two years, calling him and hanging up just to hear his voice at times, then other times I would speak, but I never gave in sexually. Through tears and prayer, I finally gained victory. We really became friends during and after this time.

He moved out of state with his wife and daughter, and we still used to call each other a lot, just to talk, and I would give him some marital advice or just listen. We were still doing this in secret because no one knew we had anything to do with each other, but then there started to be rumors of our phone calls by a family member of his wife who lived with my mom with whom I was sharing my room. One night she came home from work and I quickly said good-bye to him, but she heard me and carried the news and added to it, so we talked and mutually decided that even though we now had nothing to hide, to prevent trouble, it wasn't best to keep speaking, so we stopped calling each other. I don't know how she knew who I was speaking with because I never said his name; I think she snooped on my phone and saw his number.

While I was still battling my love for him, I had continued skipping school and got a lot of incompletes and was left back in the tenth grade. It was about to happen again when my guidance counselor, Ms Parker, called me into her office. She met with me and gave me my options, then advised me to sign out of school and take the GED. I then signed out one week later, signed up for the GED program, and got my GED the week I turned eighteen years old; at about the same year and time my classmates graduated.

I fell for my sister in law's brother when I was eighteen years old. He was seven and a half years older than I was. By the time I was seventeen years old I had left the church, although I had been raised in church all my life. I started hanging out and going to parties. I now had a clique of friends, good friends, some of which I still have today. I don't keep in touch, but when we see each other, the friendship is still there. All Jamaicans like me; we even worked together. We all went out to house parties and clubs, and it was at a house party where his younger sister introduced us. [Thank you, Cindy. I loved him so deeply and do not regret that.]

Soon after we met, whenever we were out, we would dance only with or mostly with each other. Then one night at a house party he walked up to me, took me into his arms without speaking, even saying hello, or asking if I wanted to dance, and he buried his face into my neck and shoulder area. The way he held me was different. Something in him had changed. He clung to me tightly like he needed me to save him from something he was feeling. He danced about three songs with me never letting me go between songs. After the last song he left me and said he would be back, but he never came back again the rest of the party, and most of us didn't leave till morning.

From there my feelings came into existence and developed and surpassed his. Everyone that knew us, which were basically most of the Jamaicans in the area, knew I was desperately in love with him and at times used to tease us in fun, but his feelings were not returned to me publicly. I had been in love with him almost a year when I told him as we danced at another house party. He told me he felt the same, and we left the party together and spent the rest of the morning till afternoon (checkout time) together in a motel but were not sexual (he knew I was not on birth control). We just slept in each other's arms. Another night we went back to his home (his grandmother's house) so we could be intimate, but before we were, we sat and talked a while, and he asked me if I would have his baby, and I said no, that I didn't want one right then. (In my confusion, when I was fourteen, I had wanted one but had moved past that desire.) He told me right then that if I didn't have his baby, he would not make me his girlfriend. I didn't give in to the baby idea, but I still wanted him. We then went into the bed and again he held me in his arms and we slept. Very early in the morning we both woke up filled with desire and did what we had both yearned for so long to do, but as we made love, he deliberately tried to impregnate me. He made no apologies and I didn't fuss with him about it because if he'd succeeded I would have kept it.

This thing with him was a great struggle—trying to get him to admit and show publicly what he said and felt privately. I never succeeded, but while he was in Florida, he used to talk to Lisa about me (someone I thought was a friend, but was not), and on occasions she brought me in on her three-way line (because she had her own agenda for my new friend—now my son's father) and let me hear as he told her how he loved and cared about me.

I had this male friend, Dwight, who kept telling me he was a lost cause, to move on, but I let him listen in on my three-way line during one of these conversations, and he, too, heard the professions of love for me and was shocked, because it never matched his public treatment of me. I truly believe he did love me, but he just meant what he said, no baby—no him. [In truth I don't know why Lisa did that, trying to encourage me toward him, because they were messing around. I don't know when it started or ended but I know it happened: I have a videotape of a function at the Tavern, a bar/club where we were regulars, and the camera caught them dancing with other partners while staring at each other longingly. Truth will always reveal itself.]

One night, I went to see him at his grandmother's house, and he refused to see me by sending his grandmother out to tell me things. I was angry and wanted to hurt him, and I figured out how. I wrote him a letter saying the reason I had wanted to see him that night was to tell him I was pregnant with his baby, but since he refused to see me, I aborted it.

Telling him this was vicious and hurt him more than was necessary, more than I planned, and a lot more than I wanted to. He cried on more than one occasion and probably severely as he read my words. He tried to speak to me about it one night at the club, but I walked away and wouldn't listen. He had tears in his eyes, and his voice trembled when he spoke. My heart repented for doing that to him. I couldn't let him go on thinking this and go on hurting, so I wrote him another letter telling him the truth that I was never pregnant, that I said it only because he hurt me that night, and I begged him to forgive me, that I never meant to hurt him that way or make him cry. I don't know that he ever really did forgive me because neither of us ever mentioned it again.

It's now at this time I am thinking how I devastated him, because a baby was all he wanted and dreamed of and wished for, and to this day, I don't know of him having one. That was extreme cruelty toward him, and if my love for him was not a sick love, and a love not given by God, I wouldn't have thought to do or have done that to him.

When he had moved to Florida he told me not to worry, that he would come back for me. Then he would barely accept my phone calls and would at times hang up on me, yet I remained faithful to him. For the second time, my heart was in ruin. It took years again to recover, but this time I wasn't alone, because my new friend/my son's father, who was seven years older than I was came along. There were always other men trying to get at me, and some even really cared, but I wasn't interested. Then I was tired of the man I loved pushing me away and though I wasn't ready for another love, I needed attention. I was totally honest with my new friend that my heart was taken, that the man I loved was out of state, and that he had his family watching me. My new friend didn't believe me, but I proved it to him a few times, and whenever the one I loved would hurt me deeply, like hanging up on me on my birthday, I would repay him.

When I went out to the club, I would take my new friend into a lighted area of the club, where all the watchmen could see, and kiss my new friend and snuggle with him just to cause the one I loved the same pain I was feeling. My new friend knew my purpose, because I told him, but he didn't care, because he wanted me. He deliberately took up the challenge to pursue me to win me away from the man I loved (as he later admitted) and after a few months he got my body, but not my whole heart, which he desperately wanted. At times I felt like I loved my new friend and told him I did, but I didn't, not with the passion he deserved. I treated him terribly in public at times. I never truly appreciated the wonderful, loving man he was to me, so he got tired of me hurting him and cheating on him always with my heart and once with my body with the man I loved. I would have left my new friend in a minute if the man I loved would have treated me right. I was hearing things about the man I loved that displeased me. I guess when teased by the guys, maybe about losing me to my son's father, he would say things like, "I can have her anytime I want." Though it was essentially true, I hated that he was going around saying that, blatantly disrespecting my son's father and me also.

One night, my new friend and I argued and broke up as we usually did, because every single time we argued, I would use it to break up with him. Partly because of my insecurities [and that hidden issue in me] and because I didn't know how to be in a real relationship, this time he didn't come "crawling back" (as Jamaicans say) like he usually did, and I let him go by not going to him either. He then tried to hurt me however he could and tried to interfere when I moved on with someone else, though he had a girlfriend whom he admittedly got to make me jealous. I wasn't jealous, and that hurt him even more.

I secretly despised him. I guess I blamed him for cutting off any chance of the relationship thing I had before him with the man I loved, because we were seen out together a lot, even by the guy I loved who came back to town from Florida without my knowledge. I heard he came back for me, but I don't believe it. The man I loved saw my new friend and I together in a men's store as we both exited the dressing room stall where I was helping him to try on clothes. What kind of sick and twisted coincidence was this? Out of all the stores in this very large mall (Sea View Square Mall), on this day at this moment in time, there he was. This man I loved so very much, who was supposed to be out of state, was standing there with his brother (who at times would help me by telling me what to do concerning him) and his cousin—two who were set to watch me. In their eyes I was caught and guilty, all eyes on me. The thing is, at that time I wasn't yet physically unfaithful, but it sure looked like it, and there was nothing I could say or do, so I didn't even try.

All this and more were in me against my new friend, this innocent man. All through our two-year relationship, I held the man I loved over his head, torturing him emotionally in the worst ways. I gave him no stability, no security, no comfort, no safety. I let him feel I had no need of or use for him. [That hidden issue from the childhood violations caused this; him being the first and only person that wanted me that I allowed to have me. Though I allowed him to have me, I treated him vile, like he was one of them because that hidden issue in me viewed him as though he was coming at me.] Then other times, though I hated him, I had a very strong attachment to him because he loved me, and I wanted him around, so I would bathe him in honey, trapping him, because he knew the sweetest, most caring side of me. [No doubt these were the times I felt I was losing him, so in these times I chose him and went after him and when I felt I had secured him, the sick cycle repeated itself.]

He was everything I wanted in a man and he treated me the way I wanted to be treated. Loving me beyond measure and showing it and saying it with unconditional love, though most times I treated him worse than a dog. I can't even say that, because people treat their dogs very well. I treated him worse than garbage. As I write, I realize that though he was everything I was looking for, I just didn't want it from him, and that fact probably aided my hatred for him. He just couldn't win with me.

One of the nights we broke up, we had an argument that was probably my fault because I used to pick fights with him when my hatred for him flared up. So, we argued outside in front of my gate, and he wanted to leave, but I held the keys and wouldn't let him go. I got up in his face, one of many times. I guess subconsciously I was trying to make him hit me so I would have a reason to injure him. This time, he mushed my face and pushed me hard out of his face; his thumb caught me in my eye, which later when checked, the doctor told me I had several broken blood vessels —I did hold it over his head, making him feel very guilty until my eyeball healed. He was very angry, the force he pushed me with was unexpected and I lost my balance and fell on all fours. I immediately got up and attacked him, but he wouldn't hit me as he had told me he did in previous relationships. He walked away from me up the street, and I followed him, walking behind him, cursing and taunting him all the way, calling him names with four-letter words. I followed behind him about two blocks to the main street, then he stopped and stooped down on the sidewalk with his head in his hand and cried and endured my abuse as tears ran down his face.

When I saw his tears, my heart felt it, but all my rage from my past years were coming out on this poor, innocent man whose only crime was loving me. I knew what I was doing, but couldn't seem to stop myself. After I was done, I looked at him, and seeing how I had hurt him and not knowing what to say, I reached out and touched his hand, moving it away from his head while making a wisecrack; as he looked up at me with the tears in his eyes, my heart melted for his pain, so I stroked and caressed his head, and he allowed me to touch him and comfort him that way.

I must have told him I was sorry, I believe I kissed and held him. We got up and went back down the street. I believe we sat in the car and talked, and for the first time ever he said, "You know, I think you might lose me, I don't want it to happen, but I think you might." I don't remember what my response was because I half didn't care and I didn't believe it anyway. I'm sure I sweet-talked him though, then I let him go. Yet that was not the end of us, and yet he loved and wanted me. Why? Because he had seen and experienced that sweet-as-honey side of me and couldn't lose hope, but he couldn't have my whole heart, because I was broken inside. I wasn't healed, and was still looking for the wrong thing, [Again that hidden issue, wanting who I couldn't have and discarding who I could have], wanting what God didn't want me to have, though we weren't meant to be either.

We broke up. In essence, he left me, but I guess the love he carried for me in his heart sought to protect me, so he kept telling people that I left him and I would say it was mutual. When it actually happened, neither of us really said I'm leaving; I guess we argued and neither of us came after the other. Then, he got someone to make me jealous and it backfired; that truly ended us as boyfriend/girlfriend; I moved on also, though he hated it. So, she slid from the back to the front and me vice versa, as the occasional sex continued; also, the expectation that we would eventually get back together continued in both of us for years with a few attempts to make it happen. At the time we broke up, we shared the same car, and he would take me to work. At that time, I had finished training-school and was a Data-Entry Clerk with the census bureau. He would keep the car, then pick me up and take me home because we worked in the same town, then we would take turns with the car. This was the routine, but when we broke up, to punish me, he would tell me he wasn't coming back to pick me up from work, and a couple of times he didn't. I had no other way to get home and a cab would cost me about ten dollars for a one-way trip.

So, I used sex. I started having sex with him again. He did what I needed him to, when I needed him to, because he believed I cared about him again, but it was only a weapon for me. I put no value in it because of my past that he didn't know about. I also told him what I thought he wanted to hear. In my confusion, sometimes I really believed it because the words were so convincing as I said them, though the sensible me knew it was a lie. The fact that there was no real, loving emotion involved on my part and that this was what it took to get him to act on my behalf made me hate him so much more. At times I hated his touch with every fiber of my being, but I allowed it and wished for it to be over. [It is clear to me now, though he wasn't because he was my man, and I did willingly allowed him to touch me in those times, still, because of that hidden issue, it was as if he was violating me.]

While I was hating him, because to me, it was taking sex to get him to do right by me, he was there with the thought of "she loves me," because to him, it wasn't just sex, he believed me to be making love to him. He knew me to a certain extent that I never allow anyone to touch me unless there are real feelings there. So in a sense he was right that it was love, but there was also hate, and though he didn't know it, in those moments there was more hate than love. It was during this time that I conceived our son. I knew the exact moment it happened, thinking back I believe it was a deliberate action on his part because in the two years we had been together he had never done what he did that day, which I expressly asked him not to do. I got up and angrily accused and cursed at him, he gave me a fake apology but I didn't believe him. I walked out of my room half naked still cursing at him, meeting my little sister, Denise, in the hall; I went into the bathroom and slammed the door. While in the bathroom I calmed down because some part of me really didn't care that he did that, even though in that very moment I knew what the end result would be because I knew I was ovulating—and so it was. Over the next couple of months I watched for and was aware of the changes in my body and my heightened senses. I knew I was pregnant, so I chose better more nutritious foods and protected my stomach and avoided all activities (like roller skating down that steep driveway and hill at my house) that would cause me to lose it.

When I believed I was far enough along I went and picked up an at-home test kit. On my way to the register to pay for it I ran into my friend Aisha and could not escape without her seeing what I was buying. She told me to come to her house and we would take it there and we could hang out with her son, so I said OK and we went straight there. I went into her bathroom and took the test and when it was time I was nervous so I sent her to look. When she confirmed it, she then asked "what are you going to do?" I was filled with joy but I had to pretend not to be. I lay on her couch and looked sad, then I did get a little scared because though I wanted him and was mentally ready for him, I was twenty-one years old, I had nothing and was still living with my mother.

Ever since I was a kid, I heard her say that if anyone gets pregnant they had to get out, and I believed her, so I couldn't let anyone see me happy, but God knew my heart. When I confirmed a week or two later by a doctor that I was pregnant, I was three months along. I had already stopped having sex completely with my son's father and was for almost two months into a new communication with Earl, a man I really liked. He used to call me daily, but it had to end even before it got started. I called him and told him I was pregnant, and that I was ending our communications.

I called the man I was still in love with, who by now had moved back to town from Florida, and told him I was pregnant so he wouldn't hear it from someone else. *Now*, he wanted to be with me. I didn't think it would look right, so I told him that and he said, "OK, then after you have the baby," and I said "OK." But, now I was considering getting an apartment for all three of us—me, the baby, and the baby's dad—because I told myself, "I will learn to love him," so I started sleeping with him again.

Then one day I asked God earnestly in prayer for a sign if I was supposed to be with this man (the father) or not, and days later I found out by personal evidence that his girlfriend was also pregnant at the same time, but she had lost the baby, so for me that was God's answer. "No!" I didn't break it off with him immediately though; I stopped having sex with him at about six months along.

Body

I hadn't told him I was pregnant till I was four months along and contemplated never telling him, letting him think it wasn't his. But he suspected my pregnancy because I started showing, and he tried to feel my stomach. When I did tell him, I was angry at him because of the evidence I had found, so I presented it saying I wanted an abortion, but in no way did I mean it. I had already been to the mall and bought a pair of baby shoes in anticipation. I just wanted the money out of him because at the time he owed me quite a few hundred dollars, $1,500 to be exact, that I lent him to put into his car instead of getting another for myself. After an accident where a truck rammed into my back while stuck at a stoplight, I received a very small payout from their insurance company, and since we were together and always in each other's company, I decided that my car could wait, but now he wouldn't pay me back because I had hurt him and wasn't with him.

Even though I didn't love him, he was the only one I was with sexually during the years, but he didn't know that because I had moved on emotionally, so he asked me if the baby was his, and I slapped him across the face because I thought, *How dare he ask or even wonder such a thing? He knows I can't stand his guts. Why would I even speak to him if it wasn't his?* From being with me, he knew I wasn't cheap. Misguided emotionally, but never cheap. Not just anyone could have me, there had to be some love, and when I decided they could, they had to wait a while, no less than three months, but always more, and he knew this.

I use to care for this sweet little paralyzed teenage girl who I had brought him to meet; on another day he took me by there for some reason, maybe to pick up my check, and while we were in the car he asked me if I was really pregnant and told me that he didn't want another child—he already had two back in Jamaica. I don't know if he was testing me or not (knowing that his actions on the day I conceived were deliberate), but I knew he had or could come up with the money, so I told him to give me the money and I would go have the abortion, intending to pocket the money. He never gave me the money. I kept asking and he said no, he wasn't going to give it to me.

We started attending Lamaze classes together, but I just couldn't stand him and was treating him roughly, and he wasn't crazy about it either, and that just annoyed me more, so we stopped going. On weekends he used to come by my window at two and three a.m., calling me outside to meet his friends and family from out of state. Sometimes he came by himself, slightly inebriated from a party, because he said he couldn't go home without seeing me. With the fear I already had of spirits, occasionally it was spooky to be awakened and see him standing out there in the dark and calling my name. Once I was so spooked, I poked angrily through the screen at his face and he looked at me like I was insane, then we talked and he left. He told me years later how sometimes when he would come by my window, I would be sleeping, and he would watch me from the window as I lay sleeping with the stethoscope still in my ears that I was using to listen to the baby inside me. He was glad there was that attachment between us (he deliberately made it happen), but I wasn't. I wanted *only* my baby, not him or the attachment.

There were three major incidents where I could have lost my baby. First, when I was about six months along, I was placed on bed rest because of a high-risk pregnancy, but I needed money, so I hid the fact that I was pregnant from this agency and sought work. I left this agency and was locating our job sites with a family friend because she insisted we go at that time instead of another day. While double-checking the directions, my inattentiveness caused me not to notice that a stoplight had just changed, and I went straight through the red light. I caused a car to come slamming into my passenger-side front, which totaled the car. There was a police car in the stopped traffic on the other side, so help came quickly. We told them we were OK, but I told them that I was pregnant, which shocked the family friend, but I didn't care that she knew. I just wanted my baby safe.

They got us both in an ambulance and rushed me to the hospital and did an ultrasound. Again covered, the baby was fine. I called the father from the hospital and thought he would be mad about the car, but he was only concerned with me and the baby. I stayed home and rested after that.

Second, when I was about eight months along, I was eating and had a choking episode. My airway became fully occluded. As I tried to breathe, my chest felt like it would cave in. I rushed to the room of my little teenage sister, Denise (an adopted cousin), for help but she was frightened and didn't know what to do. As she ran to the phone to call for help, it was just me and God. I banged my back up against the wall by her door in the hallway and God rescued me by allowing that plug of food to pass down my throat. Within that minute I was able to draw in the most appreciated breath I had ever breathed till that day, and I was thankful to Him. I then called to Denise who was still on the phone and let her know I was OK. Turns out she had called my sister-in-law for help and not 911.

Third, after our son was born, the night after I brought him home, at three a.m. I noticed he had a breathing problem. Satan began his attack on the baby to steal his breath and life. I sought help from family and called the hospital pediatrician, but none believed, understood, or could help, they all believed I was just a nervous mom. I was worried, seeing these repeated attacks, not understanding them myself, watching. The second day during a feeding, I noticed that he stopped breathing again. This time was different; it wasn't correcting itself. He was fully conscious and squirming around, he just wasn't breathing. I turned him over just in case he was choking, but he wasn't. I blew gently into his face, hoping to stimulate him to breathe, but it wasn't working. So, I grabbed the phone and dialed 911, then I held him with one hand under his back and head, and the other hand under his bottom and lifted him above my head and begged God for his life. Then he let out the loudest, hardest, most piercing scream, and I thanked God as he screamed, for he would not be quieted for a minute or two.

The ambulance crew entered the house while he screamed. That was the fastest response I have ever seen, though we lived only five minutes away from the hospital. He was admitted and spent one and a half weeks in the hospital, where I basically lived that whole time, in the neonatal intensive care unit (NICU).

My baby was diagnosed with apnea. They told me he was fine, but his medical records later revealed that he continued to have these episodes while there. It was difficult to see him with all those tubes inside him, but I was strong for him. When he was released, he had to drink thickened formula and wear a monitor with a sensor strapped around his chest for three months. I watched him like a hawk with many sleepless nights watching his chest rise and fall. During my pregnancy his dad and I agreed that should the baby be a boy he would name him and if it be a girl I would name her (I had chosen - Kendra Alicia Green). Though His dad named him Paul II, which was his legal name of record, during this time of his deliverance from death is when God gave me the name Sean for him, it means '*given by God*'. I took it for his nickname because I didn't want to offend his father and I truly didn't understand the gravity of the call and blessing of God Himself giving you a new name. No one took to that name easily, but Sean is who he is. So, when he turned 18 he went to court and had it legally changed; not to offend or hurt his father in any way but only to answer yes to his God.

Taking care of my son Sean intently was when I got over the man I was in love with. I was just so in love with my baby, I didn't think about that man anymore and never contacted him. I stopped going out about two months before I had the baby except for when the baby was a little over three months old. My mom kept him, and I went out on the night of my birthday at which time I saw the man I had loved and still had feelings for. We wanted to be together, but we were kept apart because my girlfriend was fighting with her boyfriend. He had hit her and she needed us (me and the girl group), so I made her a priority. We stayed with her outside the house party the whole time in case he came back. The guy I wanted to be with came outside to get me, but I told him I couldn't come in yet, that I would be there as soon as I could, but then we all (the girl group) left. That was our very last attempt at a relationship and the very last time I desired it.

I wanted to raise my baby in church, so I started taking my baby to church at two months old after he was christened, then I started to love God. I discussed it with my pastor, the same one I had left at 17 years old, then I gave my life to God in baptism one afternoon in June 1991, after a young powerful woman of God preached in Paterson, New Jersey, at my then-headquarters church at age twenty-two.

The Holy Ghost came to me that very evening after my baptism as I sat in church, but I resisted Him as He attempted to worship God through me. I literally held my lips and tongue together forcefully as He tried to speak, because I was embarrassed to shout hallelujah as it came up from my belly and entered into my mouth. I smothered Him from within me because I held the baby in my arms, and I feared what would happen if I gave in. Also being embarrassed to be stared at, I looked around me to make sure no one saw or heard the muffle of my encounter with God. I could tell then, by the way God dealt with me, that He had something great in store.

I found myself fasting a lot and for long periods. He spoke to me and gave me prophetic dreams concerning myself and situations. He answered promptly when I was in need of Him. He started me writing His words even then, though to me they were for other reasons, but He spoke into me as I wrote assignments given by the pastor—exhortations. He was grooming me, but I knew it not.

I was having a terrible affliction that would cause me excruciating abdominal pain and vomiting along with other things at times after I ate. My mom tried all the remedies she knew of during these episodes, and so did I. Some things would work till the next episode, and other times I would only vomit up what was given. But, one day while in the bathroom after vomiting much, I was weak and still in such great pain that I could not stand up straight. I had enough, and so I turned to God. I laid one hand on myself where the pain was and lifted the other hand to Him, and I prayed for healing, and He granted that healing through me and in me. The pain and vomiting left me that very moment before I left the bathroom. I thanked Him and worshiped Him, and it has never to this day returned, eternally healed.

Many other things He did and wanted to do concerning me in Him, beloved of Him, as His children are, but I fell and didn't truly rise to my feet for twelve years. Now I stand firm in Him.

So, then I asked Him to remove the hatred I had developed for my two other sisters, Carla and Denise, who were also living there. They had banded together and I felt they hated me, so I hated them more, but God cleaned that out of me, and I loved them and dealt with them differently than I had. Then, I asked God to remove the deep hatred that was in me for my son's father. I hated him so much, I could never look at him, hear his voice, or his name called, and God answered. There was nothing hindering between us. I was pure and He was dealing well with me. Then I looked away in lust and fell.

God did such a mighty work in me, removing that hatred for my son's father from me, for it was very deep, and I saw him differently, even loved him for who he was. He will always be in my heart, because I came to respect him as a person. I say this now for all to know, because though I have felt this way for a while now, I continued to let everyone think I still hated this man and that he was the villain, when it was the private pain and torture I gave him that caused in him the reactions they saw, making them think he was "a no good" who didn't care. All those years he only loved me deeper and purer than any man ever had. I put him through a world of emotional abuse and treated him like scum under my shoes, and he loved me still. I hurt him with a deepness that I don't think he will ever trust or love that way again, and he has admitted this.

Years later I wrote him a letter from my heart and a deep apology for the things I did, and the good things I remembered about him and us and that I loved him, and I did. I truly believed it with all that was in me, with all that I was capable of loving anyone at that time—I did love him. I told him to sit and read it, then I left him alone, and he did. When he was through, he ran upstairs and burst open my room door and stood there and stared at me. He was too overwhelmed to speak to me face to face, so he ran out the door, rushed home, and called me on the phone. That was when it impacted me the great extent of the pain I had caused him, and I forgave him for all he did or didn't do concerning our son. Though it was not acceptable, I understood why he behaved that way. He could do a lot better, but he's more responsible now.

For a while I thought he was my soul mate, because he just wouldn't quit loving me no matter how I behaved. Each time I needed that unconditional love and acceptance, though we were with someone else, I tugged at his heart strings to see if he still loved me, and he did. I was so insecure with every man that I was with, except him, and always turned to him when my insecurities became too great, because I could always be myself with him, no pretense. I was at ease with him, he knew the worst of me, yet to him I was beautiful always. He saw no wrong or admitted no wrong in me. I needed and wanted him to love me. He was my safe place to run to, where I drank of the strength of his love for me. Me gaining strength and him being drained and bruised. Then I would just run away or run back to the arms of someone who had no good use for me.

One year his parents came for a visit with him, and I picked them up to spend time with them, because even though I was too broken to allow us to be happy, I loved his parents and would do anything for them. They're passed on now, and I loved them so much and I miss them, but I wept for their souls, because they were beautiful, kind, sweet people who were not direct participants of the world, but I think they died outside of God, but I pray I am wrong. I know they loved Him. For their souls' sake, my heart so desires that they are both in His arms. [They are in Heaven with Him now.]

At least five years had passed since our relationship, and his father told me one day that his son—my son's father—was still in love with me, and as soon as his father began to speak on this, then his mother joined in and agreed, and they both wanted to know why we were not together and asked if I cared about him at all. I knew they spoke the truth. I knew he loved me, and everyone else around me knew it, too. It could be seen in him, and maybe also in the way he spoke of me.

For many years after we had been broken up, whenever anyone was speaking of him, to distinguish him from the other men in our group with his name, they referred to him as mine, so whomever they were speaking to would know that they were speaking of him, and somewhere in me I still liked that.

Anyway, I decided to make him say that he loved me. No longer being able to utter the word love was an issue he developed because of my abuse of him. He swore to himself that he would never utter those words ever again to anyone. I told him what his parents said and asked him if it was true, and he said, "What difference will it make?"

I said, "You never know. Is it true?" He didn't answer, so I said, "Is it?"

He said, "OK! Yes, you happy now? Yes, it's true."

I knew that was the best I would get out of him, so I told him I was giving him six months to think about it and decide if he wanted us to get married (a decision someone else had asked me to make previously), that I couldn't make him any promises, but I would try. Neither of us realized it at the time, but heartbreak was written all over that statement.

He was so happy, he grabbed our son Sean and swung him around and hugged him and said, "Did you hear what your mom said? Did you hear what your mom said?"

I meant it, but I clearly wasn't ready, and it certainly was not God's plan. I let the time pass and never mentioned it again or followed through on it. On another occasion years later, I proposed to him in a letter with all the vows written out that a preacher would ask you to repeat—vowing and binding myself to him, and he accepted and wore the token of my proposal—binding himself to me, but again I didn't acknowledge or follow through. He must have been so hurt again and again.

Another five years passed of tugging and releasing at his heart strings, then in the end, I decided to settle down with him because I thought, *Who else will love me like that so unconditionally?* I also believed being with me would make him a better father and I wanted my son to have his father. So I talked myself into loving him. When I allowed myself to remember, I did always love his lips, the way he held me, and being in his arms. It was a broken love because I was not whole but the love was real. I measure and judge the truth of being in love by searching myself to know if I would give my life to save that person and if the answer is "yes" then I know the love is real and has been sealed by my heart. For a moment in time I felt that for him so I wrote that letter of proposal. I decided to give him for the rest of his life the love and care and respect and honor he deserved from me, and I told him this, and he wanted this. He had his faults, but none I couldn't live with, but by then I had yanked his chain so much, though he loved me and wanted me, he had no trust in me whatsoever. [I recall once when he came over to my place while we were together, he slid his arms under my pillows, feeling and checking; he didn't know that I saw him because I never confronted him about it. But, this is how much he distrusted me, that he thought I would harm him in *any* way.] Even at this time I showed him no consistency with my love, ignoring him terribly at times, as I did when he wore the token of my proposal, not one word or acknowledgment of him accepting and wearing it, proving my insecure and broken love. I didn't even pay attention to know when he stopped wearing it and how it must have hurt him to take it off. He was afraid it wouldn't work, and he would be alone, something he seems to fear badly, and I saw it, so I released my hold on him because I didn't want to hurt him anymore.

He is married now, and I feel a sense of relief, because though I had released him years ago, for as long as he loved me and stayed unwed, I would have wondered if with him was where I should be, but his marriage cut that string forever, and I am grateful for my sake and his, because never was it meant to be. It wasn't a thing authorized by God, as He did tell me when I was four to six months pregnant and asked Him, though my insecurities and loneliness of heart would drive me to disobedience, taking so long to let it go.

In November 2003 God led me to make peace with his wife for all the turmoil and pain I caused her as his girlfriend over the years by giving her no thought, and to let her know that I really and truly didn't and don't hate her, though I treated her like I did. God quenched the love that was as burning hot coals between us and broke the bonds with which we had bound ourselves to each other. I also prayed diligently for peace and healing to his heart from the effects of my abuse of him. Our son was purposed to be through us but we were not purposed to be one. I believe now that through her, God gave him the love he needed, they were purposed to be one, and I have now included them in my prayers, that God will bless them and it is already done. He gave them the son He showed me in visions, so before I was told, I had seen that beautiful little one. God always opens up the womb as a sign of blessing, and so, He blessed that union. I also now love them both, and want nothing but good for them as a couple and a family; I am praying for their souls and I believe God for that too. This complete love God has placed in me is an awesome thing, "Thank You Jesus."

When I was twenty-four years old, I started seeing a man I had loved for almost two years. My mom used to bring me along with them everywhere they went, and something about him attracted me, and I fell for him, so I tried to kill the feelings. Whenever they were going anywhere, I would make excuses to my mom why I couldn't go, so I didn't go out with them anymore.

Then after almost a year, I was told that he made some repeated, lewd, unclean remarks to someone close to me, and this sickened me about him, and because this disgusted me, I tried even harder to forget him, but the feelings wouldn't leave me and later on grew stronger. This was an adulterous relationship. From the very first moment I felt the attraction, I fought it, but my feelings got only stronger till I could no longer hide it. He saw it every time I looked at him. I couldn't look him in the eyes anymore. I don't know how no one else could see it. I guess my prayers weren't earnest enough, but I begged and pleaded with God, and He wouldn't hear me and wasn't responding. I guess He left me to my filthy nature because I didn't resist hard enough.

This man asked me to come to his office one night, and I knew he knew, but what would he say? I said to myself, "There's no way I can have him, and if I can, I can't do this."

He confronted me, and I admitted it, and he admitted to his attraction but said we could not pursue it. I was relieved though hurt. We talked about other things, then about twenty minutes later he asked me for a hug, and when we hugged, we never let go; it turned into a kiss and our passion exploded right there in his office. We began our relationship that night. He was a master; he was playing me, trying to figure out if he could trust me, and I caught on real early during our talk as he occasionally flirted with me. Yet he had insecurities, thinking he could never really have me, as he admitted to me much later in our relationship.

I went along for the ride. *He wanted me. Finally I could release the feelings I had bottled up for almost two years. But how could I? I knew his wife. I loved her; she was a friend to me, she loved me. This is a dead-end relationship. If she finds out, I'll die. I can never cause her such pain. Two years, though. I'm trapped. I'll die if I walk away from him.*

All these things and much more plagued me over the next few months. I hated myself immensely for being with him. When I was delivered and God forgave me, it took years before I forgave myself. I would try to leave him, but he had a strong hold on me. I begged him to walk away from me, but he said he couldn't. We both wanted each other so much that we did very careless things, with no control between us, no one to reign in the other.

We both hated using protection between us and was behaving recklessly, at great risk of impregnating me and leaving me open to diseases, and not particularly caring. There was a really delayed period one month, and while we waited to see, we discussed it and he told me he would claim and take care of the baby if I was indeed pregnant, and that his wife would accept the baby (how he knew or believed that was beyond me, what audacity). I did not want to be pregnant because that would expose us and I *never* wanted our relationship to be public because I didn't want to hurt his wife, but these things I kept to myself. Turns out I was not pregnant, so I made an appointment at planned parenthood and started taking birth control by injections. I then told him about it and we talked about it a little and reminisced about our close call and our reckless want of each other, and again he affirmed that he would have claimed and taken care of the baby if I had been pregnant. The birth control I had been taking (Depo-Provera) was causing me to bleed, like a period, almost daily, I was told this was normal and that it would happen for a few months. [It did just that, then I had no periods at all, even long after I stopped the shots. When my cycle returned there was no real pain with it and remains so even now, so I have to keep careful track so it doesn't catch me by surprise.] I told him what the doctor said and how long I would possibly bleed, I believe they said three months. I told him I would hold off on sex till that time passed, he said he could not wait all that time to have me, and honestly I couldn't wait to have him either, so blood or not, we didn't wait. On this day we stopped by his house for something and he told me to come in. While there, he wanted me, and attempted to lead me down the hall to the bed he shared with his wife, I stopped him and said, *"No, I'm not doing that; That is completely disrespectful to her"*, so we stepped back into the living room. We really wanted each other so he said, where then, I said, *"I'm not having sex in your wife's bed"*, so we had sex right there against a wall at the top of the hallway. His activity inside me caused me to bleed even more, so when we were through, as expected, there was fresh blood, on both of us. When he saw it, maybe it was more than he expected so he was slightly surprised, I said *"See, I told you."* Now he fully understood I was being honest with him and what to expect, and from then on until the bleeding subsided as the doctor said, he knew what to expect every time he wanted me, which was often. He went into the bathroom first and cleaned up as I stood by the door watching him, he wet the wash cloth and wiped himself off then tossed the wash cloth over the side of the tub and then he came out. I asked him if he was gonna leave that there and he said she (his wife) would wash it. That's what he would call her when he was with me **"she."** I told him I needed to clean up and he gave me a wash cloth from the closet. I went into the bathroom, closed the door, and cleaned myself up. When I was through, I asked him what I should do with my wash cloth, I was privately hoping I could throw it out, but he told me to put it where his was. Most adulterers have the carelessness about them, to take their lover into their mate's bed and such other thoughtless things, but his respect for her was non-existent. Think of it, she would walk into the bathroom of her home and have to pick up, touch, and launder two wash cloths, smelling the scent of her husband's sperm on one, and the possible scent of a woman on the other. Whether or not he was withholding sex from her at that time period, what heartbreak, mental torture, and agony would that be for a wife so in love with her husband, how she would cry tears of true pain. My heart refused to do that to her, so I washed mine out as thoroughly as I could to remove all traces of me, then I picked up his and washed it out too. They were also tinged with blood, so as I washed them out with the water being as warm as my skin could tolerate, the scent of his sperm and the scent blood, not the scent of foul blood like old menstruation but that of fresh blood, rose up off them into my nostrils so strong. I washed till the blood was all gone and kept smelling them making sure the scent of sperm was no longer there. The scent of sperm would not leave them. I also thought about his wife picking up two wash cloths having that scent on them and how it would expose her to such terrible knowledge, because why would one man need two wash cloths to clean himself. With one wash cloth she may think he handled himself, but with two, she would know he brought someone into her home. So, I returned his to the side of the tub where he had it. I wrapped mine up and took it with me; I laundered it and returned it to him the next time I saw him. In my mind I wondered how he could and why he would do such a thing to her, leaving it as dirty as he did for her to wash. As for me, I was always concerned for her heart and looking to spear her pain where I could, though I was wretched, and a terrible betrayer of our friendship, feeling unable to and at times not wanting to stay away from her husband. Anyway, He sought to know why I took so long in the bathroom, I don't recall if I told him what I did; It feels like I did and we discussed it briefly, but I am not certain. I try not to make known publicly the very detailed aspects of my passions, but this one came to my mind and would not leave me until it taught me a great lesson with great understanding attached. He was more than just careless or maybe nasty, perhaps it was pure wickedness. Was he being deliberate against her? I will never know. Nevertheless, He was guilty of wickedness, but wasn't I also guilty of the same? I think, "Yes," because I was a willing participant, not speaking concerning the adultery as a whole, but concerning those things done on that particular day. She was very intelligent, and she knew her husband; she knew what happened in her home that day, but I am glad I spared her the blatant disgusting evidence that would have broken her more than she was. Now years later, thinking back, no matter how good he was to me, I was deeply in love with a very terrible human being.

Despite the fact that this whole adultery was a sin, and I could hardly pray except to ask God to remove this love that I wanted gone but wouldn't let go—couldn't fast, couldn't seek and receive the Holy Ghost with this filthiness within me—the thing that affected me most was I couldn't fellowship with his wife without this tremendous guilt eating me alive. She was such a very sweet person; I truly loved her. How could I do that to her? *I can't! I will not!*

After many trial-and-failures of trying to stay away from him, I could no longer betray her. I was determined to be the friend she thought me to be, and I succeeded for a little more than two weeks while he taunted me with phone calls to break me (he knew what hearing his voice would do to me), but I didn't give in.

Midway into the third week, my mom burst open my room door and told me his wife was dead. I was horrified. The only thing I had to console me was the fact that I had left her husband alone for her last weeks, and they seemed to be really happy ones for her. She had been radiant and joyful and just filled with Jesus—prepared. *Now* I understand. It wasn't him, it was Jesus.

I didn't have enough pride and respect to respect her marital vows, but one thing I refused to do was disrespect her marital bed. But still I had nightmares. I dreamed of her. She was in the heavenly choir; they sang beautifully, but they had on red robes, and her countenance was fixed against me. Her spirit was angry with me; so was God and His angels. For quite some months, daily at times, after I dropped my son off or when I would pick him up from school, which was right beside the cemetery, I would go sit by her grave for very long periods—at times hours—and talk to her, and clean off the site, and bring flowers to honor her memory.

She had considered me a friend. I missed her; I missed her smile. I would envision it often. I missed her laugh. I could still hear it. I missed her encouragement and had saved all her little notes to me. She cared so much for my spirit.

I loved the children also, and they loved me. I used to call them and take my son over, and we would play with them when he wasn't there, then he said he could not allow what I was doing. Because I was avoiding him he felt disrespected. If they wanted to see me and he was home, I would say hi in passing and go to their room with them, play and talk for a couple hours and then leave, telling him good-bye in passing. He got offended with that also. I still loved him and could not allow myself to be around him.

After we resumed our relationship, in our talks I would make mention only of being with the children because my heart feared the relationship with him, and I still did not want to be public with him. Though I wanted our relationship, I felt extremely insecure with him, maybe more than with any other man. So, whenever I would tell him how much I wanted the children in my life and failed to mention him he got offended or was playing more games but would tell me that I couldn't want his kids and not want him, that they were a package deal. Anyway, he needed help with caring for the kids, so he called me over one night and asked me. I had never said no to anything he asked of me, and I loved the kids beyond measure, so I was there for them the best I knew how, though I had to change the rules and now at times discipline them when all I did with them before was play, so that was a bit rough, but they were good kids and really missed their mom.

The same night he called me over, we were alone, and my son Sean had fallen asleep. The first time he moved, he called me over to show me where he lived, his children weren't there, and I took Sean with me for a buffer of protection to keep us apart, and it worked, but this time it didn't because my son slept. After we spoke about his kids and about us, he wanted me, and I could never tell him no. I could avoid him, but if he asked something of me, I couldn't say no, and I had missed him terribly, so I spent that night with him, even though I was sick with a broken great toe and a high fever. The fever was caused by the broken toe which I got because I was assembling my new treadmill and a huge iron piece fell on my foot. Now I was limping on crutches and had a soft cast on. My foot hurt when touched, but with all that, still, I couldn't say no to him.

He felt the heat (of the fever) in my body and commented about it, but I made some comment referring to him being the cause then dropped the subject, and so our relationship started again. During the night my son woke up and cried because he came to the room door and opened it and saw me lying in his arms, so my son went back to bed and cried. When I heard my son crying, I went and comforted my son back to sleep and went back to this man.

In the early morning we left, and as I drove along my son Sean told me he saw me with him, and I told my son, "No you didn't! That's not true! Don't ever say that again!" And he never did. He was four years old then, and, thank God, it seems to have been wiped from his memory, because as much as he spoke, he would have reminded me because he keeps no secrets. [I did ask him in present years and he said he doesn't remember that incident.]

After caring for the children a while and being with him, my mom hardly saw me, so she got ideas and confronted me about having a relationship with him. She kept saying, "Why do you have to be the one to care for them?" She wanted me to leave them, but I couldn't. I loved them, and it didn't seem to me that anyone else was able to do it without splitting them up and them being away from their father. Also I really liked caring for them. It fulfilled something in me. It was mostly me and them; I hardly saw their father, but we were still in that relationship. He thought of me as his woman and expected me to behave as such and showed jealousy when I didn't seem to.

I was dating another man, Martin, whom I had sought out since the moment my adulterous affair began, solely for the purpose of covering for my missing hours. But this reason I kept to myself only, so that whenever I came up missing for a while, I was hoping everyone thought I was with Martin. I made sure to introduce Martin to everyone who would be concerned or suspicious about simultaneous missing hours; I hoped they would think, so what if they were both missing from 8 till 10 it's a coincidence because she's with Martin. I even took him to church with me. Martin wanted to go (he was Seventh Day Adventist). He suggested it, and I was glad; of course, he thought he was only getting to know me better, but my agenda was very different. At church I introduced him to my lover and his wife. When my lover met Martin, he was very jealous. Martin was a slim, very tall, and very handsome man, and I never explained anything to my lover. [I have never told or explained anything to anyone until this moment, with these words of this book.] Martin, my son, and I were supposed to go out to dinner after service but my lover exerted his dominance and territorial behavior over Martin by calling me aside trying to ask questions about him, to which I gave answers that would feed his jealousy. My lover was deliberately delaying us, making Martin uncomfortable with our *very* long sidebar and I foolishly allowed my lover to do that. My lover did get his way that Sunday because he did spoil our plans; it became too late for dinner and Martin had to leave back to his town. So now, while I was caring for the children, whenever I felt mistreated I would allow Martin to call me there to make my lover jealous, and it worked every time.

    I did wound Martin terribly though, because he fell in love with me. He was a good man, and so handsome too, and he really liked my son. When I had no babysitter he would tell me to bring my son on our dates, which I did, and we all had a pleasant time. I had told him I would not have sex before marriage only as a ploy so he wouldn't expect anything from me, because I was already in love and didn't want him that way, and I don't have more than one sexual relationship at a time. The moment I said it, without hesitation, he accepted it and gave me six months to make up my mind to marry him or not. He said he was at a point in his life where he was ready for his wife. I knew he was serious about getting married and wanted it to be me, so eventually, I started avoiding him. When he would call me, I let the phone ring off the hook on a daily basis, as I also later did with others.

He was in love with me or falling in love with me and I gave him no thought, which I regretted a year or two later, so I called him and his wife answered. She gave him the phone and we spoke; he told me he had recently married; he didn't seem happy. We became friends again and called each other for a of couple months. He visited me and on the visit he tried to kiss and touch me; I told him no and he apologized. Then, I stopped calling him because it was clear that he still cared for me, and I wanted no part of that (adultery) after God had just rescued me.

Anyway, my mom did love the kids, too, but she just wanted me away from their father because she knew in her spirit that something wasn't right. But I basically did the same thing with her as I did with my son because, as I told this man, I intended to take our relationship in secret to the grave with me, and that if he told anyone I would deny it. But now God says, no more secrets!

So anyway, I got angry at my mom, saying, "We are just friends. How could you think something like that?" and telling her how filthy her mind was for thinking something like that. I put her to shame, all the while knowing I was guilty and that the filthy mind was mine, and it was me who was ashamed.

I stopped going to the cemetery after the day our relationship began again because I couldn't face her resting place. It felt very disrespectful and like such a violation to her memory, so I didn't, and have never returned.

I had no designs on him concerning a public relationship. I never thought of him for a husband and was, in fact, afraid and feeling inadequate for the responsibilities his wife would have, and I don't believe he ever considered me for anything more than what we were already. I wanted us to stay the way we were and was comfortable that way, but I knew it wouldn't last because he needed a wife. He was engaged when we renewed our relationship, but soon after that he left her because of their own personal reasons. Then he started dating again, then he got engaged again, then he started bringing her around, and I understood.

I was a little upset at him for other reasons, giving me the opportunity and way out, so one day when he brought her home, before she got out of the car, I took my son Sean and walked away from the whole family. To this day I have never really spoken to her or stood before her and looked her into the face, only to say hello and good-bye in passing. When he started dating her, he showed me a picture of her and asked me what I thought; I told him she looked nice, and she did. She was pretty and had really beautiful eyes (green or some such pretty shade). He made a comment about her weight and I told him to check himself, that he must love fat chicks because none of us besides his ex-fiancée was truly skinny; he laughed and said, "you know, you're right." So, I guess I made him realize that much about himself as to his actual taste in women rather than the idea in his head. When I left, she may have felt disrespected, but she doesn't know I did us both a favor. Also, I wanted the kids to bond with her, and with her around now, I didn't see the need for me.

I missed the kids something awful—him too. I didn't want things to change, but they had, and needed to. I couldn't have the kids (be in their lives) without him. I couldn't allow myself to stay, because for as long as I was around him, we would be lovers, and I wasn't about to meet her and smile with her and be her friend and continue to sleep with her fiancé and then be sleeping with her husband. If I hadn't walked away from the whole family, that's just the fact of the way it would have been.

He was my weakness, and he wouldn't let me go. Besides the fact of sex, he really liked the fact that I was in love with him and wanted me faithful to him no matter what he did or who he was with. After a while, occasionally we would call each other, and when I would ask about the kids, he would say stuff such as, "If you wanted to know, you wouldn't have left them." They would also ask to see me, but I couldn't go back to their father. It would have been an emotional and spiritual death to me.

I saw his son years ago in a store, and he ran over and said hello to my son and me. He had grown to be such a nice and tall young man, I thought of his mom and how proud she would be. He remembered my son's entire name well but did not remember mine, only my face. After we greeted each other, as he walked away, the boy he was with asked him who I was, and I heard as he told this boy in an exited manner that I was someone who used to spend time with them and play with them "because she really liked us." It blessed my heart that they knew I really cared and did love them. Children do know when your motives are pure.

Besides the fact that I couldn't be around their father, I was in nursing school in the last phase of learning, and because I had put them all first, I was not doing so well. His eldest child was a preteen. She used to help me study and quiz me while I was making dinner or at other times, and we had fun doing that, and she learned a few things. I really loved her, and she loved to hug me and lay her head on my neck and chest because she said I always smelled so good.

Anyway, that little studying wasn't enough. I was falling asleep in class and failing quizzes because I would study at night after I got them all to bed, then I would fall asleep while studying in the early morning and in class during lectures. It was most difficult to stay awake, and my teacher, Mrs. Konow, suspected me of sleeping, so, she would move her small podium in order to be in plain view of me. My mind adapted to this circumstance by allowing my hand to write while the rest of me slept. I would awaken from these brief moments of rest to find my hand and pen writing as if taking notes and of course the writing would be out of their proper spaces. Whenever these episodes occurred, I would have to borrow someone's notes or read chapters of what was covered in the lecture, but I loved the children and didn't regret one day with them.

Eventually, I realized I had to cut down my phone conversations with him because he was a flirter, and I was susceptible to falling back with him. In the beginning of our relationship he would tell me he loved me, then he decided to do us both a favor and stop lying to me, so he started just telling me that he cared for me, and as much as he could, he did.

Twenty-one years ago I prayed to my God for strength to walk away from him, and God had mercy on me. A very rough year followed, because he was the deepest love and deepest lust I ever had. I cried to God each time I missed them, which was a lot, and for him I felt the raw physical unyielding pain of my heart breaking—pure, piercing, horrible pain like never before.

I went for a drive to clear my head, as I usually did, but it wasn't working, so I stopped at a park (Shark River Park), and I cried out to God through my many tears and begged Him to *take this love from me and to never allow me to love another man except the one to be my husband. Only then, to allow love to return to me, and if I'm never to be married then never allow me to love again*, and He heard me. As much pain as I was in, why didn't I just ask to let me never love again, period? I didn't know why I cried those exact words, but He saw someone in my future that I didn't see; He saw His plan for me.

He was quite merciful. Immediately He comforted me, taking away the horrible, piercing, ripping pain from my chest. Then over the next few months he plucked out that love, closed up that gaping wound, and healed me without a scar. Now the love was gone, but there was a problem, the lust remained. His memory was haunting me. Every time I closed my eyes his essence was all over me. I could feel him. I wanted him out of my head, but I didn't think to give God such things, but as I learned years later, there is nothing too filthy to give to God, and He will wash it all away. I'm no longer embarrassed with God or feel like I have to hide anything, because nothing can be hidden. There is no part of me I want to withhold from Him because there is no part of me He can't handle and handle excellently.

But back then I didn't realize this, and I had to do something. I knew I couldn't let him be the last person that touched me, so I used my son's father to replace my last memory. Sex was basically a tool, a task for me, or something that was required of me by these men that I loved. It had not been something of true pleasure that I enjoyed until the end of my last relationship. That's why he haunted me so, but I was delivered from the lust also, and I don't believe I did it on my own; I believe God took that away too.

I was still occasionally being intimate with my son's father but felt a great need to stop doing that, so nineteen and a half years ago I decided to stop giving myself away and save what was left of me for marriage if God had marriage planned for me. Sick of willful sin, lust, fornication, adultery, giving myself to be used, and having my relationships be about sex instead of what was inside me. I took back control of me, took back my self respect, and learned to love myself.

I occasionally dated since then, and though I occasionally missed the feeling of love and attempted to create it myself, I wasn't ready for true love, because I would start talking with someone, then allow them to call me endlessly while I ignored the phone, pretending I wasn't there. These men were decent, but I just wasn't whole. I was broken, and my blessed Jesus kept my heart covered in the palms of His hands and kept it safe from that kind of deep love and all brokenheartedness for eight years and three months as I had begged Him. And still that kind of love has not and will never return to me because those relationships were not of God. They were so broken and unhealthy, needy, desperate, sinful, hurtful, and painful, with fornication, adultery, lust—and the list goes on.

The love God is preparing for me is built on Him and will remain pure of those evil things; no brokenness, healed, individually whole, yet brought together as one. We will like each other, we will love each other with the love of God with added desire toward each other. We will put God first in our lives and also at the head of our marriage, then put each other second. Unconditional love with no secrets, no deceit, emotionally naked before each other, being each other's comfort, each other's help, and each other's source as God the Father feeds us to supply each other with whatever needs and wants the other has. God will stand at the head of our family. This is the love and marriage I believe God for and He will prepare me for. Best of all, he will not *come at me,* neither will *any* issue choose him; God will choose, and already did when He made me. Thank You, Lord.

He will give me no less than this, because this is the love and marriage that will stand through any storm. This is the love and marriage that will stand the test of time, come what may against it. This is the love

Body

and marriage the devil may be allowed to touch but cannot and will not destroy. A love through eternity, at which time Jesus will be all the mate, comforter, king, and all in all we want and need, and the list goes on with good things. This may sound grandiose or fantastic, but nothing is too good and wonderful and blessed for our Source/God/Jesus to give us. We are His children. Anything less is a waste of time, a waste of love, a waste of your heart, is not worth having, and is not of God.

I believe and trust Him for this and much more because I know Him to be a God of works, faithful and true, and no one or nothing can now make me doubt Him. If you are not yet married, be still and wait for this love from God. If you are already married but you are lacking, give it to Him then be still and behold as He takes that marriage and makes it a new creation in Him. Children of God, it may be that He will be gracious unto you if you ask and believe and are faithful to Him.

Now, back to the past. Because my female cousin Charmaine had molested me, it gave me tendencies that didn't work their way deep down until a few years ago. It made me hate her for putting that into my head. The demon of sexual depravity and perversion had risen up and was overpowering me. Things and thoughts that were once not acceptable to me, and even things that once repulsed me, were now becoming acceptable and desirable, even pleasurable to me.

I started wondering if I was homosexual, and this made me really hate her. After a while with this fear, I thought carefully and rationally, reasoning with myself, and thought about being in a relationship and intimacy, and realized that men were who I loved and wanted. But I still had these thoughts, just in my fantasies, nothing I wanted to do for real. It just gave me pleasure to think about it. Over the years there were women who probably sensed that sensuality about me and made advances toward me, giving me opportunities to do what I thought to be this wicked thing against God, but my will, fear of being caught, and fear of God prevented me from reacting to their actions and signals.

In my teenage years, I had this friend, who was a girl, and she would always flirt with me by letting her body or her leg rest against me and it felt good to both of us but she would raise herself up from me whenever anyone came near. I also noticed that she would always try to look at me if I was changing, and would stare at my breasts. We never discussed our attraction/like of each other and I don't know that I was necessarily attracted to her physically, but the idea of her was very intoxicating/arousing to me, and my sexual senses were heightened in her presence. One night she slept over; I had twin beds in my room at my mom's house, so she was in one and I was in the other. Surprisingly, she asked me to come lay with her and I wanted nothing more than to be next to her warmth, but my mom always checked on me at nights when she got up to the restroom, it was her loving routine, so I told my friend I could not and why. I thought long about it and could not think of an excuse for being in the same bed with her if my mom caught us. I went to sleep with a desperation to grant her request and be next to her, and whatever else she wanted me there for. The point of revealing all this is to share the following experience: In my groggy state, I felt my spirit leave me body to go be next to her / with her. That's how powerful the desire in me for her was. Again, maybe weeks later, I slept over where she was, and we would finally be in the same bed with no one to check on us in the middle of the night. She made it obvious she wanted me, because after we ate dinner, we sat in the living area, and she actually put on a lesbian porno movie, her forwardness made me a little nervous, so I pretended not to be very interested in it. I wasn't really watching with the interest she'd hoped, so she turned it off and it was time for bed. She got into bed and waited for me to join her. I went to the restroom to urinate, and surprise, my menstrual cycle had begun; *it was early*. I wasn't prepared for it and was scared to now ask her for women things because she was expecting me. I stayed a really long time, trying to make due with paper towels/toilet paper. When I came out, she asked if I was okay and I said yes. She noticed I was now being weird and it got a little awkward, so she went to sleep. I got no sleep; I had cramps, and not to mention, her body was now next to mine. As she slept, she tossed and turned and her leg rested over me (I don't know if she placed it there, because she wasn't sleeping well either). Her body felt warm and good, and I lay for hours yearning to touch and caress her. The moment I got the nerve and did reach out to do it, she fully awakened and got up because it was now morning, so we got dressed and left; she had to leave town for a bit. We never discussed it and never tried to be together again, but the attraction remained between us. She probably thought I wasn't interested, having given me every opportunity to have her.

Why be so graphically detailed with my written words? Because I needed the desire/passion I was covering/hiding and trying not to feel to now be seen/known. What did I know about passion as a teenager? Yet it was there, so powerful in me that it moved my spirit toward the object of my affection. Nevertheless, I fully believe God intervened that night, not because it was sin, for it was not and is not, but because she wasn't the chosen one. I was His, even back then, and I was not to have that experience with her, though I yearned for her. Whoever you are and whatever the preference that is made in you, God has His choice for you; do not mingle with what is not meant for you and don't partake of what is not yours. Some fulfilled desires will rob you of your destiny. And, if the thing is not yours, isn't it someone else's?

Between 2000 and 2003, passion and desire for *a woman* became strong in me, as if possessing me. I hated it because Pastor-fokes and church-fokes said it's a way to hell, a place I don't desire to go; but my passion said otherwise. I found myself with the very strong desire to actually try it, and the desire was taking hold in my mind. I thought, ***if I found the perfect person with the perfect body***, I'd make myself do it to get it out of my system, but my soul knew that it was a lie, that this desire and passion would never be out of my system (I saw this as a way of escape I created for myself because there was no such perfect person; ***until*** I received that true *forever* love, **then**, **everything** about her was *perfect* to me). It was a hard fight, but I was cleansed and purified of that. I saw it as sin and asked God to cleanse me, which He did, and I made up my mind that I would never return to those thoughts and feelings, and the beginning of that healing was when I decided I will not go against God.

When God started to deal with me, I purposed within myself that I was going to live true to Him, live true to His Word. If I read it and God gave me understanding of it, I would live it. I grew up in church, so I believed it was wrong, but I allowed my want of it to convince me that the bible didn't speak of women, so it was OK.

I decided I wanted to know God completely, all truth, not what I had been taught or believed, but to start over and allow God to teach me His truth. So I prayed and set out to read the Bible from cover to cover, and God started teaching me. I saw in His Word in more than three different verses that it was unnatural and an abomination to Him—against God and against nature—for a man to lie with a man and for a woman to lie with a woman, so there it was in black and white, no more excuses, I thought. So, I immediately chose to be true to God, and He gave me strength from that very moment. My thoughts did not return to such things and desires, because I loved and wanted Him more than I loved and wanted that, but these passions would not easily be expelled and cast away from me. While I was awake, this passion and desire found no rest in me so they began to regularly express my sensuality through my dreams, where I had no control, but God does. He delivered me and expelled those things from me; He changed me and was keeping me. I was completely free.

[I truly was cleansed; I had no more thoughts and my passion and desire lay dormant 3 years, until God awakened them and showed me His choice for me. He ignited them once more forever with a great pure love, and let me know it was Him, so not to fear but embrace it. At first I felt this love and a kindred spirit but was not attracted, then, He showed me her beauty and I received it; now, to me she is the essence of beauty and no one compares. The devil was, is, and forever will be a liar, but it was not him nor his demons; it was God uncovering the hidden part of me that I kept refusing to accept, because I thought it was against Him. When He showed me it was Him, I fully embraced my whole self and loved *all* of me; I also fully embraced the one He gave me.]

I struggled in all areas of my life, I started working at a nursing home in housekeeping when I just turned sixteen years old, because I wanted to work. But, I went from job to job, not staying at one place more than three or six months. As soon as it got to that marker, I started to hate it or wanted something with more money and felt a pressing desire to leave, so I always moved on. Once I had my son, I didn't want to leave him. I trusted no one with him, especially because of his apnea, so still living with my mom and having been on welfare/Medicaid during my pregnancy, I used the opportunity and stayed home with him for six months.

Then, I felt the desire to work. I went out and got a job on the third shift because I thought at least this way he would be sleeping and my mom would be there if he woke up. After a while the company cut half of the third shift, the "last hired, first cut," so I stayed home with him again. I always sought alternative forms of work because I hated leaving him, and years later realized I was trying to be and wanted to be a stay-at-home mom so I could protect him, but how does a single parent do that?

I looked into and tried all forms of work. One way was to work double shifts (11:00 p.m. to 7:00 a.m., then 7:00 a.m. to 3:00 p.m.) every weekend, giving me four days for each week, so I would be home with him five days per week. At one time I quit a job with nothing to fall back on because I had three separate dreams where I caught the person I was leaving him with in the act of molesting and sodomizing him, and I took hold of and brutalized this person then awakened.

I rarely ever left my son; wherever I went he was always with me. This didn't always please my mom, who didn't at times want him along when we were going somewhere together, but I didn't care. I told her we were a package deal, and that he was my responsibility, that why should I leave him with other people when it wasn't necessary? Only when I occasionally worked, then I left him with my mom till he was two years old.

At that age he spoke very well with a good vocabulary, maybe because I didn't speak baby talk to him. I spoke clearly and read to him and sang to him since he was inside me and continued through his years. Anyway, I was relieved when he could speak, because now he could tell me of things that may happen, so I searched out a Christian daycare school, and he attended for years. Aside from that, he still remained always in my sight, and while he was there, I called and checked and dropped in when I could and watched him for signs and asked him subtle questions. But I did really trust the head teacher, "Mrs. Beverly," which he had, and her only did I *fully* trust.

I am to this day still very overprotective of my son, because for as long as I have breath, the devil will not have him or use him or abuse him. I taught him the necessity of his soul being saved and told him I wanted God to have him, and he agreed, so I gave him to God in water baptism at eight years old (days before his ninth birthday), and he loves God and church. But because of me, he lost the full opportunity for most of two years to grow in God.

I was always full of pride and liked nice things. By now I was a nurse (LPN), and God had blessed me for more than five years with this beautiful, very large roomed, three-bedroom townhouse. Others, because of outward appearance, thought I was living luxuriously, and maybe they were even jealous, but behind the doors I was living meagerly. I came close to losing it a few times because I did not manage my money well and often spent it inappropriately.

In the end, because of my style of paying and not keeping my receipts in order, when they audited me three different times for the same time period (two years back), whatever receipts I couldn't find, they forced me to pay again. Though I knew I really didn't owe this, I paid because I didn't want to lose it, and it was my fault for being irresponsible/unorganized, but the third time they did it within the same year I said no more. They had also raised my rent $30 per year for the last two years because new management took over and wanted to make more money.

With my new car repossessed, no food bought, no other bills paid, things being lost and turned off, every single paycheck for over a three-month period going to their lawyer for back payments God knows I didn't owe, they were also invading my privacy. The head of maintenance repeatedly entered my home without notice to me or authorization from me at or before eight a.m. when the office didn't open till nine a.m. On occasion I came home from work at eight or eight-thirty a.m. to find that my intruder alarm had been set off by this man, and leaving no work order saying what work had been done as is procedure and as they had done for all legitimate work. At times the police were still there and the manager covered for him and had probably put him up to it. In the end when management was confronted in my exit letter their excuse was that he needed to paint the apartment, which was never done.

I felt violated over and over, so I refused to give them another penny. I wrote them a letter breaking my lease and stated all their wrongful, wicked acts against me and my child, and that between then and the date I left, if there were any more illegal/unlawful entries, I would file complaint with the police. I packed up my things, put them in storage, left their key in their after-hours box, and moved to a motel. The following week my son's father told me he drove by there, and there was an eviction or some notice posted on the door.

I should have stood my ground with this whole situation because the battle was the Lord's. Had I behaved as His child and given it to Him, I would have seen victory from my Lord strong and mighty, but sin is blinding (your sins will drive you out of your blessings).

Having to pay only one monthly bill now, I planned to stay only a few months while I cleared my debts and then get another apartment, but other things were in store for me. Only a couple of months prior to moving I had changed a job of almost six years for another job with more pay that was three minutes from my home instead of ten or fifteen; I would be working with my sister, and she said it was OK there.

So now I moved, and a problem arose. My boss started piling paper work on me. With every job when I orientate and start, it's a breeze, then very soon after, it changes and becomes actual labor where burdens are piled on. Every time; it never fails. I was already on a floor that no one else wanted to work because of its difficulty. The work load became unbearable to handle with the great patient load and all my other responsibilities and charting, so I refused to do the added work, and she fired me. My sister kept me up to date, and that position could not remain filled for about one year, and after that the one that fired me got fired in the same manner. When God takes care of your enemies you should not rejoice, but I was different then, and I must admit I was very satisfied.

Before my old boss got her dues, I was without a job and could not find another because I was truthful on my applications, so after three months I started collecting unemployment and did for nine months. After that year I made a way around my old boss because she was making trouble for me. When anyone called her in reference to me, I don't know what she told them but they then refused me jobs. I know this because on one occasion I was all set to receive a job, they gave me a shift and went over with me my orientation days, the regular days I would work from that month's schedule, my days off, and pay rate, but before I could start, they had to check my reference, and after they spoke to her, I no longer received that job. But anyway God took care of her. So now I was in this job; it was part time, but it was enough right then.

I worked there one and a half years, never being able to get out of that motel, and by now inwardly had grown accustomed to it. Still full of pride and being ashamed of it, yet never really attempting to get out, like subconsciously I wanted to hit rock bottom. I let only Big Sis know where I lived, absolutely no one else, not even my mother. I would check my rear-view mirrors and surroundings each and every time I left and returned home for the whole two and a half years I lived there to make sure that no one who knew me saw me.

For this reason I stopped going to church, and mostly kept my son away too, because my son would tell everything to everybody, so I controlled the situation this way. My mom knew I lived in a motel, just not where it was located, until one day after about a year, Big Sis brought me some flowers and a couple of cards in appreciation for always being there for her. But when she came, she brought my mom in the car with her. I think she did it on purpose, and I guess I was relieved that she finally knew. Then I guess my mom drove my third brother by one day. So those three adults only and my three nieces knew where I lived. As for my son's father, he had both my phone numbers, or I took our son to him, or he came to my mom's house.

Actually, when I first moved, I was happy and relieved to get rid of the intruding maintenance man, but one night at work, Big Sis told me to remove the motel tag from the key on my key chain, then she told my nieces at another time to keep quiet about where auntie lives, and those things are what made me ashamed and start hiding it. Compared to where I was coming from, this second motel I had settled into was truly a dump and truly a roach motel in every sense of the word. I had never ever lived that way before, but it was where I had allowed myself to fall, and it was home now. I had kept my son sheltered all his life. All he knew except for the couple of times when the utilities were shut off (at which times I was very resourceful and God got us through), was a good life with most of the things he wanted, and definitely more than he needed, but a month before we moved, I was still unsure but had started packing, so I removed the veil from his eyes and told him everything. There was no way to shelter him now because I wanted out of that townhouse.

Instead of standing still and letting God fight all my battles, shutting God out of my life while becoming engrossed in what I thought was sin was causing me to walk away from my home and my blessing. But, through it all, God never took His hand off me. He stayed with me whither-soever I went, because I was His. I belonged to Him, He was invested in me, and He loved me with an eternal love I just didn't know or understand.

Besides all the main reasons, there was that other reason why I didn't regret leaving. During that time is when I thought the enemy started sorely oppressing me with what I had been taught was sexual depravity and I believed it allowed the entrance of demonic forces into my home. [The truth is, during this time, the passion I was feeling toward women, which I thought was sin, was so strong in me that I decided to leave God until I experienced being with a woman. It was the act of turning my back on God which allowed the entrance of demons into my home. I left Him and my purpose He was preparing me for, so my home was no longer guarded. Still, because of purpose, Sean and I were covered by my guardian angels, which did show themselves in that time because there was *heavy* activity in my home.] At times, I could feel their presence. (I say "they" and not "it" because one demon doesn't ever attack: they come in groups or legions to attack a child of purpose). My son also felt their presence, but when he made mention of them, I pretended it wasn't true. I told him not to talk like that and got upset at him if he did, but I knew the presence was real and was a bit afraid.

Once, I was asleep, and when I woke up and looked in my bedroom doorway, there stood an old silver-haired, seemingly Caucasian couple beside each other, side by side, touching, looking at me, and smiling in what seemed like a loving, adoring way. They were the first and only spirits I have ever seen, but strangely I was not afraid. I just turned my head and went back to sleep. I told my mom about it, and she was troubled for me. I thought they had to have been the enemy because I believed my mind was too corrupt for them to be guardian angels. But, I asked myself, "why did I feel no fear of them?" Because death and demons terrified me at that time in my life. Yet with all this, I refused to pray, for that was during the time I was refusing to turn to God because of the great passion and desire I was feeling. The great sin was me neglecting God, not the things I was feeling, which He created in me.

The whole time we lived at the motel, my son hardly complained. He made new friends and even a girlfriend, until she moved about four months before we did. Though I didn't always let him run around with them, they always came knocking for him. This was not a nightly motel, it was one used for rental to mostly families and elderly, so there were always children around.

Close to the end, I felt this great need to get out of there. I wanted my son to have his own room again. I started to get back some self-respect, which I had lost in my first few months of living there. That is why I sat there so long, and I was truly sick of the roaches and refused to live like that any longer. So, I went out looking for an apartment, just the basic one, nothing fancy. Just something with a bedroom, and a kitchen, and no roaches, or mice (which I had but got rid of the first few months I was there). After two months of living there, I had moved the furniture around, trying to make the room more of a comfort to us, and in doing that I gave the mice a way to enter from next door, but they were eliminated and driven away within the next two months.

I looked and applied for apartments, and they said I wasn't making enough, so I went to my administrator who was my director of nursing (DON); he was just promoted because the old administrator had just been fired, so he was doing both jobs until a new DON could be found. He doubled my hours, over-staffing the facility on many days. He also recommended me for a second job with another facility, but I still lost out on apartments because my credit was shot, so I turned to the department of human resources (public assistance).

By now I was about to be evicted from the motel because of privacy issues. They wanted in because they had newly instituted a mandatory housekeeping crew; I refused them and made sure they couldn't get in when I wasn't there by padlocking the door. It was wrong but I did it for a few reasons: I cleaned my own room very well and didn't need any cross-contamination; the cats were with me and I didn't want to lose any of them should the door be opened by anyone but me; also, I had fixed the room up with some of my things from storage to make it livable for my son with all his game systems, TV, VCR, microwave, refrigerator, computer, and some of my electronics, and I didn't want any of it revealed and stolen—I was allowed to have them I just didn't want them seen and stolen; And, after all I had endured at the townhouse I just treasured my privacy at all cost. They couldn't get in so they wanted me out, and I didn't fight them, because I wanted out, too.

When I went to human resources, they made me aware that they could not help me unless I was on welfare or food stamps and that I was making too much to qualify for food stamps. So, I explained to her that half those hours were like an indefinite overtime, and she wrote down for me the limit my income could be to qualify and told me I needed to drop the overtime. I did the math on my income and spoke with the new DON to reduce my hours. I explained in part why I needed this, and this woman who was previously all smiles and agreeable, turned so nasty, threatening my job, trying to force me to keep my overtime hours, even though she knew I needed to do this to find a home, and after I told her it would be only for a short while anyway. I told her I needed to do what they wanted in order to get me into an apartment, and that once I was in, I could maintain my own way so I wouldn't need them and could work as many hours as she wanted. It didn't matter to her. Though it was only a threat, telling me "I'll just have to put an ad in the paper and find someone who can work all those hours," I was angry. I asked her how is she gonna threaten my job? I reminded her of my regular hours that I was hired for, and that I requested those extra hours when they didn't even have a need for it, working out of my scope on most of those extra days, and at times being there with nothing to do.

She knew I was right, so she backed off, pretending she didn't mean it that way. She told me if I worked the shifts for her she would hold back the pay off certain checks so it wouldn't show and work against me with social services and that on those days I shouldn't "punch the clock," but I refused that way. I punched in and out for each shift and wrote her a note that I will just tell the truth. I agreed to work two more weeks of overtime and told social service the truth, that she would not release me from that schedule unless I worked those two final weeks of overtime. I no longer felt any safety in that job and wanted to leave because she couldn't be trusted. She could have still put that ad in the paper behind my back or set me up and fire me.

After all that, I was still denied the food stamps because they added in my holiday pay, so a social worker told me to reapply the following month when my pay checks were regulated to my true income, but they did help me anyway. I had stopped paying the motel where I lived for a while because I needed more than $2,500 to get into an apartment; I then began paying them installments. When human resources finally got around to actually helping me, they told me not to pay anymore money and that it was too much for them to pay off so to just let the eviction go through and they would put me in another motel. I did as they said, but in all honesty, the manager John was extremely good to me, while he was not that way with the others, and I did him real dirty' over the rent. He trusted me above all the others, and I betrayed him, though not with malicious intent. I do hold regret. Human Resources put me in another motel, which was like heaven compared to the one I left, and *no* roaches. This was about a week before I was due to be evicted. Human Resources also told me if I found a place, they would put me in it, and I could pick up from there, which was all I ever asked for and wanted anyway.

So, for a month and a half I searched *daily*: on the streets, filling applications, making phone calls, and meeting with people—but nothing; all the housing authorities in my area and its surroundings had from a two-to-five-year waiting list, one even had a ten-year wait list. When I was lucky enough to find a few places, I started being told again that I wasn't making enough. How could I go back to that evil woman and ask for those hours back after she had threatened me?

More than ever now, I searched the Internet, which I had started to do just before I moved from the townhouse. I searched all the states to see where was most suitable to live, as far as apartment quality, cost, and crime safety, and had decided on Alabama. Then, I searched to see where in Alabama was cheapest and safest and most decent. The apartments and townhouses Online were beautiful and so cheap; to get that quality apartment in New Jersey would cost no less than $1,500. So, I found Muscle Shoals, and oh, how I wanted to see if this fantasy was real!

[When I got there I was told that Alabama was a tornado state. The person I was, if I had known it before I went, I wouldn't have gone. Now that I was there, I was so at peace and knew that it was God's will and purpose for me to be there, so I didn't leave until God said, "Go!" Whatever was His will, had to be, and if His will was for me to be swept away, then He would have made ready my soul and lifted me up into His loving arms. But it was not His will, so nothing did harm me. With all that I am and all that's within me, I trust Him.]

I had wanted to leave New Jersey for years, but since 2002, I felt greatly pressed on the inside to go away. My soul was stirred up and screaming on the inside. Everything on the inside of me was crying out to get away and start over. I was greatly uncomfortable, needing a change, also wanting to leave nursing: always sick and drained and tired, with regular migraines that lasted three days at a time. I was just existing, not living; I was dying inside, but I knew I had to save first. I calculated three months' expenses with extra, and I needed no less than two thousand dollars. I needed to see Alabama for myself to make sure, because the Internet was not reality.

Three places/programs had kept me in motels for one and a half months, and I also used my own money to fill the gaps between their payments. This took me through to the second week of August, then they all passed me off to a place/program that had no room for me until the second week of September, *if I qualified*. The place that was paying mailed me a letter at the motel telling me when I checked out that week to call that other place **which had no room for me** because I had been calling them each time, and basically washed their hands of me. I knew this because the first of the three places had paid for two weeks and told me to use the time to find an apartment, but there was no success. The monthly rent for a one-bedroom apartment was from seven to eight hundred dollars or more, and a two-bedroom was over eight hundred to fifteen hundred dollars. With a child of the opposite sex, the law was that I had to have a two-bedroom, but on part-time pay, I could barely afford six to seven hundred dollars per month.

Anyway, when the two weeks were up, I started calling this first place, leaving messages for three days as to the situation, and they did not return any call and avoided me, saying the person I needed to speak with was not there and they didn't know when she would be. I called the social worker who had recommended these places, and he called this first place, and they told him they were out of funds. If that was true, they could have told me so instead of avoiding me the way they did. One thing I hate is to feel like I am a bother or impediment to anyone. If you don't want to deal with me just say so, no need to avoid me. I am very easily embarrassed (unless God sends me to do a thing), so I keep myself out of the way. Tell me clearly once, and you never have to tell me again. I protect myself. I can't find the word for how they made me feel, but it made me angry. I never beg, and I dislike it strongly in anyone else, but they made me feel that way about myself.

So, at the end of it all, it seemed that for no less than two weeks, I would be *truly* homeless. I was now drowning. It seemed I wanted rock bottom, and there it was. I had to make a decision: Do I allow myself to be homeless in the town I grew up, where everyone knows me yet has no room for me? Though my pride would prevent me from asking. Or, do I use this opportunity to go scope out Alabama? My choice was clear.

During this time my mom invited me to stay with her so I could save up the money to move out of state, because I had told her months before of my desire, but now my situation was desperate and she didn't know. She also wanted to move and was contemplating between Florida and Georgia and was looking to me to drive her down to check them out, and I had agreed to do it for her. But, when my situation got desperate, I let her know I was in no way dependable concerning her at that point, and she could not look to me for anything. I could focus only on me right then. To solve this dilemma I had, she wanted us to scout out Georgia and for me to move to Georgia with her and live in her house until I made a life for myself there, but I didn't feel the pull to live in Georgia. Alabama was calling me, and she was not planning on moving for another two or more months, and I needed to go right then. I was dying inside. I told her I would think about it, but I could not do it.

I love my mom forever and a day, but I could not live with her. She had made that same offer when I first moved from the townhouse. The motel I was in at that time was nice but expensive. It could barely be maintained. So, I took her up on her offer but could not stay there more than about one month. It was a nightmare and a danger to my health. I worked the third shift so my bedtime was during the day. My mom had no rooms available in her house, because she took in and cared for people from the State, so my bedroom was the living room and my bed was the sofa or my air mattress, but she did not like me sleeping there at that time. She knew I needed sleep, but she still wasn't pleased because it was day, especially when she had visitors, I had to get up. I could just feel the attitude from her, and resentment grew in me, and the tension was building. So, I started sleeping in my car at the gate, sometimes pretending I was doing something with the car if awakened by a passerby, or putting up the sun visors to block view into the windows, but that just did not look or feel right. Then, I started going to the park (Shark River Park), and there I would sleep in my car, but my ankles started swelling up, and I did not feel safe because it was really hot and humid so I had to leave the window down. Then, one day I said, "What's the point?" So I went and rented that motel room just so I could get some decent sleep. I then decided I wanted our good relationship back, so I just moved into that room and the love was felt between us again.

Anyway, at this time, Big Sis, who knew all the details, had made me an offer to stay with her, too. She also had no room, but she offered. The apple didn't fall far from the tree there. I declined the offer to stay with her but did ask if I could stay maybe two days to use her computer and do the searches I needed. While there, it took longer than I thought because I had to turn my searches from Alabama hotels/motels to Alabama camping grounds. So, day three, four, and five came and I was still there, but I couldn't reveal that my search had changed, I just told her the search was taking longer than I thought. Then, I started getting the *why are you still here* vibe and looks, even though I would make sure the apartment was clean for her, and one of my little nieces actually said it. I knew it was time to go, so I left and spent the last couple days at my storage unit. However, before I left, I had stayed for a week on her sofa while I finalized my plan, which was to go to Alabama for a week and a half, then come back, and by then my paycheck would be due, so I could stay somewhere in town for another few days until that spot opened up for me in the housing facility, *if I was eligible*. This social service wanted me totally broken in order for them to help me, and when I had made myself that way for them, it was a hindrance to me, and they still gave me problems.

On one occasion, after a voucher ended I arrived in their office that day just five minutes before they closed because I was running around trying to find an apartment, they said it was too late to do anything out of the office so they directed me to the after-hours department, and I got on the phone with the after-hours person. She refused to help me when I asked and then in the same breath threatened to take my son if I was seen with him on the street. I would die before I let anyone but God take him from me. The supervisor overheard my conversation with this woman and came over and intervened by taking the phone from me and speaking to this woman personally, and went beyond his duty after he hung up from her and got me into a motel that night for three days, then called the motel on the third day and extended the voucher for one more week. Again, they reminded me that when this week was over I should not call them but the other place *which had no room for me*. I made arrangements for another nurse to cover my shifts at work, and because I was only part-time again, this gave me two weeks off, It was perfect.

    On top of all my troubles, since I was about thirty-one years old, my mom kept mentioning—not in a personal talk specifically for that purpose, just throwing it out there on a couple different occasions to make sure I heard it—making me know what I always knew of myself was a big lie and a dirty secret. She told me that my dad raping her is how she got pregnant with me. I pretended I didn't hear her, but she knew I did, because the last time she said it, I told Big Sis what she did and said, and questioned how a mother could say that to her kid and in such a way. It wasn't like she was angry and said it to hurt me, we were just talking, but with her, most conversations led back to my father. [True enough, my dad was a rapist of a few women and at least one child, and a molester or attempted child molester; still, I loved him.]

    Big Sis told my mom I didn't appreciate what she said and the manner in which she did. Big Sis doesn't believe it, because my mom also kept saying she never loved my dad, and Big Sis says, "How can you have so many kids by someone you don't love then marry that person? And, that it's all lies." (They were married two years before I was conceived.) But I believe her, because I also stayed with and had a child by someone I didn't really love but felt attached to, and in a lot of ways I am my mother. The good things I will keep, but the bad things must be ejected, and a lot already has been as God works on me.

Another day years ago, as she was baring her soul to me about some of the hurt my dad caused her, she told me that after Big Sis, she didn't want any more kids, but he held her down and raped her, but that once she was pregnant, that she loved me. If this was true, I wonder why she couldn't bring herself to discuss my childhood or her pregnancy with me. If she could tell me about the rape, why couldn't she speak of the rest? What could be worse than that?

So now, no longer was I a loved and desired child for a playmate for my sister, but a by-product of rape. It's icing on the cake of my disturbed messed up life, I thought. Of course, if you spoke to my father, he had a mouthful to tell you of my mom, which contained truths, so in thinking how I did my son's father, I wonder just how my mom caused my dad to feel and all the ways she hurt him. He did hurt her a lot though, and there is *no* excuse for that. [Our ages also witnesses to me that the rape was true. All her children are two years apart except for Big Sis and me. After Big Sis was born, my mom was indeed dreaming of a little sister for Big Sis to play with but there was trouble between my mom and dad when Big Sis was 10 months old; one month later he married my mom. The trouble between them was my dad had a baby two months expecting at the time he married my mom (in order not to lose her). I believe my dad spoiled the family plan of a child every two years and made my mom decide she wanted no more kids by him (still, God saw I needed to be born). That sister between us is one and a half years younger than Big Sis and one and a half years older than me; so, Big Sis and I are three years apart. I was conceived from the rape of my mother by my father (her husband) during the month of her birthday, when Big Sis was two years and about three to four months old, and was I born two years and two months after he married her.]

Anyway, Alabama was calling me; a new and wonderful life awaited me. I had three hundred dollars, but I had to use two hundred to prepare for the trip. I didn't let anyone know how much I had left in my pocket, because they would have tried to talk me out of going, but I knew it was now or never. I felt the call, and I had to answer yes. There was nothing left in New Jersey for me, only my family, and I believed they would be right behind me (and they were), so I wasn't worried about not being close. I would go back only to make money to move permanently, and that was all.

I packed the car with all I thought we would need for a week, including food and an electrical pot, but the car was too full, so I had to repack it. I kept only three changes of clothes plus what we had on and had removed the pot, but Big Sis convinced me to carry it, and it turned out to be extremely essential. I trimmed our supplies and made us all fit, but we were still packed to the roof. This trip was definitely designed, everything packed was by God's direction and purpose. It was time, God was ready to move, He was now in full control of me, and I was following His lead. I was allowed to do life my way and had failed miserably, now it was time for God's way and I was willing.

On August 29, 2003, at 3:00 a.m. with ninety-five dollars in my pocket, directions I printed off the Internet, some music for the drive, my portable stereo because my car didn't have a CD player, and a book I had bought two months prior that I was interested in reading, my son and I and our family of cats all left for Alabama. I just had to see if what I was dreaming of and had promised them was real.

We had a family of seven cats; my son, Sean, named them all. First we had a brother and sister, Max and Misty, that we got when they were one-and-a-half months old. We got them from a cashier at our neighborhood Shoprite supermarket. One day we went food-shopping and as the cashier checked out our groceries she asked me if I wanted a cat, we said, sure, so she gave me her number. My son and I went by her house and met them and had a liking for those two, or rather, those two chose us, so when they were weened from their mom she gave them to us. Then, when they were six months old, my son and my nephew (Sis' son) found 3 baby strays (two boys and a girl), and to save their lives because we instantly loved them, I took one and so did Sis and Big Sis. They were about three weeks old, but we thought they were one week. I took them all home and bottle-fed them with cat milk formula and cared for them, and they thrived. I encouraged and helped my two cats to mother and father them, and they did very well and were gentle and protective. When the babies were ready, I taught them how to drink from a bowl and how to use the litter. Then, I gave them to their owners. Big Sis wanted the boy (Dusty - a white and gray cat) she had chosen on that first day, and my nephew (Sis' son) wanted the girl (Gabrielle - a leopard color cat) he had chosen. My son and I kept the other boy he wanted and named him Figero, like Pinocchio's cat, because he looked *just* like him. I was a bit of a dunce in the spelling of his name but I kept it that way because it was already on his doctor's records. So, my son and I had three, Max, Misty and Figero.

When Figero was six months, Max and Misty had a litter, so I neutered Figero and Max. It was a litter of five, and she had a difficult time, but she had come to me when she was in labor and let me help her. I had done a lot of reading and preparation, so I was able to help her. She was very inexperienced, so I had to help a lot, pulling out some of them, helping her break their sack and holding them to her mouth so she could lick them to stimulate their breathing. She had five boys, and each of them took their first breath while lying in my hand. She didn't make enough milk to supply them, and her breasts and nipples were sore, swollen, and raw because of their nursing. The babies lost weight and were not gaining it back, so on their fourth day of life I started supplementing them with the bottle. I had made them a kittening box of wood with inner levers the babies could crawl under for shelter, just as the book had said, but she still would lay on them accidentally, which would frighten her because she really loved them, so I watched them intently. The first night I left them and went to work, when I returned home that morning and all day, I noticed one of them, King, previously a vigorous eater, would no longer eat, even though I put him to her breast. About the fifth day of his life, he was listless and I fed him, then about an hour later I decided to weigh them, and he was limp. I picked him up and worked on him for a half hour but he was dead.

I don't deal well with death. I can hold a person's hand till they take their last breath and even care for the body after life has left it, but once the body is cold I have a problem with it. [Maybe it's because of my brother Alli. At his funeral here in the states, I touched his hand and it was so cold I felt the chill shoot up my arm to my elbow.] I had become attached to the babies, so I paid for King to be cremated and returned to me. After about three weeks I heard nothing back, so I called; they told me they accidentally discarded his ashes, sprinkling it over a cemetery with the ashes of other pets no one wanted back. I distinctly requested him back when I took him in, they realized their error and apologized to no end, but the damage was already done and nothing could be undone at that point. I was so angry, I couldn't say what they had done out loud. For months my son kept asking "when we were getting King's ashes back?" And I couldn't bring myself to answer for a while. The other four thrived, and we had grown very attached, so we kept them all.

Once I got to Alabama, God never allowed me to leave, until He sent me. He brought me there and kept me there. He stripped me of everything I had and had known, cut me off from all I was used to and depended on, and stripped me of this independent self (thinking I could ever live without Him). I was becoming naked before Him, so I would rely on Him only and trust Him completely, teaching me to rely solely on Him. From the moment I entered the state, He gave me peace and started dealing with me, bringing me close to Him and healing me.

We also were dealing with my weight issue. Since my male cousin Richmond tried to rape me, and other people coming at me, I developed issues concerning that. Those issues, I have accepted, is the cause of all my weight gain, steadily since eleven years old when I went back to live with my father. I thought it would protect me and keep perverts away, but I now want it all off and have turned it over to God because He has shown me and I have accepted that it won't matter to a sick mind what I look like. I trust only God now to protect me from such things and all things not meant for me and to strengthen me through what is meant for me.

We got to Alabama on the night of the twenty-ninth with thirty-five dollars in my pocket and a plan of God I was not aware of. We spent the night in the car, then in the morning we continued driving and got to the town I wanted on the afternoon on the thirtieth.

I have to halt here a little, so I can go back for a moment.

I had basically stopped praying, because my thoughts had become of the flesh of a sexual nature. I had also not cried in about eight years. I held in all emotions. I started getting teary when watching programs on TV, which was not like me, but I would hold it in then, too. I had a terrible respect and fear of God, and knowing that I wanted these, as I believed—unholy sexual things I was thinking, how could I turn to Him? But I could have; this is when He would have done His best work in me, proving to me that He was truly my God. I thought, After I experience this thing I want, I will then turn back to Him. How extremely presumptuous of me—a thing which God hates, but I gave no thought to it, because I thought evil was working in my flesh, so I stopped praying. This was my crime against Him, making what I was feeling number one; *No one and nothing is above God.*

I began to believe in Him in a different way though, never questioning Him, always accepting everything that came my way as His will for me or something that He allowed. I still believed on Him and would thank Him when He blessed me. I even thanked Him in my trials for the experience and strength it would give me. He was preparing me, pouring faith into me, though I didn't deserve such a blessed gift. I believed in Him strongly, trusting Him to provide, and He did, but I just refused to turn to Him in prayer. When things looked bad or went bad, I refused all the more to pray, because after I had neglected Him, I did not want to now turn to Him with prayers of need. I wanted to wait till my life got better and I wasn't needy. Then I could start praying again, not because I wanted something, but because I just loved Him. But He was always waiting, still loving me, and though I was allowing myself to fall, He was at every turn sending angels to catch me to a soft fall.

I did turn to Him for a moment about two months before I moved, while my god-children's mom went into distress from her pregnancy. They had delivered the baby from her prematurely and she was in a coma for a few days. Oh, how I prayed for them and went to her daily! I felt God listening, I felt his *full* attention. I guess that's when my change started, but I was still in too deep to notice.

When I saw her lying there, dead to the world, is when I knew the depth of my love for her, that this friendship was really important to me. God did a great work in restoring her. Even though we lived in the same town, I hadn't kept contact with her except on holidays to drop off the kids' presents, and she would give my son his presents, because she is his god-mom. This last baby is also my god-baby, and because of my drastic move, I never even got to hold her; she was by then released from the hospital. It disappoints me, and I still long to hold her, but all in God's time and purpose.

God had used this same friend to save me in my late teenage years. I met this Rastafarian young man, Ragga, who was older than me by maybe ten years or more. (Ragga is short for Ragamuffin, meaning in Jamaican lingo a tough guy, bad boy, rude boy, able to handle your business). We met outside the Tavern (a Jamaican club) one night after it closed because he boldly walked over to the car where we girls were standing and made a crude remark concerning himself and my breasts. Over time I got to know him and that he was all right, and he came to respect me because he saw that I wasn't a loose woman.

We became friends, and we got to love each other as friends, and I really loved him. There were five of us girls, three of the girls were not a part of the other girl group, Ragga was the one who named us five girls the *Girls' Posse* and sometimes called us the *"A" Posse*, because all our first names had A's (Andrea, Sophia, Aisha, Keisha, and Towanna). He was there for me emotionally and would do things to help me with the man I loved when I asked him, even getting up and leaving his girlfriend alone to help me, which made her despise me. When we were at the club she would try to get back at me by dancing with the man I loved, but I didn't care because I knew she was just jealous of my friendship with Ragga, and I knew I wasn't guilty of anything.

He set me up with one of his new friends once because he thought the guy I was in love with didn't deserve me. His friend was a nice person who kept his nose clean, but we became nothing more than friends because I was already in love. When I was brokenhearted, I would hang out in his sound studio basement, and this Rastafarian friend I loved would dedicate and play me music to cheer me up.

He was a small-time producer I guess, and he had connections with more famous Jamaican artists, like Rula Brown and Frankie Paul whom my friends and I got introduced to, and others. He handled a few local Jamaican aspiring artists, so he had set up a huge sound system like they had in the clubs in his basement, where they would sharpen their skills, and he had produced a record for a couple of the guys from the male group; all us friends would hang out at his house.

My wonderful friend seemed to have a little secret life that I had looked away from because he respected me and didn't put it in my face. The police suspected he was a drug dealer (of marijuana, I guess). One day I had plans to stop by his house, but first I dropped in to visit my friend and my first god-baby. We hung out a while, then I wanted to leave to go by Ragga's house, but my friend urged me to stay with her till her husband got home, so I gave in and stayed with her.

While we were there having fun with the baby, the news came. I don't recall if someone called her or if her husband came home with the news, but the news was that everyone in the house where I wanted to go had just been arrested. There had been a raid on the house, and the police had dragged off everyone to the station. Some got questioned and released and some got arrested. I would have been right there in the midst of them had God not used her to save me, and I thanked her over and over. After that, I knew the police would still be watching, so I stayed away from his house, but Ragga and I remained the same friends. Now when I think of my friend (my god-kid's mom) I have such great respect and admiration for the woman, wife, and mother she is.

Years ago, I was told that Ragga was in Jamaica and had died there of a stroke, but I don't know if it's true. If it is, I weep for his soul; if it is not, then my soul will rejoice that he still has the chance to hear and obey

God, and this is my prayer for him. [He is with Jesus now]. I was told that my old friends, a girl from the A-posse and her boyfriend from the guy group were saved and got married. I pray they are living in truth to God, and I am joyful concerning them.

So, during the whole trip to Alabama I could feel the powers of darkness working against me, just a very heavy presence I cannot explain. The enemy didn't want me there, but God did. Usually if I have directions, or even if I don't, I get there, because I love driving. But, this time was different. To this day, if you ask me how I arrived or what path I took, though I never had to turn around for going in any wrong direction, I still cannot tell you, because halfway here, my directions just didn't make sense. God led me there, at times literally holding my car on the road at seventy miles per hour while the enemy closed my eyes, even at times when I didn't feel sleepy or had just rested. I was just drained. God used my son to talk me through the day, and He used my music to keep me through the night.

When I arrived in the state, I called my family again, and because of the rough trip, I was feeling what needed to be done, so after speaking with Big Sis, it was confirmed in me, and we agreed that I would stay and tough it out in Alabama. There was nothing to go back to, because in either place, I would be homeless. Also, being there with a cheaper cost of living, it would be easier for me to get on my feet, and I already felt much peace that I couldn't explain.

We all made it, but it was an extremely rough trip, especially for the cats. They were overheated: The air conditioning had caused the car to overheat in Virginia while trying to keep us cool when I had stopped for a nap, so I could no longer use it. Anyway, I had decided that we would go camping for the week, but I didn't tell my family because I didn't know how they would receive it, so I let them believe I was staying in a hotel, which was the last thing they knew I was checking on the Internet. I went and viewed the apartment I had decided on from the Web, and it was not all they said, but it was OK, so I went on.

At about 3:00 p.m., I was driving around trying to find the park where I intended to camp, when a police officer pulled me over thinking my tags were out of date, but when he checked, he realized they were fine. I had them in my glove compartment instead of on my license plates.

I must say that I had developed a real hatred or let's say, a real strong dislike, for police officers. I felt they harassed me; though I was an occasional speeder, at times they would stop me and give me tickets for speeding other things at times when I really was innocent. It rarely ever happened when I was guilty, so this made me ~~hate~~ strongly dislike them. Anyway, to myself, I would curse at them whenever I saw them stopping other people, believing they were harassing them, too, but since I had entered Alabama, a peace had overcome me, so there was now no ~~hatred~~ strong dislike.

He asked me some questions, and we got to talking and I liked him, which was a first for me with any officer, so I told him what my plans were. God used him, and he told me to hang on. He went to his car and made some phone calls then came back and told me he got us a bed at the Salvation Army. He then drove in front and led me there to show me where it was, we got out of our cars, and he walked me to the door, showing me which door I was supposed to use (they would not be open until 5:30 p.m.). We walked back to our cars and stood there talking for maybe an half hour. He told me a little bit about the area, and the job prospects, and that his wife was also a nurse (she is an RN), and how it was for her as a nurse when they moved to the state. Then, he told me where I could find him if I needed his help for anything, and we said good-bye.

I left, went to the park, and gave my cats more water. They were not doing well. They wanted out of the car and I wanted that for them. I wanted to open out the other carriage and put the babies in it to give everyone even more room so they wouldn't be so hot, but there was just no space in the vehicle. I rearranged the car a bit and set two fans on them that I had packed for that purpose. It was a little better for them.

It was time to check in, so I went back to the Salvation Army and was processed. I told the guy who processed me that there was no way I would allow my son to be parted from me to their male quarters. The women's side was empty, so he gave me a large room with four beds just for me and my son. The TV had no cable or antenna, so it didn't work at all, and my son wasn't happy about that, but I was grateful he had a bed. The shower was the most disgusting I had ever seen, with green mold growing everywhere, but it was better than nothing: at least we could shower. My son and I went to the room where I read him their rules from a sheet of paper, then the guy came and got us for dinner. As we stepped outside the door I thought I would be honest and ask if they allowed pets. To my great disappointment, he said, "No." I wanted so badly to get them out of the car. I had promised them a home where they could run around freely and sit on the windowsill hammock, which they loved to do. I promised us all a better life.

    We ate dinner, then I decided to go feed the cats and give them water for the night. I had rolled the windows shut to prevent the car from being stolen because the policeman had told me that this was a problem in the area; the cats had the fans on them so I believed they were OK. When I opened the car, they were not. With the windows closed, the fans were circulating pure hot air, nevertheless, they were blocked from it and they were in heatstroke. My son and I sprang into action, and I grabbed the gallon bottles of water I had in the car and poured it over them, wetting our clothes and the car, but I didn't care about that. There was no more water, and the bottled water we had used was warm, so I sent my son dashing repeatedly to the room to fetch water in the empty bottles as I grabbed them one at a time by whoever was worse off and saturated them from head to tail with water, but it was too late. Only five of them were in distress. Of the two that were OK, one (Precious) was separate because he was sickly with his bowels and I didn't want him to mess on the others during our trip, and being separate did save his life; the other was Figero. He had sat in the entrance of this huge carrier getting all the air, though hot, and blocking all the others from any air circulation: the fan was right up against the gate of the carrier.

    By now my son, Sean, and I had double-teamed, each of us holding one, trying to cool them down, but each one we held started going into seizures. Then, one by one as I held them, they stopped breathing. I did pet CPR on them, but two of my babies (Ray and Matt) died, and my son cried. Then as I held the dad, Max, cooling him off, he had a seizure, and I begged him, "Please don't leave me." As I did so, he locked eyes with me as if he understood my plea but couldn't stay; he had to be with his babies. Then he died. I worked on him to no avail, then held him tight in my arms as my heart broke because he was the best, most well behaved, caring, and loving of all seven, but the others needed me so I continued. The mom, Misty, and the third baby, Tai, hung in there, but they were weak and still having seizures. The seizures they all had were not violent ones: their legs would extend and stiffen. I let my son hold the two sick ones, Misty and Tai, while I quickly cleaned up the mess I made.

By now, it started raining a little, and it was getting dark, so I took Misty and Tai from my son and sent him to bed inside the room. I stayed in the car with them lying on my chest while I watched the door to the room where my son was. As I sat, my mind went back to when I was at my storage unit, packing for the trip, how God told me what he would do.

I had bought a few home-veterinary-care books to learn how to care well for them, and as I packed for the trip, I wanted to take one of the books with me, so as I flipped through them, comparing to see which one had the most information, one of the books fell open to a page telling how to handle grief from the death of a pet. I immediately closed the book and said, "Forbid it, Lord," but now here I was; it was fulfilled.

I cried to God for the first time in years, and I talked to Him. I begged Him, saying, "No more deaths, Lord," but He wasn't through. I saw my son coming back out, so I stopped crying. He didn't want to be away from us, so I let him stay. He took Tai and held him; that baby was his favorite.

About ten minutes after he sat with us, Tai started gagging, so I gave Misty to my son and took Tai, and he vomited up something that was not recognizable. Then, moments later as he lay on my chest, he took his last breath. He looked so peaceful, I didn't bother working on him. So, three babies and the dad were dead. I later had them cremated together, as the family they were, and returned to me (each of them, and all of their ashes). Misty was weak and had a couple more seizures. She was in worse shape than the others that had died, but I begged her not to leave me, and I cried and begged God for her life, and He responded to me.

I took her to a vet, but they referred me to someone else, and I didn't have the money for a vet anyway, so it was up to me. I nursed and cared for her and never left her unattended for a moment because she was extremely weak and could not take one step without falling over. She fought hard as we encouraged her, and within two weeks God had *fully* restored her.

Three days after the others died, Big Sis called me, and as I started telling her the horrid details, I broke down crying in front of my son. Then because I was crying, Big Sis started crying because she knows I love them greatly like kids. Except for the dad, Max, whom I got at one-and-a half-months old, they all took their first and last breaths in my hands.

The pain was unbearable and haunting. Because of the promises I had made us all of a wonderful home, I felt like I betrayed them. I didn't ask God why, I just told Him I trusted Him and prayed, for the first time in years, concerning myself. I prayed for him to take the pain away, and He did, but I still miss them and always will. I also broke down sobbing when I handed them over to the person who would cremate them; as I watched him walk away with them, it broke my heart. The man was worried about me driving, but God held me up. My son and I missed them and talked about them, and at times imagined how they would look running around our home, but we understood that God knew best. [In hindsight, who would receive a person with seven cats into their apartments? No one].

We stayed at the Salvation Army for three nights over the holiday weekend. Their hours were from 5:30 p.m. to 8:00 a.m. That's the only time everyone was allowed on the premises. At 8:00 a.m., all had to leave, so my son and I spent all day at the park or driving around to try to get familiar with the area.

On Labor Day, when we went to the park and as I cleaned out the car, there were some church people having a picnic. They all were extremely friendly and kept inviting us over to join them, but my pride prevented me from going, besides, I wanted to clean the car and rearrange the things in it to make more room for us, but I let my son, Sean, join them.

They saw my out-of-state plates and inquired of my situation, and I found myself telling them my plans and where I was staying—something my family didn't even know, but I felt no need to hide it from them, and I have been telling the truth ever since. The only way I escape is by avoiding being asked, or give no comment because if I open my mouth, nothing but truth comes out; unless, of course, if I'm playing around. It seems God won't allow me to lie or be dishonest, and troubles me greatly if I try to do otherwise. This came about because I purposed in my heart to be faithful to Him because of how He cared for me. The temptation comes, but my soul is greatly troubled if I try to do or say anything other than what's true or right.

It was about 4:00 p.m., and I needed gas, so I had to go. The gas tank was on E, so I couldn't keep the car running while cleaning; but, when I was finished, with the fan going for my cats and vacuuming the car and pumping up the tire with the air compressor I had bought for the trip, I had drained the battery and my jump pack was not working. One of the church ladies passed by again and asked if I was OK, and I said, "No," that I needed a jump, so she got her car and gave me the jump and told me she would bring me an application for food stamps the next day. We said good-bye, they gave me their numbers and a very heavily stocked plate of food, and my son and I left.

On the first business day of the week, I went to one housing authority and applied for housing, and then to all the facilities I saw and filled out job applications until it was time to check in, then I headed back to the room, but when I got there I was told I couldn't stay because I was supposed to see their social worker that day, so that was it. The guy also told me that the woman from church had come by, and he gave me the applications she had left for the housing authorities—one of which I had already been to that day, and the food stamp application. I called her and she came right over within five minutes, also bringing her husband to meet me, and they gave me more phone numbers to reach them. Turns out the couple is a pastor and his wife.

I went back the next morning to speak with the social worker, but she seemed firm and unreceptive, even though I had explained that I was out hunting for a job and a home, which could be proven. I also told her I did not recall being told I needed to see her that specific day. She didn't seem inviting and repeated a rule they had which said, once you are cast out, no matter the reason, you must wait thirty days before you can reapply for shelter; because of her demeanor, I didn't beg. I just asked for any job leads she had, which was none, then I left.

We slept in my car for two nights, then I got my last paycheck from New Jersey. We went camping for ten days and nine nights, then I ran out of money. While camping, I was resourceful to keep us somewhat comfortable. I had packed our fishing poles for activity, and we went fishing a few times, but we caught nothing.

Someone who was fishing with us caught a big catfish and gave it to me. I prepared it and cooked it, but it is not something I want to do again: I didn't like the smell or slippery feel when I was preparing it. Though it did smell great cooked, I still had that memory, probably also because I saw it die—panting as it lay there. My son expressed the same feeling about watching it die, and I just listened.

The campsite had decent showers and we had privacy. We had a laundry room with a washer and dryer to wash our clothes, a picnic table with benches, a water pipe and electrical outlets—all by my tent at lot number forty. We both were relieved to get out of the car and lie down. I had brought my air mattress and air pump, so it was somewhat comfortable for us to lie down; the cat had sunk its claws into it previously in New Jersey, so it had a slow leak that I just found out about that night, but it was manageable.

After a couple days, it did start feeling kind of spooky to us while we were outside the tent because during the week we were the only tenters there. We would turn in the minute it got dark. When we turned in for the night, I plugged in the light and the stereo and brought them inside the tent, along with the cats, and locked us all in—then we felt safe.

Every day, I bought two bags of ice to give us cold drinks and water; I also cooked what I had packed, daily, in the electrical pot I brought. I realized, that through God, I can make do and have peace in any situation, making it work until I can do better. I am a survivor, and my son, though I caused the situation he was in, is now stronger for it.

On the day I left the campground, I was relieved; I believe it was a move of God, and He never allowed me to go back there to sleep. The reason I was relieved is because of someone we had camped with over the weekend. The following Saturday morning, he came back with a friend. They came fishing at the park, and he remembered me from before. He said he came over to see if I was OK because I was still there. He and his male friend were both intoxicated. As we talked I let it slip, in error, that we would probably be there over the weekend, and he said he would probably see me, because he was *"planning to drop by"* or come camping again. After he left, something about the whole conversation, and the way he said what he did, made me grow quite uncomfortable, and I regretted telling him I would be there. I felt unsafe, like they could not be trusted, so God removed me from that, and I have never had cause or need to drive back into that park since I left that evening at six (except when I showed it to my mom and brother).

That Sunday, after the creepy visit from my creepy visitor, I quit my job in New Jersey. Then on Monday, I took out a post office box and filed for unemployment. This same day (Monday), the pastor's wife found me at the park; I had called her a couple days prior, to let them know where I now was. She came by and took me and my son to the supermarket and bought us some groceries, and I gave her the applications for the food stamps and a couple of housing authorities, which she turned in for me. I went to the other housing authorities myself.

Another woman, Susan, I met camping, came back to the park to check on me shortly after the pastor's wife had arrived; she gave me her number and the names and numbers of housing authorities, also a safe house, because she said she didn't know if I had needed protection from physical abuse.

The campsite manager also allowed me to camp for three days while I was waiting on Big Sis to put my check into my checking account. When the check cleared, I paid the manager all I owed.

Two days before we left the park, my son was there playing around, and there was a broken concrete bench, exposing the steel, onto which he accidentally rammed his shin—it was really bad. I was dressing it myself from the first-aid kit I had bought and packed, but two days later I knew it wasn't enough, so I took him to the hospital and he received six stitches. Though he had received one less than two years prior, I insisted they give him a tetanus shot.

During the week, I had received a letter from the Department of Human Resources, from a county and department I never filed any papers with, telling me I had an appointment with them that Tuesday at 8:00 a.m. We slept in the car for three nights, then I went to my appointment. Through the hardships I never lost the peace God gave me and believed God for a better home and a better life. I gave all concerns to God and did show my faith with works, but through nothing I did or could explain, this blessing came to me.

When I called to check what the appointment was about, they said someone from the other county where I had filed the food stamp application (the one the pastor's wife had gotten me and dropped off for me) had contacted them about me, because the park I had been staying in belonged to their county.

When I went to the appointment, I first met with a woman, Ester, from Assistance/Aide to Families with Dependent Children (AFDC). We spoke at length, and I hid nothing from her. She told me I needed to make a choice, because by now I was spending my days in their parks to cook and wash, and my nights in a different town which was just across the bridge/border in a different county, so I needed to choose and declare a county as my address. Though I was homeless, I still had to declare homelessness in a specific county or I couldn't be helped.

God prompted me to choose their county because He made me feel a liking for and a certain trust of her, so she asked me a few more questions and discovered I was not eligible for the AFDC because the child support I was receiving was $200, and the maximum income I was allowed was $190. Was this déjà vu? Did not another social service say the same words, which brought me to rock bottom? But, she told me she needed me to speak with an intake worker, so I did, and we also spoke very openly, and I hid nothing. She asked me what they could do for me, and I told her I needed a home and a job. She left me a couple times, I guess to make phone calls, then she left me for a few minutes to speak to her supervisor, and when she came back she said, "Would it help you if we put you in a hotel?" I said, "Yes it would," and they put us in a hotel that night. It was the nicest we'd ever been in and also clean. Also, it had ice machines: no more struggling and counting change to buy ice. They served a continental breakfast every morning, and they had a phone in my room so I could receive calls and make calls—no longer cut off from the world for lack of minutes on my cell phone. I discovered that we could speak to my sister and the kids for hours for free via our computer, hearing each other's voices (I brought my laptop along for the trip).

We had a large TV with cable, and my son was thrilled about seeing his cartoons again. I was a regular ABC soap watcher, but since I got to town, a TV had not been available to me, so I kept listening to my gospel music, and by then I preferred it, and it also uplifted me. I didn't know how long this blessing would last, so I let my son have the run of the television, to his delight.

We had air conditioning now, which felt good, but we were upstairs, and the three kittens had to remain in the car. The hotel would allow them in but at ten dollars each, and I had no money. My account had sixteen cents in it. I was very worried about them but could not leave the windows open, especially now, because when we were checking in, there was a prison break from the prison that was about two blocks over.

The police were all over the streets in cars and on foot and had come to the hotel lobby inquiring of everyone if we had seen the escaped man, and I don't believe they ever caught him. So, even with what happened to my other babies, I was still trapped: having to shut all the windows. When it was day, and hot, we went to another park and would let them run around while we played with them to keep their attention, so they would not stray. We would always stay at the park till dusk; when it got cool, then the kittens would be OK locked in the car.

The voucher DHR had given me was for one night and I was supposed to return to them the next day "for more help if needed." When I checked out that morning, the place I had parked my car was right in front of an empty room. I looked in as I got into my car and thought: *This room is so prefect; the parking space is three feet from the door; it has the huge glass wall where I could pull the curtain back and see the car so I could leave the windows open and they would be OK.*

I went to DHR, and they gave me a voucher for seven days. When I was checking in, I wanted to ask for that room so badly, but I stifled the urge, as I often did; never speaking up for what I want, and never wanting to be a bother to anyone. When she was finished, she handed me the key card to my room, and it was the same room my heart had desired. God had blessed me, and I thanked Him where I stood. I knew it was a blessing because other rooms were empty and the one I had checked out of that morning was still empty. It would have been very easy for her to put me back there, but God intervened on my behalf.

While I was still at DHR I met with the real intake worker, April; the other woman had filled in because April was not available. She told me they could not help me further unless I agreed to **"open myself up to services."** I felt like walking away because this was the government, and I didn't want them in my life—not that I had anything to hide, but once I signed their papers, I would be in the system, and they can be so invasive and intrusive.

I am (or was, before God called me to do this) such an intensely private and proud person, I would rather have died than be back in the system again, having a social worker in my life, but I looked at my son, and my heart had love and compassion for him, and my pride melted away. How could I keep him on the street when he could be in luxury? There was a fight within me, but I chose my son and said yes to the social worker, and it was the best thing I ever did. They were angels sent of God to me. He used them to care for us so well, and they were not at all intrusive, but I guess they didn't need to be because God was changing me. Every time we met, I laid myself open and revealed all that was in me.

That day when I agreed to work with them, God immediately caused them to set in motion a plan of deliverance for us. Along with the hotel voucher, I was given a gas voucher for a full tank of gas and a food voucher for groceries. Also, because I was new to town and did not know my way around, instead of just giving me directions, this social worker, April, left the building and drove in front of me, taking me to one of the gas stations where I was authorized to use the voucher. She waited for me, then showed me to the Food World supermarket I was allowed to shop at, she inquired of me if I would be able to find my way back to the hotel, then left me to shop. I thanked God from my heart for these blessings.

When the week was over, I went back to the social worker, and she gave me another hotel voucher for ten days. I had called the hotel and confirmed the reservation so I wouldn't lose that same room; then, when I got there, the manager informed me that the hotel was filled up because of a biker convention. I told her I had called ahead and who I spoke with; she made a phone call to that person who was on duty when I called, and she confirmed what I said, then she gave me my room.

On Sunday, the twenty-first of September 2003, the pastor's wife came and drove in front of me, showing me the way to their church. I marked it at about twenty-eight miles from the hotel, so I would know when to look for the building. God caused it to rain that day, making it cool, so I didn't worry about the cats.

They are Baptists. The experiences I had in their services were very different from what I was used to, being from an Apostolic/Pentecostal background. Now, being called of God through a dream, He gave me to be of the Apostolic faith/Christ's faith, and has anointed me to be an Apostle and disciple of Jesus, which I now profess and declare boldly. God did use this pastor at certain pivotal points to speak to my soul.

After a while, I was very reluctant to stay with them because there was no manifestation of the Holy Ghost in their church; it's to me like they mock and are embarrassed by such things as when the Spirit gives utterance of speaking in tongues with individuals from other churches, even of their denomination. There is power in the presence of the Holy Ghost. There is change in the presence of the Holy Ghost. When the Holy Ghost is present He will be felt, He will be heard, He will be known. The presence of God will be evident, for the vessel must give witness to the Spirit of God abiding within it, for He is too great to be contained with normalcy within our mortal bodies. He will cause God to be glorified, He will speak, He must perform a duty. The gift cannot lie dormant unless something is wrong. They all believe they have Him abiding already; even the very little children are taught and believe this. Not that God won't fill and use children, He will, but I am concerned for all their souls (the church body) and keep them in prayer to God concerning this. Because they all believe they already possess the Holy Ghost, they are not open to Him, and therefore will not receive Him in truth. So, I await God to open their eyes and do a great work in them. There are sheep of other folds that belong to God and the body of Christ, but whatever fold, denomination, or doctrine they are, Jesus must be their center. And, before He should return, they must adopt His faith and His doctrine and live according to His gospel, coming into apostleship and discipleship with Him, in order to reign with Him in eternity.

 I was very afraid of receiving strange teachings and believing a lie, but God has told me to hold on to what He teaches me and not to be afraid. He will put the truth within me, and I will know it. In my terrified state, I turned to God, and He gave me Proverbs 22:17–21. The great fear I felt left me after I read His Word to me. He had shown me with a strong hand that He wanted me to go to their church. He reproved me when I didn't obey and blessed me when I obeyed. He had shown me that He loves them and wants to do a work in them, and that I and my son would have been cursed if I was not obedient, and that His purpose is to be fulfilled in them. [His purpose was in the wife, she was chosen and beloved.]

 I do love them still, and was obedient, though I didn't know exactly what would be done or when or how. He only said, "Go!" So I went without fear, because I believe God concerning me and concerning them. His Word is true and not one word falls unfulfilled, but I need to abide in Him to receive of His promises. I am so joyful about what God will do, because I love them, and God used them to care for me, not just with things, but inwardly. It was ordained: I was given to their care and that they should love me; though we have now been released from that command, I will carry them in my heart.

After church, everyone greeted me with loving, open arms and hugs. The pastor told me how his wife was continually worried and concerned for my well-being. She invited me over for dinner, and it was a good fellowship. I felt extremely comfortable, and it was a bit surprising to me, but that comfortable feeling brought me pleasure because we talked and laughed just like I was with Big Sis, and she reminded me very much of her. The kids flocked around me like my nieces and nephews would, as if they had known me previously, but they had only met me that day. I love children, so this was good and made me feel more at home. My son had a very outgoing personality that he sure didn't get from me or his father, because we are mostly quiet. Maybe, he got it from his aunt (Big Sis): but, he was sure at home. Anyway, it was a good time.

They had introduced me to all the ladies of the church, and I made plans with a church sister to meet with her the next day. On the twenty-second, I left my car in the church parking lot, and we went with her to view apartments. She also took me to the apartments where she lived. The property was nice, but I didn't get to see the inside. We met with the landlord, and I filled out the application right away, but I had to wait to hear from the unemployment office, because this two-bedroom apartment was $260, and I had only two hundred coming in, that didn't belong to me, but would now have to be used for my storage payments anyway. I was not even thinking about the utility bill I would have with this apartment or living expenses, but the manager said as soon as I heard from unemployment, to let her know and give her a copy of it.

During the rest of that week I received a message at the answering service of my cell phone from one of the nursing homes I had applied to.

I called them immediately after listening to the message; they seemed very eager to hire me. We made an appointment for 1:00 p.m. the next day, then I went over to find the location again so I would be sure where I was going and how long it took to get there so I would not be late. [This is something my mother taught me: always locate the destination ahead of time if at all possible.]

After I found the nursing home, I drove around looking for an apartment close to the job so I would feel some safety for my son. There was a housing authority / apartments across the street, but they had previously refused me because they needed my green card and my birth certificate and a couple other papers I didn't have with me. My trip to Alabama was not meant to be permanent at this time, and all my belongings were packed away in storage. I had the only key with me on my key chain, so my family couldn't even help in getting these things to me even if I had given them the security codes.

There was also a small group of lovely apartments on a property next to the nursing home. I thought it was perfect, so I wrote down the number to call and stopped looking because I believed that apartment would be mine (and it was—for a price God wouldn't allow). I then went to my post office box and had received mail; my unemployment was approved. I didn't call the other manager who told me to call when I heard from unemployment because that apartment was more than forty miles away, and I wanted something really close. I called the number and made an appointment to view the apartment the day of my interview at 10:00 a.m.

On another note, when the seven-day voucher had ended and I had checked out of the hotel, I saw the maintenance guy and a housekeeper. I don't remember what got us talking, because we never held a conversation before, only to say hello, and they would ask me if I needed anything. They were really nice to me beyond their jobs. In our talking, it came out that I was looking for an apartment, and the maintenance guy told me there was an empty apartment next door to him. We agreed to meet at 2:00 p.m. when he got off work because he said he had a connection with the landlord, and I could have the apartment that night. But the housekeeper, in a subtle way that I picked up on, was encouraging me to keep looking and told me she would bring me the classified ads the following day, which she did. That was the first time God said no, but I wasn't hearing. When I got to DHR, I was hesitant and afraid to ask for what I wanted, but got the courage from God and my son, so I asked the social worker if instead of them paying for more time for me at the hotel, if they could use the money to get me into an apartment. She inquired how I would maintain it, and I told her about the unemployment. I told her about the maintenance guy's offer and asked her for the directions because I had decided it wasn't a good idea to go with him in case I wasn't pleased. She went to her supervisor and came back and wrote down the directions for me but then told me her supervisor said, why don't they pay for more days at the hotel and I can use the time to look around instead of taking the first thing that I find. I think when she was told where it was, she wanted better for us. I understood but I was still sad, which was the second time God said no, but still I wanted to at least see it. They gave me the ten-day voucher. When I left there, it was about 3:00 p.m., and I was relieved to have missed the maintenance guy, so I went and found the apartments myself. I wasn't pleased with it and didn't feel it safe for my son to live there, and it was so far away. For the third time God not only said no, but showed me no. Only then I listened, even though my son was urging me to take it just so we could live somewhere, but God spoke to my heart, and I listened to Him for the home He had in store for us, instead of listening to desperation.

 The day of the interview, I met with the apartment owner/manager I had made the appointment with, and he showed me the inside, and it was beautiful with a lot of new appliances and two bedrooms for $395. I couldn't find this beautiful thing in New Jersey for that price. The roach motel I was staying at in New Jersey was two hundred per week, six fifty per month, with no offered efficiencies. He was all set to give it to me, but there was one more detail: "Do you allow animals?" Answer: "No." But, he suggested if I gave them away, I could have it. I thought of everything to keep them, and even called him back with an offer to add one hundred dollars monthly to my rent, so they could stay with me. He was very moved to do this because of my love for them, but still could not; he said it would show favoritism, and my neighbors who had to get rid of their animal would be very displeased.

I went to the job interview, and they were very excited to meet with me. We agreed for me to orientate that Monday, Tuesday and Wednesday, from 10:00 a.m. to 3:00 p.m. and agreed on the pay rate I would receive. For my son's sake I knew what I had to do concerning the animals, but it tore at our hearts. I had repeatedly promised us all a home and believed God for it, and it felt like such a betrayal to now dump them somewhere in this new place. They had known only us all their lives; they are not just animals to us, we truly love them. They are a part of our family, so I was also looking into boarding homes to keep them there so I could accept this apartment while still looking for an apartment that would accept us all. I spoke with my mom at length about this job and this apartment, and she made the same suggestion before I mentioned it, so we agreed that was the thing to do, but God had something better for me.

The next day I drove around the neighborhood again, and it was late and getting dark, and my son was getting bored and hungry and urging me to go back to the hotel, and I almost gave in, but my heart said, "Just one more drive around." God directed me down a street that looked like a dead end. The street is barely noticeable; no one would think anything is back there, but God directed the car there, and lo and behold, one block away from the nursing home around the corner, there stood a lovely brick apartment building, fairly newly constructed, containing four apartments, two downstairs and two upstairs. In one of the upstairs windows was a "for rent" sign. My heart leaped with joy. I parked quickly, and my son ran out of the car, up the stairs, and read the number to me. I wrote down the number to call, and I just had to see, so I joined him on the balcony. There were no blinds or curtains, so we peered through the window—We loved it. I felt more peace within. I knew it was ours. I had a feeling of trust and faith like I had never felt before. I thanked God for it right there.

I called the number and made an appointment to view it the next morning. At 9:00 a.m. on Friday, September 26, 2003, the owner/landlord showed me around, and it got better and better with every step. It was a two-bedroom, it had a laundry room, it had a dressing room, and it had a balcony outside my bedroom in the back. Also in the front was another balcony that was not shared, either.

I filled out the application, we talked, and she said I could have it that night if I got the utility turned on. I then went and spoke with the social worker. I told her about the job interview I had, the drug test I was to take later that day, my orientation days, and the apartment I viewed that morning, so she set things in motion. But, while filling out the application, my son drew my attention to some little tiny hoppity insects crawling on my chair. When I looked down, they were all over my pant legs, shoes, and on the floor. I thought them to be fleas but knew I could get rid of them and would not allow them to hinder this blessing, so I wanted the apartment anyway. The landlord left for work, then when we were leaving, we stood outside by the car, and I told my son to strip down to his swim trunks. I checked him and got them off him and gave him clean clothes (all our belongings were still packed in the car), then I did the best I could with myself and covered my cats' carriages with a sheet so they would be protected from these insects. I suspected they crawled on me when I went out on the rear balcony, and I was right.

It was a very close call in getting the apartment that day. We set up another meeting with the landlord at 5:00 p.m. to sign the lease, and by then it was already after three, and the landlord had told me if I didn't get the utilities turned on that day, she couldn't hand over the keys till I did. I needed to move in by that night because the utility company is closed on Saturdays, and I was to start my job on Monday morning. For my son's sake this needed to get done. Also, I couldn't have the cats locked in the car all day while working; they would die for sure. For all concerned it needed to get done that day. The social worker met me at the utility company with the voucher to pay them, but there was a problem. They needed a copy of the lease which I wouldn't have till the meeting with the landlord at five, at which time the utility company would be closed. I couldn't think straight; everything was a blur. It was all moving so fast, I just trusted God to take care of the details and keep me from something regrettable. I made some phone calls to the landlord with my cell phone, she signed and faxed over a copy of the lease to the utility company while I waited, and I filled it all out and signed, then quickly skimmed over it to make sure I didn't just sign my life away. The social worker paid them, and they rushed through the work order right then just minutes before they closed. It was already 4:00 p.m. or minutes after. We then left, and I showed the social worker where the apartment was so we could meet at five. I also showed her the nursing home where I would be working, and she was amazed and agreed with me that the location was *"just perfect,"* as all God's gifts are.

I was about ten minutes late to the meeting because a cargo train held me up, I have never seen trains that long (approx. one hundred or more cars). When I got there, they were already inside. I walked through the door and said, "hello," and that angel of a social worker looked at me and said, "It's all yours, and the utility is on." I signed the official copy of the lease, and the landlord briefly went over a few things, then she handed me the keys. I thanked both of them, and I remember wanting to give the social worker a great big hug but I held back. I hugged my son tight and just thanked God over and over. Without a credit check, without a reference check, no red tape, just like that, handed to me by God. My God is all that, awesome in every way, and a true provider. We had a home, no more streets, no more parks, no more motels, no more hotels, a real home, able to take bubble baths, a kitchen with appliances. Everything was pleasant and precious to us, even the smallest, simplest things. The social worker and the landlord (the wife; a husband and wife were joint owners) were both filled with joy for my son and me, and they just smiled at us. I couldn't stop staring at the key in my hand, then my son took it and held it, then I took it back and just stared in amazement because I couldn't believe it: it was surreal. Yet, I believed and just thanked God. The landlord left, then the social worker left after we spoke very briefly. I stood on the balcony—*my balcony*—until she left.

Now, it was darkened and cloudy outside. I came in and closed my door and walked from room to room, corner to corner, thanking God. As I did that, rain started pouring down, hard, like never before since I got to Alabama. As a matter of fact, God held back the rain all the days we were tenting at the park; but, it had occasionally rained while we were in the car, at the Salvation Army, and at the hotel.

I called my mom and let her know I had gotten a home. I then checked the back balcony, and what I thought about the insects was right. They were all over the leaves that had fallen off the trees onto the balcony and also on the outside of the glass door to the balcony. These insects had come from the trees, but they looked like and behaved like fleas. Until this day, I'm still not sure what they were; I hoped they wouldn't return the next summer. They were present all the years I lived there, but less; I kept the balcony clean and they were never a bother to us. They were a tree insect though, because when my mom moved, she told me of the same insects on her deck at the back of her house; she lived in Georgia, but had a lot of trees in her back yard, so I guess it's a southern pest. A pestilence that God drove out of my home.

Anyway, I measured the windows and my bedroom door because they had no blinds or curtains, and I also needed some insect bombs, so I gathered the small offering the church had collected for me and went to Wal-Mart. The church had done this on two occasions for me, and it was greatly appreciated, though my pride caused me great embarrassment, because on one of these two occasions they called out my name at the offering table. I begged God to forgive the way I felt, and that He not see it as my being ungrateful, and that I thanked Him. I'm glad they never did that to me again. They did also fix my car a few times; they are good people. Anyway, by then the rain had eased up and had completely stopped by the time we got there. When I parked the car and we got out, I looked up at the sky, and there were two beautiful rainbows, side by side, stretched across the sky, and I hugged my son and showed them to him and told him they were for a sign because God loved us. As I pointed to the smaller one, I said, "That's you," and then at the larger one, "That's me." I had never before in all my years seen two rainbows in the sky simultaneously, and have never since seen any such thing. There may have been some, but they have not been seen by me but once. [Until 2015; but, never quite like that first set. In 2015 He also made a rainbow cloud for me and my son to view; additionally, He also made a rainbow in the atmosphere directly across our doorway over our front porch for my son and I to view. They were all beautiful, magnificent sights to behold, to remind us of His promises to us.]

The next day, Saturday, I called a church sister, Sis Roach, to let them know I had gotten a home, and I told her of the rainbows and how I believed they were a sign of His promise to my son and I. Then, I said, "It may sound like I'm crazy, but I believe it." She said, "Well, that's your testimony right there," so as I have written, I have testified of God's love, and goodness and mercy to us in bringing us all (animals included) home: a place prepared, a place of refuge, and a place of peace. But, there were more trials and strength to be gained.

The nursing home called that same Friday we got the home. They needed me to take a drug test before I started the job, so I went and took the medicine I was on with me. The person that hired me drove in front and showed me where the lab was, then left. When I got out of the car, I realized that they were out to lunch, so I waited in the car an hour and a half until they opened back up. I went in and showed the person drawing my blood the medicines I was on, and she said to wait until afterwards, so I took the test, and it came out positive for narcotics. I showed her again what I was taking, and one of them was a narcotic. She faxed over the results and told me to go by the nursing home and show them the medication. I went there and met with the guy who hired me and another woman. She mentioned off-hand that I *"may"* need an Alabama license, then, immediately focused on the drug test. I explained the whole details to her: While I was at the hotel, I had developed an excruciating mouth ache that I thought was a toothache, but went to the dentist and he discovered that it was an ulcer on my gum. So, he prescribed the narcotic and the mouth rinse (which DHR paid for to help me). The medicines were just barely helping (I think a mouth pain is arguably the worst, most maddening, ungodly pain to ever feel). [The narcotic, if taken at the minimum dosage, was a six-day supply, and maximum four-day supply—this was day seven.] They were at times non-effective to my pain; I only took them when I felt pain, if it was time, and if I felt no pain, I skipped doses, so I still had a few left. When I showed her the bottle, this woman offended me in the worst way by saying, "Oh! And they're almost gone. Couldn't you try Tylenol or something?" Thank God I'm a Christian and a professional. I let her comment go by without responding. Me, a person who looks for and prefers the natural remedy, who prefers to nap away a headache or use herbal remedies and had tried using clove oil on my pain for days before going to the dentist, being looked on and suspected of being a pill-popper! I had to let go my desire to put this woman in her place, and give it to God.

Anyway, I was still to start on Monday, but she had to speak with her supervisor, and I was to call before I came in. I had no doubt my innocence would be seen. I guess she had to be that way, because she didn't know me. When we got to know each other a little better, we did see each other differently. She then seemed really nice. I also learned she had previous reasons to be suspicious because of other people she had to let go; a nurse does have access to narcotic medicines and some do abuse that access.

I didn't move into my apartment right away because of the bugs, and I wanted us to enjoy a real bed one more night. When we left Wal-Mart, we went back to the apartment, and I set off the insect bombs, then we went back to the hotel where we both washed in chlorinated water, as this will keep flees and bugs off you for a while. When I looked at my son, I realized they had gotten to him and bitten him up terribly, so I put medicated lotion and Hydrocortisone on those areas. On Saturday morning, I decided to stay at the hotel one more day because my son had been after me to go into the pool, so I decided to stay and let him enjoy it. The pool had chlorinated water, so it could only be good for him, but the pool pumps weren't turned on, so it wasn't pleasant and the water was cold. The bitten areas on his body still looked terrible and swollen. I had to take him to the hospital to have the stitches removed from his leg, so while there, I showed them the swollen bite marks and they gave me an instruction sheet concerning it, which contained some of the things I was already doing. The doctor said his leg wasn't healed enough to remove the stitches. My son waited almost two more weeks before the leg healed enough to remove them.

When we left the hospital, we went to the apartment and I put up the blinds we had bought at Wal-Mart. We then went back to the hotel, showered, ate, and slept. On Sunday morning, we checked out and were headed for the apartment, but if I had gone, I would have missed church, so I pulled off the road and we got as decent as we could, then I turned around and we went to church. I caught the message, and I believed God had a word for me, though there were things about the pastor's faith that wasn't with mine, concerning the things God had taught me. After church, I came home, and the whole family was now indoors. What a blessed day! I cleaned up and wiped down everything—walls, light fixtures, ceiling fan, counters, floors—everything.

On Monday morning I got half dressed, then I called the job and spoke to the same woman who informed me that her boss agreed that it was OK that I was on that narcotic, but that they needed me to have an Alabama nursing license before I could start. They offered to fax the application to the State for me, but there were a few fees to be paid with it that I didn't have, and I didn't see how I would get the money without first getting a job. Nothing could convince me that she was not being biased against me because of the medication, because the license had never been an issue during my hiring process, and the man who hired me knew I didn't have one, because I told him, and it was also written on my application. Later, as I continued looking for a job, I realized that no facility will hire without one. I was in a bind: no license without money, and no money without a license. I looked in other fields besides nursing, but being a nurse was now an impediment to me, because nursing was all the job experience I had for more than eight years, and no one trusted to hire me because they knew I wouldn't stay with them but a few months. I searched for the next four months for *anything*: I signed up at the employment office, an agency, applied at McDonald's and other fast food restaurants, and applied at gas stations; at times walking many miles when my car was broken down, and walking over five miles one way to an interview that went nowhere; but, I never complained or murmured.

In everything that went right or seemed to go wrong, I believed and told my son it was God's will and purpose, and I was right. He was preparing me for a purpose with other things and with the walking. I fell in love with walking, and when I wasn't going anywhere, even when the car was fixed by the church, I kept walking a little over two miles both ways from home. [When I received our things from storage, my son and I also rode our bicycles a few places.] It felt good because I found the town so peaceful and lovely.

My mom had moved to Georgia in October. It was a blessing; she was close, and God had blessed her with something I had dreamed of giving her but couldn't—a beautiful house and no mortgage payments. No more struggling, no need to continue working at her age, able to enjoy her early retirement. I was so happy for her and hoped she was feeling peace.

In mid-November she called me. She wanted me to drive over to Georgia, then use her car and drive us up to New Jersey so she could finalize some business. She also said that while we were there, maybe we could get my stuff out of storage and bring them home to Alabama. I was joyful because, even if I couldn't bring them home, maybe I could at least get the documents I needed out of there. I could also go talk to my son's father, because I had told him that I wanted to move down South but not that I had already done so. Once I arrived, and God held me there, I couldn't tell him over the phone; it was not appropriate. I had to wait until I saw him face to face, so I was glad to be going back to visit. In addition, I was dying to see and hold my god-baby. Going, and coming back home, my peace was disrupted as the enemy made attempts at my life again.

I must first say that my mom was a stickler about keeping her car in good shape, always taking it in for service even when I thought it was a waste of money because there was nothing wrong, and she was always getting on me about caring better for my car. I made sure we left before daylight so that by the time it was night, we would be on familiar roads.

In the early morning light I made a wrong turn, and when I turned back and got back on our path, on the side of the road at the distance where we would have been—had God not taken me off this path—were ambulances and a wrecker and three or four wrecked cars, and someone being loaded into the ambulance. When we saw it, I prayed within me for healing to them and no deaths and thanked God for our lives.

Going and coming, I felt the heaviness of the enemy, but I didn't tell my mom, because I didn't want to worry her, and I trusted God to keep us safe. I knew it was meant for me, but the whole way from start to finish, I kept God in my heart and sang along with the Jamaican Christian songs my mom always had in her car.

When we were going through South Carolina, it was about 9:00 a.m.; thank God there was barely any traffic because it would have been a very different ending. As I drove along in the middle lane, I felt a change in the car. I was pressing the gas but the speed of the car wasn't changing, so I turned down the stereo to listen; the harder I pressed, the engine would roar but the car was just rolling along; I steered it to roll to the side of the road and tested it again. This time, the car wouldn't even budge from that spot, and the engine just raced. The transmission was dead.

This was still a fairly new car, that my dad had bought (cash) for her, and if my old car that badly needed a tune-up made the trip, something was wrong. I took out my mom's cell phone, and as I pressed the buttons to call 911, I saw a truck pull up behind us. It was a road safety patrol person. He asked us what was wrong, then called a garage for us; he waited with us until their flatbed tow truck came.

When we got to the garage, the owner told us that they had other cars ahead of us; he said it would take about three days and we would have to stay in a hotel. I pleaded our case to him, and God touched his heart concerning us; he said OK, that he would work on it that day. He started seeking a used transmission, then, I pleaded down the price with him. I asked my mom how much she could afford to spend and she said no more than seven hundred dollars, so she offered him that, and he said OK. But, when my mom actually checked, she only had six hundred dollars. She wanted to wait until he was finished because, I guess, she was worried and afraid he wouldn't finish the job; but, I prompted her to tell him so he wouldn't feel betrayed, like she was trying to cheat him. He had been so nice, fixing the car right then, when he could have made us wait for days. So, she told him that she only had six hundred dollars and asked if he would take that and a check for one hundred, and he said, "Sure, no problem." Then, I started thinking that if she gave him all six hundred dollars, how would we get to New Jersey. She and I discussed it and decided it would cost maybe forty dollars in gas to get there, so, she would take fifty dollars from the money and add it to the check, or better yet one hundred dollars. But, she decided to let that wait until the car was done, since we already knew he would take the check.

We sat and waited, and I napped on and off the best I could, to rest up for the drive. While waiting, I spotted an article about him on their wall and read it. Turns out God brought us into the hands of one of His. The man and his wife, who ran the garage together, were Christian people. My mom talked to his wife about it a little. The car was finished about 9:00 p.m. They took it on the road and it ran great, but some light came on, so they worked on it some more, and flushed it. It was the only car they worked on all day—they dropped everything else.

Now for the payment. We went into his office, and I explained our dilemma to him, that we were going to need "some money" to get to New Jersey, and asked if we could take it from the cash and put it on the check, and he said, "Sure, I'll take five hundred dollars and the rest on the check." He allowed us one hundred dollars; this was the exact amount we really wanted but were afraid to ask for—What an awesome God!

They asked us to call them when we got to New Jersey so they would know we were safe, and we did. We got back on the road about 9:30 p.m.. We didn't get there until about nine the next morning because I missed my exit twice; first I ended up in Washington DC (near the protected streets of the White House), then later I ended up in Atlantic City. But, I sang with God in my heart all the way to our destination, and pleaded the blood of Jesus every time my eyes closed—It was really bad, but God brought us safely.

Now, coming back home: I took two 2-hour naps, but it was still rough. The heaviness was still there; not just tired or sleepy but drained. Nevertheless, there were no wrong turns or missed exits, until I stopped for gas, then I drove down a street trying to get to a building I saw, where my mom could use the restroom. It was a one-way street / on-ramp, that took me onto a totally different expressway. I never got back on my planned path, but this was an alternate route. Yet, I didn't murmur or complain. I held onto God to bring us safely, singing my way there.

We finally got to my mom's house with our lives, at about two in the morning—the heaviness had lifted. I stayed with my mom about four days, doing stuff for her around the house; she and my brother and me working together to set the house in order because she still had many things to unpack. It was finally looking like a home the way she wanted it. I had to leave and get back to job hunting; I felt guilty that DHR was paying my way and didn't want them to think I was off having fun, so I had to go, but my mom didn't want to let go. She kept creating things for me to do around the house (I'm handy that way) so I wouldn't leave; she wouldn't have minded if I moved in with her. My brother didn't want me to leave, either, because he loves to converse with me, but he understood that I had to go; he also saw through my mom's attempts to make me stay. A part of me wanted them too, but Alabama was my home until God said differently, and I needed to get back to seeking work there. I packed up myself, my son, and the cats which I had taken to my mom's house. My brother had offered to care for them until I came back from New Jersey, which he did. Misty and Precious mostly hid, but that traitorous Figero was all over my brother, sitting on his lap as often as he would let him.

Of course, my mom was not an animal person, which was one of the reasons I couldn't live with her, and was another reason I had to go home;

because, she wouldn't allow any animals in her house. I had to keep them in her garage, and I didn't want them to live that way. I had bathed them before we left home, and they were all cuddly and smelling so sweet and good: But, in her garage, I had to keep them mostly locked in the carriage, so they wouldn't eat her plant and get sick, or mess up her stuff, or run away if the garage door was accidentally lifted. So, by the time we left, the Misty and the Figero, being locked away with the sick one (Precious), were all smelling horrible, which required another bath when they got home.

Anyway, my mom had loaded me up with many things. The car was so packed, I couldn't see anything out the rear, but that's my mom; no one ever leaves empty or wanting, and God just kept providing for her. We left at 4:00 a.m. because, with not being able to see out the back of my car to change lanes safely, I needed to have very little or no traffic on the road; I didn't know then how that would save my life.

By my calculations, I was supposed to be home by no later than 10:00 a.m.; I was well rested, but there it was again, something just not quite right. To make it worse, my son's portable stereo wouldn't work *'for nothin'*: not the CD, not the tape, or the radio. My car stereo wasn't working either, not even the car radio, so I was facing over five hours of driving in silence. But, I was doing OK singing my way through. My son slept most of the way home, so he wasn't speaking to keep me alert.

At 5:00 a.m., while going about fifty miles per hour, my headlights caught view of something in the road: It was a big deer lying in the street, in the middle of my path. I had a *very* worn right front tire: If I slammed on the brake, I would have skidded into the ditch, and somebody, or all of us, would be dead. There was no place to get around it and no time. There was no hard choice to make: either we die or go straight up over it; I chose for us to live, and went over it and kept driving.

Everything seemed OK. I kept singing and going, but in the midst of singing, my eyes were closing for periods of time. I just kept calling on God. Then, at 6:00 a.m., all my dashboard lights came on, and my steering got very stiff: it took much effort to turn the steering-wheel. Immediately, I noticed my car had also shut itself off, so, I rolled into a gas station and was able to roll to a nicely parked stop. I tried to start the car again, and it would turn over but wouldn't start. My eyes were extremely heavy, so I took it as a sign to get some rest. Even though I had slept all night, I slept there for three hours, then woke up. The car started, so I thanked God and got going, trusting God to just get me home; then, if the car died it would be OK by me. I just didn't want us all stranded or have the car far from home.

A few miles down the road and one hundred miles from home, I stopped at a red light, and the moment I came to a complete stop, the whole car shut down. Nothing worked, not the windows, not the flashers, nothing. All I could think about, was when I was twenty years old: a friend and I were going somewhere, and I had a Mustang that was always overheating, so on that morning it had overheated and shut off at a stoplight. I put on the flashers, and we got out, looking to push it somewhere, but it was too dangerous because the highway was very busy. A couple of guys working at the gas station across the street yelled to us offering help, and we yelled back that we needed it, so they called for help. My friend and I got back into the car to be safe because my flashers were on. Everyone saw the lights and went around us, except this one inattentive person, who crumpled my car at full speed. [I guess it wasn't his fault alone because there was a box truck in front of him that swerved around me at the last minute and he was going so fast there was no time for him to do the same.] The guy was hurt and bleeding from the head, but my friend and I were basically OK. My passenger door was sealed shut, and the seat I was sitting in was broken in half—the back separated/broke off from the seat where they were joined—and had it not been for God, my back would have been broken in like manner. The impact sent me straight upward, slamming the top of my head into the roof, and had it not been for God, my neck would also have been broken along with severe brain injury, leaving me, as a result of this accident, either crippled and non responsive or dead.

I thought out loud that the car may blow because the tank was located in the back, which was now all crumpled and rammed into the back seat. I shouldn't have said it, because it made him panic, trying to force the door open with his body, but I told him we would be OK, and we started to talk, and he was calmed. God covered us, and we walked away with only minor aches and pains. In thinking about this accident, all I could now see was one of those giant trailers, very popular on these southern roads, rolling right over us, crushing us all to nothing. I had no peace, only fear, because I had walked away from peace into the arms of fear, and it did embrace me, but I kept calling on Jesus for help and pleading the blood.

 I got out of the car and directed some traffic to go around me. Thank God, there was very little. Standing outside the car wasn't safe either. I just pictured someone running over me. I thought of pushing the car myself, which I could have done (I have pushed cars by myself before - self reliant), but I was just afraid of getting run over by someone, leaving my son alone in the middle of nowhere. So, I sat back down in the car with the door open because there was no power to roll the window down. I kept directing the little traffic around me, all along picturing this big Mack truck rolling over us like butter. I was so afraid for my son and tried to waken him, but he was so sleepy and would not stay awake. I just kept calling on Jesus to rescue us. Then, this time when the light changed to red, someone rolled to a stop beside us. It was a woman driving a black four-by-four-type SUV, and God prompted me to reach out to her. So, I got out my car and motioned to her, and she rolled down her window; I asked her could she please push me off the road, and she said yes. She backed up and got behind me; then, she was very hesitant to do it because she said the height of her vehicle would most likely break out my rear lights. But, I made her know that I didn't care about the lights and would not hold her in any way responsible. I just wanted off the road, and I convinced her; she said OK, so when the light changed, she pushed me. We stopped for another light, then she pushed me again. I expected her to just push me off to the side of the road but she kept pushing me over a half mile right into a gas station. I thanked her and told her God bless her, and she left. I thanked God, also, for covering us, and He also covered the car because not one light was broken.

My mom had given me one hundred fifty dollars for my nursing license, more than one hundred for my pocket, and I had also gotten the one-hundred-dollar child support money from my son's father when I saw him. All together, I had a little more than three hundred fifty dollars, but had spent almost one hundred on something I really liked, which my sister told me to go ahead and buy and she would give me back the money. When she got home to New Jersey, within the same week, she replaced that money to my bank account; the thing I got was her early Christmas present to me. So, I had about two hundred fifty dollars, and that was all. Now, I would have to use it to fix my car.

I went inside the little food mart and asked the gas station attendant if he knew anyone who could fix my car well but cheap, and he called this person; I thanked him. I waited in my car about one hour for the person who was called. When he got to me, he had his daughter with him. He loaded up the car while I told him what happened. While loading the car, he noticed and showed me how that tire was worn down to the silver wires in the threads. He said that tire wouldn't take me home. I asked him which was cheaper: for him to tow the car the one hundred miles home or to fix it. When he told me the prices, the tow cost more than I had, so I said "fix it."

He took me straight to a tire place, got me five dollars off the cost, and they put on the new tire; because, he said his heart couldn't let me drive with the one I had. I told him I didn't have a lot of money. When we pulled out of the tire place, he told me the company he worked for, which was a reputable name and he was driving their truck so I knew he wasn't lying, but he said if he took me to the company, it would cost me a lot and that he had a home garage, and he could fix it there for a lot less. Normally this would be creepy, but something made me trust him, so I agreed, and he turned around and took me to his garage by his house.

It was a professional place. He printed me up an estimate, and I said OK, so he got it up on the lift and called me under it and showed me what was wrong. The steering column and some adjoining pump fixture were broken, so he just replaced the whole thing. Looking under the car gave me chills because it had pieces of the deer's bone stuck in crevices and its blood all over the bottom of the car. He said he would remove the bones for me. There was also a broken transmission line that was leaking fluid which he replaced. He lent me his cell phone to call my mom, because the battery on mine was dead.

The daughter that was with him was half of a set of twins, which I found out once we got there. They were maybe ten years old. While waiting, they befriended me, and we played a game on their cell phone. They were impressed with my skill level, and they shared their little girlie perfume with me, then they and their brother and my son ran around playing until the car was ready.

There were a lot of things he fixed and did not charge me for. It cost me $168.20, from start to finish. God provided him for my help, and I thanked him and God. We said good-bye to him and the kids, then left. The road I needed to take to get home ran right in front of his property.

It was a struggle very soon after I left them to finish that one hundred miles without music, so again I sang my way through, again missing moments of time while going fifty to seventy miles per hour, always calling on Jesus and pleading the blood of Jesus. Jesus and His angels covered and defended me with a strong hand all along this entire journey, from when I left Alabama until I returned home, overcoming this enemy/darkness/heaviness, and evil that were sore against me.

When I got into the area of Alabama, I knew it even before I saw any city sign because I felt relieved and more awakened; but the enemy was still against me. I was less than five minutes from home, but the enemy entangled my mind, and I drove back and forth and around for half an hour. I then pleaded the blood of Jesus and called on His name as He led me out of the enemy's snare and brought me home. Peace didn't return to me until I got home at 7:00 p.m. on November 26, 2003.

When I got inside, I just fell before God and worshiped and thanked Him for His mighty hand of protection that was over me, over us all. I then called everyone that cared about me in all the states that they lived, to let them know I reached home safely.

The night before he got to me, the delivery guy dropped off more of my mom's stuff in Georgia to her that he still had not delivered, then on the morning of December 1, 2003, he brought my things to me. My mom also sent with him, one hundred fifty dollars, to replace the money for my nursing license which I had to use on the car. She had trust in him because she knew the family and had used their services for over twenty years. Anyway, I still used some of the money for living expenses. My mom used all her money blessing me in these ways; she said she did it to fulfill her promise to my brother Peppem: During the time he was stationed by my school in Jamaica he had instituted a life insurance policy with me and my mom as beneficiaries, which he showed to me and explained to me during one of my visits to him. As time passed, I never thought about it. After his death, and the insurance company's investigation, they paid. My mom said because he was murdered, as per the policy double was paid out, but the money never made it to us here because my dad took it for himself. She said she felt the burden to fulfill my brother's desire toward me, so she gave me these blessings as my portion. God knows and sees all, all is planned, all is perfectly designed, and all is laid up until the time of need. Anyway, the pastor had promised to help me with my things, but everyone was at work, so I paid four of my next door neighbors twenty dollars each to help me bring my things off the truck; I was left without a dollar, but it was worth it. We worked really hard for a few hours.

Between working in the storage unit and the work I did here, I was in full and complete understanding that God had prepared me for this with the walking. When I left New Jersey on August 29, 2003, I weighed more than three hundred seventy pounds. It was affecting my heart and my breathing. In walking swiftly and after a good flight of stairs, I was only a breath away from respiratory distress. I knew I was killing myself, but I felt a safety and comfort in the way I was, until God made me see differently. In walking, as a bonus, God took off over one hundred pounds, but the real purpose was getting my heart and lungs in shape for the great task of bringing my things home. If He hadn't conditioned me, there is no way I could have done it. Either I would have ended up in the hospital or something much worse would have occurred.

The beginning and end of the trip are spoken for, so now, the middle. We were supposed to stay in New Jersey for about three days, but Sis (a really close family friend, considered my mom's daughter, by us and all who know us), also bought a house in Georgia, and she had to go down to the closing. So, we had to leave the next day because my mom wanted us to travel together, to help each other drive. I borrowed my mom's car and went to speak with my son's father. He said he already knew I moved, but I don't see how, when the only ones who knew were my mom and Big Sis, and I don't believe they told him because they knew I wanted to do it myself.

Anyway, I gave him our address and house phone number (he already had my cell phone number), and I gave him my checking account information so he could deposit the child support. Then, I called his wife to the car and made peace with her, as God had put it in me to do that—nothing between me and Him; no hindrances. We spoke, then, I held out my hand in peace and she took it; God was pleased. I left our son so he could spend time with his father and sister for the day, then I drove by my friend's house to see my god-baby. I was told that my friend was at work, and the baby was at her grandmother's house. I left word with my god-son to tell his mom that I hadn't been by for these two months because I had moved, and I gave him my address and phone number to give to her. The last time I saw them, I did tell her that she wouldn't see me for a while, thinking it would be only for two weeks.

Anyway, when we had first gotten to town, my mom had paid what was owing on my storage, so when I left my friend's house, I went to the storage unit to get started. I had a ten-by-fifteen-foot storage area, literally packed to the roof and full to the door. Half the things were disrupted out of their boxes and bags from me digging into them over the last two and half years, and I had less than one day to get them together for the truck, which God blessed my mom to bless me with.

While there, my friend called me on my cell phone. I wanted so badly to go see and hold the baby, but a good portion of my things lined the hallway of the storage that were ready to go on the truck. I couldn't put them back in, and couldn't leave them in the hallway for that kind of visit; because, that visit would take a while. So, we agreed on noon the next day because I just *knew* I would be done—I was wrong.

About 10:00 p.m. I went to get my son. His father would be going to work at about 6:00 a.m., and his step-mom wasn't that kind of step-mom, so his dad said he couldn't sleep over. When I picked him up, he wanted to be at storage with me instead of going to Sis and his grandma, so I kept him with me. He wanted to help, so I let him. I stayed there all night cleaning up and packing. I had a mattress laid out on top of some things, so I made my son go to sleep at about 1:00 a.m.; then, at about 4:00 a.m., I took a two-hour nap.

In the morning, I wasn't even half done. I dropped off my son at Sis' house and my mom came with me. She dropped me back at storage, then took the car to a mechanic because the light came back on and wouldn't go away. Turns out, in the rush to get us back on the road, they didn't flush out the transmission *before* they put it on—they did fix it in January 2004, free of charge. At this time however, it was flushed to no avail.

I kept preparing for the truck, then my cousin came over and brought his son so I could see him again; we talked, then he helped me pack. The truck came about 2:00 p.m., then my cousin went and got a couple guys off a street corner wanting work, and they helped us. We worked hard from 3:00 p.m. to7:00 p.m. loading the truck. Because the truck came so late (it was supposed to come at 9:00 a.m.), Sis couldn't wait for us. So, both Sis and Big Sis, and their kids, and a friend went down to my mom's house in Georgia. Once my mom, my son, and I got there, we were all together at my mom's for two days, while Sis closed on her house and Big Sis got a change to view Georgia. Then, Sis, Big Sis, and their kids, went back to New Jersey; the friend went back with them also.

My mom paid the truck guy half the money and he left—everyone left (my cousin and the guys he got to help). I continued to work until 11:00 p.m., cleaning up, and taking out the garbage; also, packing the rest of things I wanted into my mom's car, that the truck couldn't wait for. I still didn't get to see and hold my god-baby, and now I had to leave, but God knows best. I needed some sleep before I set out, and both my sisters were gone, headed for Georgia, so I was not able to sleep at either house. It didn't make sense for my mom to rent a motel for such a short time, so I napped in the car until 1:00 a.m.; I was then awakened by some movement or noise. My mom and son had fallen asleep, too, but I was just ready and eager to get home, so we went to a restroom, then got on the way.

Now, back to the job thing in Alabama. Within the next couple of weeks, after the nursing job fell through, so did my unemployment benefits. They investigated and asked me if the *only* reason I left the job was because of my homelessness and my moving, and if not for these would I still be there? I said yes. After the interview was over and I thought about it, I realized that answer wasn't accurate, because I didn't feel safe there with the new DON. Anyway, I did answer yes, so they decided that my cause for quitting wasn't *"just cause."* Never mind that I was trying to save my life; because, I believe if I were still in New Jersey, I would either still be on the street or God knows where, but it would not be good.

Because I quit, they were holding my benefits indefinitely (***"pended"***) until I got re-employed and worked at least one month and made a certain amount, then they would release it—they said. That was the most ridiculous, senseless thing I ever heard, but again, I was not angry or worried because God allowed everything for a purpose.

I believe He wanted to prove to me that He could care for me all by Himself, without a dollar to my name, so I couldn't claim any credit. He *brought* people to me left and right: clothing me, feeding me, giving me shelter, caring for us in an indescribably magnificent way. He brought people I didn't know, and some I never saw again, to assist me in all my needs. I never once went seeking these people—they were all **brought** to me, offering themselves. They gave such love and provision, even though, all along, I was putting up a front like everything was fine because my pride won't allow me to look or act needy, and I didn't want any pity (God doesn't like pride, but He is working on that.) Regardless, none of them did make me feel that way. Even though I never asked of them, they gave, and I received with my dignity intact—nothing but the work of God, my source.

[I know without a doubt that He is able in all things, spiritual and natural. This knowledge is forever locked within my heart. *I trust Him, always, and completely, come what may.* I wish someone would come to know Him this way, or admit to the world of all He is and is capable of. Please, just come to Him and love Him; let Him love and care for you. He can! If you need to, stop reading for a while, and just wrap yourself in Him right now, please do it. He is waiting and ready. Just give Him all of you. He wants you right now. Nothing that you have done matters; give yourself to Him now, and don't go back to those things anymore. God also has a plan for you. There is nothing extra special about me more than you; the mighty love God has for me, is the same love He also has for you, when you are true to Him. I am special because I belong to God, and in *Him* is my everything. He is all that I am. I am His treasure that was once hid, but now, He has revealed me in all His glory, refined for His purpose; to God be the glory, *I love You, Jesus.* Before you are finished with this book, cry out to Him from deep within your soul, and let it come out through your mouth with all sincerity. Let Him in and let it be God and you to *your* deliverance.]

OK, so, I held off telling the social worker, April, about my financial setbacks for almost three weeks. She was supposed to meet with me to close out my case. How could I tell her all that happened? I really didn't want to have to tell her this news. I finally got up the courage one day and called her and was glad when I got the answering machine. I felt like such a failure, but I still believed God for better things, and still do. She called me back the next day and we talked. Even when I'm in great need, I don't ask any but God for help, unless it's *extreme*, and I guess she sensed that about me, so every time we spoke she always asked me: "How's your gas? Do you have food? Are you OK?" That's when I would tell her what I did or didn't need; because, once asked, I could not lie to her. I thought I would have to transfer to a different DHR because I was now living in the other county I had rejected before, but she asked me: "Do you really want to transfer?" I said, "no," because I *really* didn't, so, she said I didn't have to. She consulted with her boss, and they paid my rent and utilities, and gave me vouchers: for gas about twice per month, and for food once per month until the food stamps were approved. They also assisted me in whatever ways they could in getting my nursing application in order—notarizing and faxing things. They *don't* normally do these things, and it is in *no way* their responsibility, but out of the goodness God placed within their hearts, they went the extra mile for me and my son.

About two weeks before Christmas, April called me and left a message asking me to call her. I called her the next day, and she said, "Do you want some Christmas for Paul (my son, Sean)?" Joyfully, I said, "Yes." She told me to make a list of the things I wanted for him; I was not greedy in the things I listed. I wrote only necessary things, like clothes, and shoes, and one video game he said he wanted. I took the list to her, and they approved it; they gave me two hundred dollars in vouchers, and we (April and I) went with Sean in tow, and shopped for him.

A couple of days before Christmas, I went to the office to have a document notarized for my nursing application packet and saw this lady at the desk talking to the secretary; we said hello and joked and laughed a little. Then, she asked me if I had gotten everything I needed for my son, and I said yes, and told her thank you, not knowing who she was. I began to tell her that he got a lot of things (and he did, triple times the amount on the list) and how grateful I was. She said something about him being surprised, and I said, "He won't be, because I had to take him with me." She said they would have kept him in the office for me; but, I didn't know that, and being over protective as I am, I don't know that I would have left him. But, I told her he was happy with all we got him, and so was I. Then, she told me to come with her; I still didn't know who she was, and I didn't know what she wanted or where we were going, but I felt no hesitation.

Body

As we walked down the hallway, she introduced herself and told me that she was their boss, and we joked and laughed as we walked. I think I said something about how nice she was, and she said, *a lot of people don't think so because she says no a lot, to a lot of people, and they think she's mean*. I knew right then, the extent to which God had caused her to bless us. This was also the department that will take people's children away, probably for situations like mine was; which was probably the intent of the one who initially contacted them about us, but God caused them to care for us instead. I *now* understand, the person that contacted them, whatever the intent, was being used: everything was allowed or set up that all things/help concerning me (this family) be fulfilled.

So, I didn't know where we were going, but I walked with her, then, she stopped beside a huge closet and opened it. It had a lot of things inside it, which I think she said people donated. She gave me a CD Walkman (which had many features and a cassette adapter for vehicle use), and a really cool watch, and a couple other things—all new, and she told me to hide them from my son, so I could surprise him on Christmas day. I hid them and wrapped them on Christmas morning before he got up—he was surprised and happy. Because I had received the CD player for him, I had also gotten him some CDs out of the money Mom had given me, which I asked God to help me choose to bring/draw him closer to God. That was *my* Christmas present, and a joyful one, to see him have a really decent Christmas; also, renewing in him the *true* meaning on the season—Jesus Christ.

I wanted and planned to drive to Georgia for Christmas, but God said no, by allowing a problem with my car. It was still drivable, but not for a five hour trip. I acknowledged and accepted right away that it wasn't God's will that I should go, and He dealt with me greatly over the holiday, bringing me yet closer to Him, and anointing me for purpose.

I came to the end of the road with DHR. They were allowed to help me only for three months, and they helped me for six and a half months and helped me to obtain my Alabama nursing license, which I had in my possession. All that was left, was me stepping into the nursing job God had prepared for me. DHR didn't leave me blowing in the wind; they made preparations for me by providing things to sustain us for awhile and left me contact information. Our social worker, April, transferred to a different job, and she closed us out the day before she left. I didn't want to be in the hands of anyone else, and she didn't want that for us either. God *truly* placed her over us, and she cared for us extremely well, and He touched the heart of her boss concerning us: in that she went beyond limit, for us. After April closed out our case, we said good-bye, and I gave her a hug of thanks and appreciation, then called my son, and told him to give his "guardian angel a hug good-bye," which he did. She told me where her new job was, and told us to drop in sometime and say hello; I had *every* intention to, but never did. I had learned that she was a church goer, and I kept her in my prayers for blessing, caring, and prosperity to her.

Ester, who prompted me to make a choice; April, our social worker; and Katy, her boss—three people engraved on my heart: because out of nowhere, God caused them to reach out and call to me, and equipped them to lift up and rescue this drowning family to safety and restoration.

At no time, except once, over the last six months did I ever have any money in my pocket to do as I wished or to even spend on basic things, yet I lacked *nothing*. God provided *all* my needs, and even my wants, by positioning me in line of help from the angels he sent; also, closing doors of danger, and opening doors of help that did not cause me to be ashamed. Since I moved there, and until He sent me, God had brought only people who were beautiful to me—to my path; except for the woman at the job that was questioning my use of drugs. Though she offended me, I accepted that she was just doing her job, and because she didn't know me; but, she was forgiven.

God is awesome. All I need is Him. He is truly able in *all* things. Now, that I know Him this way, it would be abominable if I ever turned away— How could I? I don't want to; I don't ever intend to. I pray He walks with me till I fall asleep and wake up in eternity with His arms wrapped around me. I am so in love with Him, all of Him, Blessed Trinity. It breaks my heart with pain—literally, just as a mate in love can feel wounded on occasion—whenever He is displeased with me. I don't ever want to lose that bond with Him that causes that feeling in me; because, knowing how my heart will hurt when He looks upon me and cannot smile, will cause me, even more, to love and serve Him in truth, with no deceit or falsehood; naked before him—nothing between.

Going back a little: When I was still in New Jersey and living at the motel, near the end, still rejecting part of my sexuality because I thought it sinful and still rejecting God, thinking who I was and am wasn't OK, I began to embrace psychics. The psychic thing was a careful trap set by the devil, and it worked. When I first learned of those things as a teenager, and up until this point of embracing it, I knew in my heart that it was the devil's work and avoided it, but at this time because I had shut God out, I began reaching for this thing for direction. I was getting letters from them in the mail about my "lucky period," and these letters came at a time when I was in need of *this financial windfall*, but I tossed them all away, ***until***, these two letters started talking about *god this*, and *god that*. Silly me; when someone says "god," I think only of the *God of Heaven*, but they served something else. These two *entities* kept writing, three or more times, urging me to respond, and the *god thing* hooked me, and they *seemed* genuine. "There is a way which seemeth right unto a man, but the end thereof are the ways of death" (Proverbs 14:12).

My heart knew it was wrong, but again my head made it OK, so I responded to them both, and they sent me readings and charms. When I got them, I read them all. They had done write-ups on me and daily readings. There were some accuracies about me in the write-ups they did on me, but the devil knows us almost (but not quite) like God knows us (because he gains his knowledge about you by eavesdropping when Heaven speaks of you), and will tell you facts about yourself and also facts twisted with lies, only to get his hooks into you. The devil is a liar and cannot change. If you allow him in, even when he tells you things about you that you know are real, he's still a liar because there is always deception behind it, and there is no deception in truth. Truth is pure and the devil is not.

Eventually, you will start believing his lies about you, and see yourself as he says you are, which is a lie, instead of who you really are—who God says you are. God is truth. If you believe God, you believe the truth. Anything else you believe, other than God and Jesus Christ, is a lie, and is the devil, because the devil is lies and a liar; he is to be resisted and trodden underfoot. He cannot add to you; and, he cannot take away from you, unless you say yes to him, or it is allowed by God to prove the content of your heart or to make you strong for some later purpose. As long as you stand in God, the devil (evil) is powerless.

The more I write, the more I feel God speaking, and my eyes are being opened as I write. It's being revealed to me how insignificant this enemy is, and how I have allowed my fear of him to dominate, rule over, and intimidate me most of my life. *All* power belongs to God, and every event of my life was allowed by God to prove me or build me. If I choose God, I will prosper in abundance. If I choose the devil, yes, he will consume and destroy me, but only by the allowance of God because I didn't choose Him—then I am not His. I would then belong to the devil, and evil would now receive power to do with me what it will.

There are only two choices to ever make in this world—good or evil, or in other words, God or the devil. There are not three such as God, the devil, and self (one's own way), because to choose self is to choose flesh (selfishness, gratifications, elicit pleasures, elicit (to entice, lure, deceive) sensuality, and all ways contrary to the Spirit), and to choose flesh is to choose sin, and to choose sin is to choose the devil, so there are only two choices ever to be made. You choose God and in Him is good judgment, etc.

In everything I do, no matter how simple, in everything I think and speak, and allow myself to feel, in all areas of my life, I need to choose God by asking myself, would this be pleasing to God? And, if my answer is yes, then I should embrace it, even if it seems unpleasant to me. Because of self (ultimately the devil's way), not every right and good thing will be comfortable for me; but, if I love and trust God and just do it, I will be blessed. God is love, and everything pleasing to Him is on the side of love. Is what I am about to do or say loving myself and to the good of me and my soul? Is what I am about to do or say loving another and to the good of them? Am I being true to Jesus (the love of my life) or am I about to betray Him with selfishness, lust, perversion, depravity, anger, violence, hate, lies, thievery, envy, denial, distrust and disbelief in Him, etc.? Am I about to speak or act against myself and my soul or against another or against Jesus? Am I about to build up or am I about to be guilty of blood? Love yourself, love others, love Jesus, feel love, show love, live in love: this is pleasing to God because He is love. If my answer is no, that it will not be pleasing to God or that it is against God, then I must resist, because it is sin. If I resist, the need to do or say or feel or think whatever it is will leave me. It may not leave me the first or second or third time, but if I love and believe God and am as persistent in my resistance as the devil is persistent in his temptation, he *will* flee from me, as promised, because he has no power of himself.

Matthew 22:37-40: Jesus said unto him, "Thou shalt love the Lord thy God with all thy heart, and with all thy soul, and with all thy mind. This is the first and great commandment. And the second is like unto it, Thou shalt love thy neighbour as thyself. On these two commandments hang [attach] all the law and the prophets."

Romans 13:10: "Love worketh no ill to his neighbour [and to his God, and to himself and his soul]: therefore love is the fulfilling of the law [and all things towards God]."

If you love (from the heart), you will not act against God. If you love (from the heart), you will not act against another. If you love (from the heart), you will not act against yourself and your soul.

The devil is cunning (the master of cunning), and he uses trickery and fear to gain power, when you say yes to him. Sinful things are designed by the evil one to feel very good, in the desire of them, and while they're being done. No matter what form they take: lying, stealing, cheating, slandering, of a sexual nature, gluttony, abuse, killing/murder, whatever it is, small or great, it feels wonderful while we're in the midst of it. There is some form of gratification, somewhere in you. That's why it's so hard to resist.

We don't want to resist, but where is the deception? We know there is one: the pleasure doesn't last. So, we find ourselves doing it again, and more frequently, and moving on to greater acts of sinfulness, and more unthinkable things become acceptable and OK to us. And, where is the destruction? We know there is one. But, as long as we hear that voice inside that questions why we behaved that way, or feel that feeling of guilt or wrongdoing, or feel that sense of low from that height of the sinful pleasure, or feel that sadness from what was done or said, as long as we feel these sorts of things, *know,* that there is hope for us, we are not yet all his. This is the good in us fighting to survive. Feed that good and let it prosper, by choosing the right things and actions and words, and victory will come. It may be an excruciatingly sore battle, but believe and fight. God will also fight for you, and deliverance will come. But, if sin is continuously chosen, the devil will consume every bit of good left in us and claim us unto himself: therein lies the destruction. And, God will allow this, and also take away our peace because we chose sin and not God.

God needs something inside us to work with, no matter how minute. He searches our hearts for even one tiny drop of good or willingness. If He sees the desire or hears the cry of our heart, though we may not yet feel it or know it, He discerns it, and gets to work on us. But, if we are consumed by the devil, when God searches, He finds no good but only wickedness in His sight, and no desire for change, so, He has to leave us to our corrupt nature, vile thoughts and deeds, and immorality. If we are wicked and corrupt, we are His enemies, and how can He allow His enemies to have joy and peace flowing like a river? He will not. He will take it away. If you have never had it, then it probably won't matter to you; but once you have had it, and experienced the beauty of it, then it was taken away, it is an unbearable state to be in.

Have you ever been without joy and peace? Confusion, hopelessness, loss, fear, hurt, pain, sadness, depression, emotional turmoil—these and more were my feelings.

What are yours?

Have you ever had joy and peace? Calm, worry free, loved, cared for, more joy, more peace, protected, content, nothing-shakes-me-because-I-know-a-door-will-be-opened-or-closed-according-to-my-need—I can't find all the words to describe it. It just feels wonderful; and, if I always choose Him, this feeling will never leave me. Even on the occasion when He needs to prove me and allows the devil at me, if I resist and choose God, He will maintain and even increase this joy and peace within me. And, after a while, when He is satisfied with me, He will wrap me up in Him and give me rest from my enemies: I speak not of Heavenly rest, but while still here on earth. I long for the day when the devil and his workers of iniquity cannot approach me, and cannot touch me. [Thank You, Jehovah.]

How about you? Choose! Choose now!

[Oh, my Lord, that was unexpected, but God must have His way. Thank You Lord, I love You.]

OK, back to the past. So, I read what these people had to say, then laid it aside. I didn't follow their daily plan, but once in a while I read it and heeded it as far as controlling my attitude and not arguing back in any situation. I really did have a great temper that only my family saw, and God was dealing with it and was still cleaning up the remnants of it, and the devil knew that about me. I also kept looking for my big *lucky period* that never came.

When I packed for the trip, I packed the plan. I think the reading was for two months, and I think I still had about one month left, so I brought it with me. Now that I think about it, maybe this was the dark force I felt against me on the trip, because it is witchcraft, and it does bind its misled believers. Satan saw or heard God's plan for me, so he raged against me and the truth because I was in his clutches: I had chosen him and his witchcraft.

When I got to Alabama, I did not follow after or read it or desire it, because I had tasted of joy and peace, but I still had it with me packed away somewhere. It's a great and rewarding thing to let the sin in you die or be killed, but it needs to be plucked up by the roots and cast off—all remnants of it, lest there be some hidden life in it, and it be nourished and spring up again. Also, staying away from all that got you into sin in the first place and all that kept you there or will cause you to fall. Learn your weaknesses, and protect yourself with the blood of Jesus Christ, through prayer and laying yourself in His hand. He will pluck up what needs to be plucked up and strengthen and straighten what needs to be strengthened and straightened. He will wash and cleanse what needs to be washed and cleansed, and teach you self control—but only if He searches your heart and find willingness.

You can't fool Him with your lips/lip service; you only fool yourself because He knows and judges your heart. He knows even what you're afraid to uncover within yourself. He knows the truth of the lies you tell yourself that you have come to really believe. Don't be afraid of Him or be ashamed. Stand before Him emotionally and spiritually naked, with nothing between. He loves you beyond measure, messed up though you may be. Bare all before Him and get a glimpse of how He sees you. He will show you how beautiful you really are. God is speaking to somebody: because I can't seem to finish writing the past. He keeps taking me places—for you, but I follow Him willingly. He is in full control and knows exactly what He needs of me and what you need of Him, and I say "yes" to Him.

So, back we go again... On the first or eighth of October 2003, I went to Bible class, and God again used this pastor to speak a word to my soul. He gave us an assignment to have completed for the next Bible class: "Write the definition of witchcraft and what it consists of. And, what are the repercussions of witchcraft?" I knew what it was, and I had one kind of it in my possession; I knew I needed to get rid of it: pluck it up and cast it off. The next day, I thought carefully, remembering all they had sent me, and I unearth them—every charm, every single page of reading. I tore them to bits and tossed them into garbage bags, then immediately carried them away because I didn't even want them at my gate. I then erased the digital one that was on my computer, then immediately went into the "trash bin" and deleted all traces of it.

Everywhere you see sin in you, pluck it up and cast it away, or it will cause you to fall and feel ashamed. Don't cover for the enemy. You're not protecting yourself or another; you are covering for the devil. You don't have to share with the world as I have, but don't hide from yourself, and don't try to hide from God because you can't. Don't hide from those that *truly* love you; stand emotionally naked before them and before God, and He will clothe you in newness and cause you not to be ashamed. Only, when you speak to Him, whether silently within or from your mouth, if you are turning your life over to Him, please be sincere; know what you say and promise to Him. Speak to that loved one and to Jesus from your heart and not your head, that your words will be honorable. He will hold you at your word, and His Angel also bear witness of your words, so if you do anything other than that which you speak, it is an abominable sin in His sight. He is a God of His Word and a God of kept promises, and He expects the same of you, but since we mess up a lot, to our help, there is grace.

He is also merciful, so if you fail Him by not choosing Him in any situation or circumstance, or fail to be true to any promise, no matter how terrible the thing you chose instead of Him was, just turn right to Him. He won't reject you. If you are sincere and truthful, He will forgive you, and right away, you have a new fresh start with Him, and if you believe, there is nothing He won't do for you. Only, don't be presumptuous or wicked; don't tempt Him and make Him angry at you by deliberately going back to making the same wrong choices over and over. He is *very* patient, but even God has His limits, and sooner or later, if you show no desire to change by resisting the devil's choice, He will give you over to your filthiness and let you suffer. And, He will not hear you or listen when you call Him, until He discerns that your heart is ready and willing for change; only then, will He move on your behalf.

Section III:
Spirit: The Call

The chorus "Higher Ground" was brought to my heart and memory as soon as my eyes beheld this section for review, on May 24, 2004. A chorus describing my heart's plea for more of Him, and so He responded—calling me up hither and planting me on higher ground.

One month in my new home, God had been blessing me, providing for me, preparing me with walking, and preparing me for what He wanted of me spiritually. All my belongings were locked away in storage in New Jersey, including my Bible, and now going back to church, I needed one, so when I was returning my key-card after checking out of the hotel, I got the courage to ask the receptionist if they had an extra Bible I could have.

She said, "Sure, why don't you take the one in your room?"

I told her I had already locked the door, so she let me have the key-card back, and I ran to the room and got it, returned the key-card to her and thanked her greatly, and also thanked God. There came in me a great yearning for knowledge of God, and to be real and true to Him with all my heart and soul for all His goodness to me.

So, I started reading the Bible from the beginning, and He began teaching me. Then, I felt the need for more. After living all my life with one foot in the world and more than three years of consistent rebellion, I was now seeking Him personally, one on One, heart to heart. He had already started to cleanse me by taking lies from my lips and taking cursing from my mouth (which I started to do again over those rebellious years), taking deceit from me, and giving me morals and character in Him. He just kept refining me, but I felt in need of a purging, even of possible hidden things, so I knew it was time to fast.

Written on Monday, October 27, 2003
Concerning Sunday
Early yesterday morning as I began my fast, I thought it was only for cleansing me, lifting my burdens, and to loose me from anything binding me. After I prayed, God moved me to ready a book and a pencil, and I thought to write down whatever He showed me, through Scripture or a dream or any other means, so I would remember and work on them. But, He led me to seek Him in Spirit, and to record my way to receiving Him. Hallelujah!

I didn't go to church, because God needs me to seek Him and they don't believe, so I needed to be alone with God. I spent the day fasting, listening to gospel music, reading the Word, talking to God, and being in His presence. I feel something going on inside me. I don't understand, but I know it's God dealing with me, and I need to be alone with Him.

Mom called this evening. She's coming to Georgia on Thursday, God willing, for the closing on her house. She'll be staying a while.

My heart and soul feel deeply troubled, my heart is yearning for God. My mind is yearning for knowledge of Him—how to live, how to be more like Him, just to know Him fully. My soul yearns to be filled, to be one with the Holy Ghost. After my son ate dinner, I kept communing with God, then sent my son to bed at 11:00 p.m. After that I settled in bed, read His Word, prayed, and started talking to Him. My CDs were still playing, and a song came on that touched my heart, so I set it on repeat and continued talking to Him, and God was dealing with me, stirring me up inside like I had never felt before, ever. I felt the need to praise Him, so while lying there on my back with my eyes closed, I raised my hands and arms to Him and praised Him, and He kept increasing the yearning and desire for Him within me, but I didn't feel His presence.

It was now about 3:00 a.m., and I pleaded with Him to bless me, saying, "Why won't you bless me Lord? If there is anything within me standing in the way of my blessing, show me Lord and remove it. If there is nothing in the way, Lord, then bless me, bless me Lord."

And, instantly, He touched me; this was different. He has touched me before, but never in this manner. On other occasions, I felt only the electrifying sensation of His touch. I expected to feel the same, only this time, prayed He would abide within me. But, this was new, a different touch. It was like He reached down His hand and said, "You want a touch? Here you go." [Because it was new, it made me afraid, and I wondered if it was punishment, but it was a deeper touch, as my desire for Him reached His heart.]

Instantly, my eyes were sealed shut: total darkness, no shadows or glow from the light in my room; just looking into a sea of darkness. I was searching for His light but could not find Him. But, instead of pressing through the darkness to my blessing, trusting the God that has been with me, keeping me, who has never hurt me, I became afraid that He had blinded me. In my fear I looked away from the blessed Spiritual Light that was about to be upon me and sought desperately for the physical light of my room by stopping my worship and trying desperately to open my eyes. So, He released them, and when I found it. I stared at the ceiling and the light all around me, and my heart and soul gravely repented for what I had done. I wept with all that was within me, for He had passed me over, again, because once again I resisted my blessing of His promise. I sought Him again and felt His presence, but I still wasn't ready.

Why do I fear the power of God? It's what's been keeping me; how can my faith in Him be so strong about *everything* else, but be so weak concerning this blessing—the blessing and promise He has wanted to and tried over and over again to fulfill in me? I begged Him to let morning find me with my soul blessed, but in my fear of my destiny, I failed Him again; but will not give up. I will not let go, I *will* be blessed! I will move everything out and make room for Him to dwell within me. I love You, Lord, Hallelujah!

Written on Tuesday
Concerning Monday

I spent most of the day listening to music, reading the Word, praying, and talking to God when I was moved to. I settled into bed about 10:00 p.m., read more of His Word, prayed, then began to talk to Him. While lying on my back with my hands and arms held high, I began to worship Him and call on Jesus, and He began to touch me. The more I felt His presence, the more I praised and called upon Him with all that was within me. The presence of the Holy Ghost was *very* strong around me and upon me. It was a greatly strong current, the strongest in my hands, going through my arms and into me. I felt Him touch my face, my left cheek, then searching me for a place to dwell. He stayed with me a long time, then He began to leave me—again. I begged Him to stay, saying, "Bless me as You promised Lord; ask and it shall be given, knock and the door shall be opened, seek and ye shall find, believe and have faith and it shall be done."

"I have surrendered all—heart, mind, body, and soul for You to use me according to Your will. I have, through You, removed the fear. My soul yearns for You to fill me with Your blessed Spirit and abide."

"I love You so much," I felt Him calling me.

"I am ready, Lord, I am willing." I had never hungered after Him so much, but He left me—again. "What is it, Lord? What is hindering my blessing? You want to bless me, and I want to be blessed. My heart, my mind, my soul, and my body are available to You, Lord. I surrender, Lord, I surrender all. Bless me now, Jesus, right now. I am weak, and I am tired of being alone. It's been long enough. Not another day without You. Let the morning greet me already blessed and rejoicing. I don't want to be alone anymore. I won't let You go, I won't turn back, I will press forward till You bless me, I won't give up. I want my new life with You to begin now. Yes, Lord, my soul says yes, my heart says yes, my mind says yes. Yes, Lord, yes to Your will, yes to Your way. I offer my body a vessel to You Lord. Fill me, use me to Your purpose and Your will. Have Your way, Lord, hallelujah!"

"I love You, Jesus, You are my one and only true God and Savior. God the father, God the Son, and God the blessed Holy Spirit. Thank You, for dying on the cross. Thank You, for washing away my sins. Thank You, for Your mercy. Thank You, for loving me so much. Thank You, for Your grace. Thank You, for covering me. Show me, Lord, show me the hindrance, shine Your light into me and search me. Is there something in me that in my ignorance I have not seen and know not? It's me, Lord, You know me better than I know myself. If there is anything within me contrary to You, not of Your will, not of Your way, cast it out Lord. My will is strong, Lord, but my faith is weak. Give me one-hundred-percent faith, Lord." [Thank You, Father.]

"I love You, I trust You, I trust You, Lord, You are worthy, Lord, You are worthy, Jesus, and I thank You. I surrender all, Jesus. Shine Your light into all my dark places and make them light. Reprove me then prove me, Lord. Wash me, purify me, cleanse me, make me whole. Make me worthy, Jesus, make me acceptable in Your sight, then bless me, Lord, as You promised. Show me, Lord, reveal the hindrance. Am I standing in my own way?"

After pleading with God, I felt the need to open up my Bible. He guided my hand and showed me Ecclesiastes 5:4. God wants me to pay a vow I made, to fulfill a promise I made to Him before He can bless me. I am not an offense before Him. I just need to keep a promise I made.

"What did I promise, and when did I promise Lord? Please remind me so I can fulfill it. Forgive me, God, in my ignorance, forgive that I have sinned against You. Remind me Lord. I feel so weak. There is a sleepiness over me. My eyes and spirit are very heavy. I can't keep my eyes open. My body feels completely drained like I'm about to take my last breath. Lord, if this is a spirit of sleepiness not of You, cover me, Lord, cover me, Jesus. I love You, Jesus."

Written on Tuesday morning
Concerning Tuesday
I woke up with praises in my mouth, which I gave to Him even before

my eyes were opened. Then, I spoke to Him saying, "My heart aches because I'm still without my gift. Nevertheless, I thank You for another day, Lord. Have Your way, Jesus." God took me right back to the verse He gave me, and again I read Ecclesiastes 5:4: "When thou vowest a vow unto God, defer not to pay it; for He hath no pleasure in fools: pay that which thou hast vowed."

I am still ignorant of my promise and when it was made, so I read the whole chapter, but God had selected the verses above and below that which was given to me—three above and three below—to open up my understanding (verses 1–3 and 5–7). I thought back on what was said out of my mouth, and they seemed nothing that I had not given Him or had said in truth, so, I thought this vow may not have come from my mouth, but from my heart. "It must have been said in my heart, but when was it said, Lord?"

Then I got up. When I was almost done in my dressing room, God revealed to me that it was last night when I had made the promise, and that His angel was with me and with Him and heard the promise as I spoke to Him, even as He tried to bless me. Now I know when, so now I have to search myself as to what.

As I write, I believe it has come to me. I said in my heart, I will spend all night till morning worshiping Him. I will let morning find me on my knees. This is what I thought in my heart to myself, but God in His glory, who knows the deepest part of me, heard it and expects it of me. "I will give it gladly because you are worthy, Lord." I sinned against Him last night, because when the anointing touch of the Holy Ghost left my body, my soul felt His presence strongly still—the room was full of the glory of God—and He stayed, waiting for me to worship God as promised, but I had stopped because I allowed the spirit of sleep to overcome me. In my dozing as I fought it, though not hard enough to gain victory, I still felt God's presence around me, beckoning me to praise Him.

I my soul was crying out; "Worship God! Praise Him! Get on your knees!" But I allowed weakness and sleep to overcome me. I don't know how long the Holy Ghost hovered over me through the night, but I know

He was there. I felt Him there when I barely read the verse with heavy eyes and began to search myself. He was still there as I begged Him to cover me and told Him I loved Him, which were the last words I spoke before weakness and sleep finally overtook me for the night, leaving the blessed Holy Ghost still present in my room. Thank God for extreme grace and mercy, that though I was disobedient and had broken my promise, He covered me so that no evil entered me.

I am aware that this kind of sleep is a weapon of the devil, to infringe upon you at your weakest and most vulnerable point as your heart, mind, and soul are empty, swept clean, open and ready to receive God. If you take your eyes off God, the devil will bring sleep upon you and fill you with familiar spirits. You need to be careful of familiar spirits when you have need of God and when receiving prayer. Not just anyone should be allowed to lay hands on you or guide you through your need. If they are not of God, whatever they are of, you will be open to receive it also. Whenever you are open to receive of God, whatever your need, wherever you are, alone or not, you must focus on God intently so that the enemy may not come upon you, because here is where he seeks opportunities; because you are open—mind, heart, and soul—easy access. If you are not focused on God, you will receive of the enemy instead of your blessing. If you are focused on God then His Spirit will be with you and cause the enemy and his seeds and fruits to flee. "Thank You, God! My body was weak and afflicted through fasting and drained from seeking You, and though I had forsaken You by not worshiping You as I had promised and as You later bid me to, You had such great mercy and compassion on me and kept me safe from the evil that wanted to possess and devour me. Thank You, Jesus. Hallelujah!"

[Reading over the daily record written those months ago in order to now write it in this book, God has revealed to me more clearly my errors, His Word to me, and my problem, which He has been wanting to fix. My errors: I didn't understand God. I rambled on to Him everything that came into my heart and mind. Every part of me that could speak was pleading with Him simultaneously. Words were coming out of my mouth, but with it, my mind was also racing with thoughts to Him, and my heart was also speaking to him a mile per minute. I was trying to judge what came out of my mouth so I would not be false to Him in the things I said, but I failed, all in an act of desperation for the Holy Ghost to remain and abide within me. God already knew my desire and yearning for Him. I didn't need to go on at length telling Him all those things—just to get my way, and He didn't need to be reminded of His promises. And, not only did my heart speak that vow to Him, but so did my mouth, saying, "Let the morning greet me already blessed and rejoicing. I won't turn back. I will press forward till you bless me. I won't give up."

    God is not like us. He is Holy and true all the time. Not one Word falls unfulfilled. Yes, we can and should tell Him everything, but there is a way and a reverence in which to speak to Him. *Not* just to get your way, but seeking His way, His order. All gifts from Him are given and received because of Love only: His love for you, and your love for Him. Because you love Him, you show your love for Him by being and living true, and because He loves you and discerns that your heart is close to Him, He receives your love for Him, and He showers you with His love by His many blessings and gifts. It is all about Love, only Love. You have to think well about what you say before you say it, making sure it is the truth of your heart (the sincere things of your heart). The truths of your heart are the words and meditations God has placed there. Those only should you speak. Those only are His will. Those only will He act upon, for they are His spoken words and His desires placed in you, for you to feel and utter and ask, that His Spirit may perform them. Only a fool speaks without first thinking (from the heart: from that sincere place, not the evil; you must allow that evil place in your heart to be killed and cast out. Then only, will you possess the heart and mind of God—fully containing truth and sincerity and love—a child of light. Then, ask, seek, and knock and all will be received because it is already created and planned, already in His will, already His desire, already promised, already done; only to be released to you and received by you; activated and manifested by asking, seeking, and knocking). To speak as a fool will cause you to lie. It is unintentional but still a lie, and to lie is to sin.

His Word to me:

1. "Keep thy foot when thou goest to the house of God, and be more ready to hear, than to give the sacrifice of fools: for they consider not that they do evil" (Ecc. 5:1).

Be still and show honor and respect in the presence of God. Be more ready to listen and obey (submit), than to offer something you don't understand and are not able to give. Think about what you are promising and make sure it is the truth and that you can and will deliver. Don't you know it will be a sin (evil) if you don't follow through?

2. "Be not rash with thy mouth, and let not thine heart be hasty to utter any thing before God: for God is in heaven, and thou upon earth: therefore let thy words be few" (Ecc. 5:2).

Don't be so quick to speak. Think first, and be in control of the meditations of your heart. Keep foolishness from your heart and mind, for God is above you; He is Holy, all seeing, all knowing, a discerner of hearts and minds, not like you, and you are in His care and created by Him. He knows every part of you, He sees you, so there is no need to always speak, or when you speak, there is no need to utter everything, because He already know your heart, so *don't ramble on or be repetitive*. "Speak that which I give you, it is enough."

3. "For a dream cometh through the multitude of business; and a fool's voice is known by multitude of words" (Ecc. 5:3).

For the desire of your heart comes by great serious engagement (love—giving yourself to Me, commitment in serving Me) and diligence (steady application and serving God). Give diligence to make your calling and election sure. Keep your heart with all diligence. Much talking will only show you as foolish; no commitment, no purpose, just full of talk, no action, *no substance*.

4. "When thou vowest a vow unto God, defer not to pay it; for He hath no pleasure in fools: pay that which thou has vowed" (Ecc. 5:4).

When you promise God something, do it. He dislikes 'double-mindedness' and lies; someone not serious, not dedicated. Do what you say, do what you promised, when you promised.

5. "Better it is that thou shouldest not vow, than that thou shouldest vow and not pay" (Ecc. 5:5).

It's better for you that you don't make Me any promises, that you shut your mouth, than for you to make a promise and not keep it. I will require it of you; there will be consequences if you break your promises.

6. "Suffer not thy mouth to cause thy flesh to sin; neither say thou before the angel, that it was an error: wherefore should God be angry at thy voice, and destroy the work of thine hands?" (Ecc. 5:6).

Don't allow the foolish, careless words that come out of your mouth to cause you to fail God. You must do what you say, and don't say it was a mistake or you didn't know (ignorant) or you didn't mean it that way, or that you didn't say that, because the Holy Ghost heard you and was a witness, so don't you stand in His presence and deny it. What you say in the presence of the Holy Ghost is binding. You must hold true to it. Why would you be disobedient and cause God to be angry at you, and not hear you or respond to you when you call, and destroy your purpose in Him and everything He has called you to be? He will destroy you and raise up someone else in your stead if you are not true to Him. If you are not committed to Him, He will not be committed to you. You will lose your blessing.

7. "For in the multitude of dreams and many words there are also divers vanities: but fear thou God" (Ecc. 5:7).

For in the many desires you have and the many words which you speak are various useless and meaningless things: things of pride and selfishness and satisfaction of gaining this blessing, and He is not pleased. But respect God.

The Holy Ghost was present with me that night, discerning my heart and mind, wanting to abide within me, proving me, every thought and feeling; knowing how much I wanted Him, but seeing I was afraid. Hence, my problem. He had touched me in the manner I was used to, I may have still been afraid or may have been OK; but, when He touched me in a different way, I was even more afraid, even terrified. I realized that I have been afraid of the Holy Ghost, and afraid of familiar spirits. Every time He attempted to bless me, He met my fear and underlying resistance to Him. I fear (respect) Him, but I am also afraid of Him.

Since I was twelve or thirteen years old, I have been in a warfare with the evil one and his demons, and an intense warfare with them since the past few years. They have oppressed me, and I have been in a battle to keep them from possessing me. The enemies made themselves known to me on several occasions.

First, there are sexual demons that attempted on no fewer than three occasions throughout the years during my sleepy, groggy state to lie with me, and they were rebuked each time in the name of Jesus, and each time they fled. The last time was recently, and I believe they are finally defeated forever, eternally.

Second, there are the restraint demons that seemed to work most times with the sexual demons. They have attacked me with the sexual demons, those three or more times, and also by themselves as many times as they did with the others. What they did was try to restrain me. I wasn't quite asleep, but I couldn't move, couldn't fully wake up, and couldn't get up. A tremendous exhaustion; drained, fighting, struggling, conscious, aware of this force, trying to shake it off, trying to shake myself awake. And so, each time I called on Jesus, and He enabled me to shake them off, and I rebuked them. The last attack of these restraint demons was very recent with that sexual demon, and they also were rebuked and bound in the name of Jesus. I also believe they are finally defeated eternally.

Thirdly, there are the terror demons. They have brought me nightmares throughout the years, and at times would almost be caught or heard upon waking, but they left me with a feeling of fright. For this purpose I have my home lighted at all times. It seems darkness gave them the opportunity to enter and affect me. Those who have been attacked know it is not a thing of the mind, as I have proven over and over. All areas in my home remain with some light and always something playing, be it TV, radio, or music. I never sleep in the dark, and have not since this began in my teens, unless, I was not alone in the bed. My son, since birth, was not allowed to sleep in darkness, though I have never admitted these things to anyone; they just know it's a thing I do.

My sister, though I'm sure she doesn't know or understand why, supported me in my teens by giving me a large teddy bear night-light as a gift, because my mom didn't appreciate me burning her light. So, that was when I first started sleeping with the TV on, not for watching it, but for the light it gave, but mom didn't appreciate that either; though, for whatever reason, she did the exact same thing. Anyway, all I have told my son is that the devil loves darkness within and without. Though he doesn't know of my reasons, he doesn't appreciate the darkness either and never did. Since I have been on my own, all areas of my home stay lit with some form of light.

While asleep, at times, I would wake up frightened of these terrors I just had, only to find that I was in darkness—at times because someone had switched the light off or there had been some cause for a power outage—so I deduced the terror demons were real. Their existence was evident because I had fallen asleep with the lights on and was fine, and I had no knowledge of the lights going out until after I was attacked and woken up. These demons have also been rebuked, but of them I am still afraid, so God is working on that. The sexual and restraint demons attacked me whether the lights were on or off, but are now permanently defeated through God. Nevertheless, they and the existence of familiar spirits caused me to be afraid, protective, and resistant to all things spiritual possessing me, controlling me.

Therein lies my great fear of the Holy Ghost. Though blessed and Holy, He is still a Spirit that I *must* let in to abide, but something (fear and trembling) in me, that I want gone, is still in battle mode / protective mode. So, I resist this blessed Holy Spirit every time He tries to abide within me. I didn't understand Him and didn't know Him, so I could not embrace Him. He is teaching me about Him, all of Him, because when I understand, I will not be afraid. I was terrified of Him taking control; this fear is my only hindrance. In every other area, He has all of me, and I trust with no doubt, but to allow the Holy Ghost to abide in me, I desperately want Him but am terrified of giving in, so He is gently teaching me about this part of Him. The very gift and baptism I desperately need, my portion of living water, my soul was resistive to Him. But, I await the day my knowledge of Him will be perfected, in that I will be one with Him. For now, He seems very patient with me and is very gentle and encouraging to me; and for now, He rests upon me, overshadows me, anoints me, lets me feel His touch, lets me feel His presence, and is greatly with me and speaks to me in many ways to let me know it. He has promised me deliverance from this great fear and trembling, and has already begun. I can feel it. He also promised me that the time will come when He will abide within me, but He beckons me to be patient. [Thank You, Lord.]

I was also filled with vanities concerning this blessing, because I pleasured in the feeling I had under the anointed touch of the Holy Ghost and was looking forward to having that feeling abide with me. I sought the satisfaction and pleasure and accomplishment of knowing the Holy Ghost was dwelling in me. I thought it would be time to sit back and relax, but not so; time to get to work! Time for more teaching, and renewing, and witnessing, and labor, and showing and giving the love of God.

As I was just now writing about the previous experience of that Tuesday morning and the revelation received, God placed these songs in my heart and memory. I jotted them down on a sheet of paper each time He spoke to my heart, and now I feel the need to make mention of them because the words are of such significance to me, a communication between my Savior and me, like much of this book, shared with you, just the way they were given:

1. "The Solid Rock." As I sang it to Him I was giving myself in commitment to Him, and Jesus was telling me that I had now been planted firmly in Him. I was delivered from all that would cause me to sink. I had made Him my all and I was accepted of Him. He was telling me "I am the Lord thy God, forevermore."

2. "I Have Everything." He gave me this chorus to seal the commitment I had just made to Him—with Solid Rock. Confirming that He is my everything and all I need is Him.

3. "Remind Me, Dear Lord." These words were placed in my heart with the melody, but the rest could not be remembered. These words would not leave me, so I tried to find it in my song books but could not, then I called my mom, and she told me what she could remember; as she spoke, the words were the most beautiful to me because I heard my Jesus speaking to me. In due season Jesus then connected me with someone who gave me all the words to this blessed anointed song. The words are in answer to my heart's cry: that though He raise me up, and exalt me, and lead me through open doors, and bless me, and give (lend) to me things natural and spiritual, to please always remind me of the mighty work He did in me and with me; to remind me where I would and could be if not for His exceeding love, mercy, and grace, so I will never be puffed up, but always acknowledge Him and give Him glory, honor, and praise. Also, that I will love Him with all of me, and allow Him to reign in me till I draw my last breath in this mortal body, and even beyond—in my immortal body. Knowing all things belong to Him and come from Him, only because of love.]

Written on Wednesday
Concerning Tuesday (continued)
I read His Word most of the day and talked to Him. My son fell asleep in my room at 8:30 p.m., so I sent him to bed and settled in, read some more and talked to God some more, then prepared myself to worship Him. Within myself I said to Him, *"I love You, God, but what will I do or say for all those hours? It's such a long, long time till morning."* I was very worried I would fail Him, but I knelt and prayed. I asked Him, "Teach me to worship You, Lord, and teach me to praise You. Place the joy of prais-

ing You within me that I may be pleasing to You, because my God, You're worthy. Teach me to glorify You, Lord, cleanse my heart, mind, and soul that I may be worthy of Your presence. I love You, Lord, teach me to honor You." And, so I prayed. When my prayer was through, I began to praise Him, then I worshiped, and as I worshiped, I felt such love and such joy within. I never knew it could feel like that. I had to control myself from smiling, out of reverence to Him; I just felt so good, and it surprised me. I felt so lightened, and so free; I can't find enough words to describe the feeling. He just fed me, and I worshiped and praised and loved Him. Many, many tears flowed from me as I thanked Him, by name, for *all* He brought me through and had done for me—everything that I could recall. I adored Him, talked to Him, sang to Him, and talked and praised some more: just wrapping myself in Him.

Then, it was morning light, 5:30 a.m., on Wednesday. My body was drained and tired, and the tempter came, but I was full and strong in my spirit, so I rebuked him. God brought me through. I thanked Him, then prayed and ended my fast.

I got up from my knees about 6:00 a.m. and got a bottle of water and drank. Then I picked up my Bible, and God gave me Proverbs 4, and great joy was still within me, because God was pleased. Jesus had just blessed me.

[In retrospect, and in reading it again just now, I see that it was a blessing and a warning. I had received the blessing, but failed to recognize the fullness of and heed the warning about the enemy that was seeking a way to rob the blessing I had just received. I kept running heart-first into things when God wanted me to just wait on Him and let Him handle everything. He had been ordering and guiding my every step, and counseling me, but I would not hear.]

Feeling this great, cleansed, refreshed, and spiritually strong, I thought, *Why don't I seek Him now?* So, I knelt again, this time, to seek my blessing of His precious gift: the baptism of the Holy Ghost. I prayed, then I began to call on Him. I called, and called on Him, and He did not touch me; I called, and cried to Him, now feeling desperate, but He still did not touch me. He was present, and listening, but did not allow me to feel His presence. He was listening intently, proving me worthy or not. I thought I was ready, but I was not, and He knew it.

My heart was still sorely afraid, causing my mouth to be deceitful in calling for Him, all which He just warned me of. Also, not "putting away perverse lips far from me," as He warned me, seeing I would betray and deny and curse Him. Because, I did not do as He said, to "keep my heart with all diligence" (great, painstaking effort in steady application to God), for out of it my life flows.

My body was extremely weak, I could not even bear kneeling, and I had to lean on my chair. Then, the tempter came, the very enemy God had just warned me about, and he caught me by surprise because I did not obey God's words. I was not patient to hear and receive what God had just warned me of—stubborn, stiff-necked, and rebellious.

The enemy brought great despair to me and I let him in, causing me to say things such as, "Where are You Lord? Where are You? I need You."

The moment I said that, the tempter said in a clear voice not of me, just like someone was right beside me speaking, like I never heard before. (He must have been desperate too—not being able to rest unless he caused me to fall, just as God had said). The evil one said, "He doesn't come, because there is no God." And, for only one second, I let that find rest in me—a deadly error with deadly consequences; then, I rebuked him in the name of Jesus Christ until he left me.

I then stopped seeking and prayed and got up. I went and lay in my bed and opened my Bible to read it, but because of great exhaustion, I fell asleep before I could find or read any thing. The Bible was left opened while I slept. Minutes later, God woke me up; my Bible lay open just as I left it when I had fallen asleep, with one difference. My left hand was holding a group of Bible pages on the bottom right corner of my Bible; my hand was lifting them up, a quarter of the way up, just enough to expose what God wanted to tell me. He let my eyes fall right on the verse and nothing else. Still sleepy and groggy, it most certainly woke me up. To my horror and disbelief and certain death, I was cursed.

Spirit: The Call

With my hand still holding the pages up, I reasoned with God. "God, what did I do for You to curse me this way? I just finished praising You, and You blessed me and gave me that scripture with encouragement. How did I go from that to being cursed? What went wrong, Lord? What did I do?" He told me to read again, so I did: He showed me the verse above it and said, "Read!" And, I did. The curse referred to Him putting me in a land not known by my mother or father, where I will be made to serve other gods all the rest of my days. The reason referred to my heart being vain and filthy.

I lay there feeling so lost (and I was—forever). He allowed me to sleep, but before I fell into that sleep, I revealed the whole page so I could remember the book and the chapter and the verses. He allowed me to sleep about two or three hours, then I awoke with the most despair I had ever felt. No joy, no peace, and an enemy of God. I tried to find the verses and book again, but could not: He had wiped it from my memory. There was no sound or activity from the enemy, for he had succeeded in causing me to fall because I let him in, so he was now resting.

I started to talk to God again, and He brought back to my mind the moment I failed Him, so miserably, by letting the devil in. "God what will I do? Where will I go? How can I live? I will not survive without You. I love You. There is only one God for me. I don't want to serve another. Please, don't let me be lost. I believe in You. You're holy, the only true God. I know who You are; that was not of me. If I didn't believe in You, who has kept me all these months? All those years? No one but You, Lord. I know You are real. I have felt Your presence and have felt Your touch. Please, forgive me, have mercy, Lord. Please, have mercy on me. I cannot be without You, I will serve You only for the rest of my life, even if I remain cursed and lost. I will serve only You, but please, forgive me. Don't allow the devil to have victory over me. That's what he wanted, because he saw how much You love me and how much I love You. Please, God, restore the joy to my soul; please, forgive me. I'm sorry. I believe, Lord, I believe."

I cried, and cried from the deepest part of my soul. I had never felt so hopeless and so lost. It was the most indescribable feeling. I was paralyzed with fear and doom. I couldn't move an inch. I felt like if I moved, I might fall off the face of the earth. I just wanted to lock myself away, forever, and waste away. How could I get up? How could I go out my door into the world with no protection, without Him? I was horrified. I couldn't even be around my son in that moment.

I just lay there with my door shut. I thought, *What will I do? Wait a minute, If I'm cursed, my home is cursed. What about my son, Sean? Will he be lost forever, too? That can't be! What will I do? God, please don't let him be lost; He loves You. The man I love; I can't bring this curse near him: I have to stay away; I have to let this love go. I'm terrified. I can't move; I can't move!*

Then, God led me to open my Bible again, and as I did, it fell open to what He wanted to tell me. He brought my eyes directly only to Micah 7:18–19, and nothing else. "Who is a God like unto thee, that pardoneth iniquity, and passeth by the transgression of the remnant of His heritage? He retaineth not his anger for ever, because He delighteth in mercy. He will turn again, He will have compassion upon us; He will subdue our iniquities; and thou wilt cast all their sins into the depths of the sea."

I read it and thanked Him from the bottom of my soul, and worshiped Him. Forgiveness was on the way. He still loved me, He was still listening, and still hearing me. He didn't turn away forever. I won't be cast away and lost forever. Though God spoke to me with deliverance, I still lay in shock of what had happened to me. My heart was still heavy, but through it and through tears, I thanked Him for His kindness and mercy.

My son had now been awake a little while (I heard him moving around in his room), so God sent him to me to comfort and reassure me. God had given Him a dream to which I listened intently. I knew it to be of God, because he had never come to me with such dreams before. His dreams always contained his cartoon characters or some childlike thing.

His dream: He was outside playing, and suddenly the whole sky turned red, and the sun turned red—the redness signifying the great anger that God had against me—but, nevertheless, He forgave and saved me. Then, he saw Jesus coming down from Heaven: first small, then larger and closer. He ran home, and came in to tell me Jesus came back, but he saw me lying dead on the floor, and he watched my spirit as it floated away and disappeared. As he was finished telling me that portion of his dream, God brought me to His words in Matthew 24:29–31, how He would send His angels to gather together His elect. As I read His words my heart, mind, and soul thanked and praised God; yet, I couldn't show it in front of my son, because he had no idea of my private turmoil/hell. I then explained and taught my son well, that if he sees the signs of the times and Jesus descending, to look for no one—not mommy, not daddy, not auntie, not grandma, no one—just stay where he was and look to Jesus and worship Him.

Then, my son left me, and I cried and thanked God for His mercy, and just talked to my Savior. I felt I needed further cleansing, so I went back to fasting. I read the Word and prayed and talked to Him all day, except, to care for my son. As I spent the day in God's presence, the tempter was back, speaking as clearly as he did previously, working hard against my mind trying to corrupt me, to cause me to be cursed again, coming at every angle and with every imagination, just messing with my mind, because the mind is the window to the soul, and that's where thieves enter. Guard your mind in Jesus, people of God.

Each time the evil one came, he was cursed and rebuked. He would leave, then return a second and third time, then would leave for a while, then come back; each time tempting times three, again, and again, and again until he was defeated. The closer I got to God, the harder the liar worked trying to rob me, but I'm still saved, and I let him know he cannot have me, that I belonged to God. God gave me power and strength to trample him under my feet. I felt God dealing with me all day and night. I stayed most of the night reading His Word.

[Recently one morning after devotion, the scripture we discussed reminded my son, Sean, of the dream, so he told me about it a second time. It seems he had lost my attention after he spoke about me being raptured, as God had immediately taken me to the scripture in Matthew. This time I was attentive to the whole dream, and in it, my son was also raptured, almost immediately, along with me. I rejoiced in my spirit for him. I pray we both *live,* that in the end, all will be fulfilled and we will reign with Jesus, our Lord and King. Hallelujah!]

Thursday
In the morning I prayed and worshiped and cried and thanked Him. I prayed ending my fast, got up from my knees, drank some water, got something cold to drink, and put a different music CD on. Then, a song came on about Jesus being the Lamb of God, and immediately, God demanded praises of me. It was something I couldn't control or stop if I wanted to. It was compelling, and powerful. It came from very deep within me, from my belly: *"Hallelujah!"* Over and over, continuously, my soul cried out; it came out with such strength and boldness through my mouth; with tears of joy and appreciation streaming down my face that I didn't notice had started. My ears, along with the rest of me, were quite shocked at this thing happening to me. I could not hold my drink. I had to put it down quickly, and I gave way to God, raising my hands and arms high to Him and dropping to my knees until He was finished with me and had justified me, and redeemed me.

I have never felt Him that passionately and compelling before. My joy was restored, Thank You, God. I was joyful all day; singing, reading, praying, and praising Him. I feel the change. I was still not with the gift of the Holy Ghost within my soul, only at times upon me, but He had not yet abided. But, I was assured that God was working on me. There was a lot of work to be done, and most was accomplished this week. God is teaching me all His ways, if I only obey. No longer am I in darkness. My eyes are opening, my ears are hearing, my heart is no longer hardened. Wisdom and understanding are being imparted to me by God, and through them I will gain knowledge. Knowledge of how to walk, how to speak, how to sit, how to stand, how to think, how to behave, how to pray, how to worship Him, how to care for myself, how to read His Word daily, how to love, how to live, how to be, and how to stay in His will.

["Thank You, Holy Father, I ask in the name of Your Son Jesus Christ that You shine Your blessed light into every darkness within me and make them light. When You bless me, Lord, bless me also with boldness to do what is required of me, that You may use me to Your glory. Fulfill Your promise and purpose in me, Lord God, and help me to be fruitful. I love You; You are holy; You are worthy. Cleanse me daily—heart, mind, and soul—of all vain, filthy, and perverse things, all things not of You, Lord God. Let me never be ashamed, let me never quench Your spirit, Lord, and if I try, remind me, Lord, of my promise before I sin against You, so I will allow You to have Your way with me, Lord. I am Your vessel, Jesus, keep me meekly and humbly at Your feet, Jesus. Crush to naught under Your feet all feeling, desire, and imagination within me that rises up against You, and fight my battles against my enemies in this world and beneath. Keep me true to You, Jesus. Hallelujah, Amen."]

[Just now, as I finished writing that prayer and sat back in my chair to rest, God brought this chorus to my heart. I had to stop and find the whole song in my hymnal.

"Near the Cross." A prayer answered in an instant. I have been drawn near to Him. I was a lost sheep that has been found and is being kept by my Master's love, mercy, and grace. I am healed. I am in Him and He is my everything. I love You, Jesus.]

December 2003
Satan and his demons tried to steal God's Word out of my mouth by attacking me on three separate occasions, trying to possess my mind with the spirit of laughter. I am a lighthearted person who loves jokes and loves to laugh, and he tried to use it against me. Just as I would wake up praising and worshiping God, on these three occasions when I woke up, I heard myself laughing. It wasn't as if I had a dream or a thought, it was just this laugh; not weird sounding, but nevertheless inappropriate, and my spirit was not pleased with it. There was just something about it not of God. I recognized it as an attempt of the enemy to rob me, and this third time was all he would get away with without severe action to put him in

his place. This third time, immediately after I woke to hear it, I pleaded the blood of Jesus against it and rebuked it with all power in Jesus' name, and ordered it bound and cast into the pit of hell in the name of Jesus. Then I gave it to God to cleanse and purify me and to cover me that no such evil would ever come near me again. I spoke to God telling Him I didn't like it and wanted it gone from me, and God was merciful and has given me eternal victory over the demons whose job it is to rob the mind, for if they had succeeded, they would have stopped God's Word and purpose through me, but Satan already is eternally defeated, because *when all else fails, the* Word *abounds.*

December 19, 2003, 9:00 p.m.
I had previously read the book of Revelation with my natural eyes, and so, as could be no different, I was lost. At two this morning I desired to read this book again and prayed for heavenly understanding. Just days ago, God blessed me with such understanding for Revelation, chapters one through three. I intended to pick up where I left off, but God had other plans for me. I settled into my place of sleep, picked up my church hymnal, and God directed me to three songs: 1) "The Unclouded Day," 2) "Hold The Fort," and 3) "Where the Soul Never Dies."

All were songs I had heard in my younger years but had forgotten, so God reminded me of the basic tunes with some small understanding of the musical notes, and I sang them to Him from my heart. My intentions were then to pick up where I left off in the Bible, then to pray and go to sleep. But, God said, "No!" He desired me to pray first, *then* read, so I prayed.

Almost immediately, as I began to pray, I felt the Spirit of God overshadow me, moving through me, searching me or doing something. A different touch [an anointing touch]. At first, I thought He was about to fill me with the Holy Ghost. As I continued to pray earnestly, He revealed it to my spirit and allowed me to understand that He was just giving me a blessing [He was filling me with His purpose]: another wonderful gift—though I knew not what gift [Apostle of the Lord], or its purpose. His

Spirit continued to move in me, searching me, cleansing me, purifying me, preparing me, and doing a complete work in me; an unusual touch, working through me. A touch I can't quite find the words to describe at this moment, but I felt His work in my hands, in my mouth, in my tongue, in my belly, just all through me, and I thanked Him and received it in the name of Jesus.

I continued to ask of Him in the name of Jesus and received of Him until this blessing [this anointing], was complete in me. The initial blessing [anointing] that He gave me flowed within me for what seems now like no less than five minutes. I never kept track, because I was wrapped up in Him, but He took quite some time. I kept praying through it and continued praying after He was through. Then, in praying, I asked Him to "give me a deep abiding love" for Him, "deeply rooted and grounded, anchored in my soul, unconditional, just like the love You have for me. Let me love You like You love me, Lord."

As soon as those words (that last request) were completed from my lips, immediately, He touched me again, and I thanked Him and received it in Jesus' name. I continued receiving of Him, praying and asking to let me be true to Him always. (As I write, now, I feel His anointed touch on me.) Asking to let me never turn away from Him, to let me always make time to read and pray, and if I don't do it daily, to trouble my soul with a yearning desire for more of Him till I do. Asking that it never be my way, but always His for me, to make His path straight before my face and guide me through. Asking Him to cover me from the attacks of the enemy, keep me from falling, uphold me, and let Him be glorified in me. Asking to let Him be always pleased in the things I do, say, feel, and think, and to never leave me.

[He has fitted me with the yearning I asked of Him but has been merciful and has now taught me a better way: open communion/communication. He revealed to me the purpose, the need, and the benefit of this way, and has planted this way in me. He has made me aware that the moment I slack off, I leave myself open to the enemy, giving evil access to me in all forms—be it cares of this life, bad behaviors and attitudes finding a place of rest in me, being affected by a person being used against me, or by direct demonic attacks. He has fitted me with the love and desire to seek Him early, that I may be armored daily.]

I prayed earnestly from my soul. It was a most unusual prayer for me and I received greatly in an unusual way. I thanked Him with praises and closed my prayer. Then, I got up, sat on my sofa, and picked up my Bible and writing book, but instead of picking up with Revelation 4, my Bible fell open revealing chapter eight, and He drew my eyes to it and told me to read. In reading, it confused me and I felt like reading something else; but, I said, "whatever You will have of me, Lord."

I looked to Him, again, and prayed for *"heavenly wisdom, heavenly understanding, and through those impart to me heavenly knowledge. Speak to me, Lord, and let me hear You. Be not angry with me for my lack of understanding. Open my heart that I may receive You, open my eyes that I may see what You want me to see, open my ears that I may hear and understand what You want me to know of You. Reveal Your truth to me, Lord, not my words but only Yours. Feed me, Lord, give me to drink, Lord, let me eat of You and drink of You and be full. Show me my purpose, Lord, teach me and let me learn. All these things I ask in the name of Your Son Jesus Christ and receive it in the name of Jesus. I thank You Lord. All these things I have asked of You, Lord God, bless and grant them. Whatever I have failed to ask of You, Lord, You know my heart, only You know what You want for me. Bless and grant them, that Your purpose for me may be fulfilled. In the power of Jesus' name I ask, Lord, that You bind the devil and his workers of iniquity. Keep them bound till You are through with me, Lord, that they will not interfere with what You are giving, Lord God. Loose me in the name of Jesus, that You may be glorified in me, Lord God. All I've asked, I receive in the power of Jesus' name, Amen."*

I prayed such an ending because the closer I get to God, the more I find lately that the devil has been trying to interfere when I turn to God. He attacks my mind with filth or tries to make me lose focus with thoughts of the cares of life, and I know it's an oppressive attack, because it comes only when I am reading the Word or praying, so I keep having to bind the evil, because replacements come.

After praying, I turned to my Bible again. Since my first prayer, when I asked God for a love like His and He touched me, He touched my eyes also in that same touch, sealing my eyes to see into that sea of darkness again. [I believe this was done that I may not see His face because I was brought into the presence of God the Father Himself.] Since that prayer ended, I felt an unusual feeling in my eyes that stayed with me until I closed my Bible in the morning.

This time I decided to read the whole chapter through first, and I did, then I picked up my writing book and pencil and started reading verse one again—Nothing. Verse two—Nothing. Verse three—Nothing. I stopped reading again, put my book and pencil down and just talked to God—not praying, just talking, asking Him to speak to me that I may hear, because I was reading and understanding with natural eyes, and I needed more to break through His mystery. I was perceiving it with natural eyes not spiritually, so it wasn't making sense to me.

"I trust You, Lord. Show me the truth." I talked to Him for about two minutes. I started to read again, then the work He had begun in me during my initial prayer manifested. I was now open. In a very quick moment, as quick as lightening, God revealed His thoughts to me. In the moment of revelation I could no longer read. I became filled with great emotion: first joy of receiving of God, and I glorified Him with thanks, but in an instant, *great* exceeding sorrow was also within me, and I wept sorely and uncontrollably. I begged God to save His people, to let them turn to Him, to let them accept Him that they not be lost. I begged Him to deliver them, to reveal Himself to them and harden not their hearts; to let them know and experience how wonderful He was, and cause them to accept Him.

I cried and cried for all the lost, that they may not be lost. Then, I remembered a teaching that a messenger of God, Apostle Smith, gave from a taped convocation in 1999 (my mom gave me copies of them). The teaching said that God will not reveal His thoughts to you if you cannot handle it. I didn't want to lose this open connection with God, so I controlled myself and stopped crying. I got my writing book and pencil so

God could continue imparting wisdom, knowledge, and understanding to me concerning this scripture—His thoughts to mine. I read chapters eight and nine, and step by step He revealed to me what He needed me to know and what I could handle concerning the seventh seal—the seven angels and seven churches—and what will be, which will be placed after this testimony later in this book.

Through the revelation, evil was bound at every turn so as not to interfere, and I spoke to God and said small prayers between passages and revelations. At the end of chapter nine, I thanked God from my soul in a small prayer, closed my writing book, and put down my pencil. I desired to read on, but it was 8:00 a.m., sleep was my enemy, and I fell asleep.

At 11:00 a.m. I awoke, and the Spirit of God was still with me as He spoke to my heart in my grogginess. I got up and did a few things, then sat on the sofa with the Bible under my right hand, which I intended to read when I had finished listening to and learning from a teaching tape from the same man of God. The teaching was on "releasing your potential" in God. I leaned my head back on the sofa and closed my eyes, concentrating on the teaching, but in my exhaustion that was still with me, I fell asleep about 2:00 p.m. During my sleep I had a sexual dream, which I believed was an attack of the enemy because the dream was homosexual in nature. From what I heard and was taught in my younger years, homosexual things were filthy and a sin, even *all* things sexual were deemed filthy.

Let me go back a while. I used to have these *"filthy"* thoughts and dreams and took pleasure in them, making excuses that it wasn't wrong because they were only thoughts, so when God called me back to Him, through God, I started emptying myself of all uncleanliness so God could use me. I have committed myself to live by the truth of God's Word and whatever is revealed to me, so when I read in His Word that female laying with female was a sin against Him, I instantly gave it over to God, and my thoughts and feelings were cleansed. As long as I was awake, I no longer had use of or for those thoughts, and they no longer had a place of rest, so they did not enter me or come near me. In my conscious state they were defeated, but occasionally when asleep, the enemy gained access to my mind and attacked me through my dreams—a different form of sexual demon that works in the mind but still about the same business and duty—to defile and condemn its target. [Because I had fixed my mind against it, the enemy now used it as a source of torment/attack against me.]

This kept happening until a couple months ago one Saturday night. The enemy attacked my mind through a dream, and I awoke that Sunday morning having derived pleasure from the dream as usual. I got dressed and headed out for church. In the car on the way (a drive of more than thirty miles), the dream came to my memory, and I was very displeased and disgusted with the whole thing, so I started talking to God. I told Him that I hated those dreams that came to me and hated that I awoke feeling pleasure from it in my flesh, which I didn't want in me. I begged Him to bind it and cast it away from me. I told God that I was on my way to Him (church) for a deliverance and that I would receive it, that I knew He was able, then I sang songs of victory the rest of the way.

When I got to church, I thought the message was for me—concerning the man living in the tombs that Jesus cleansed—touching on what I believed my part about evil and sins that dwell inside a person. I remember the pastor preaching that you can't have something inside you that you don't really want there; be it hate, envy, hell, demons, backbiting, anything not of God. So, when it was altar-call time, I was focused on what he was saying, because I believed God was using him to speak to, as I believed, this sexually perverse oppression I *wanted gone*, but when he was finished speaking, the altar call was over because no one went to the altar.

I said to God, "This cannot be. I *will* be delivered!" So, with boldness I walked right up to the altar anyway and asked for prayer, and through faith, I left it right there. I was delivered of those dreams. Only now, because of my breakthrough anointing from God last night, I believed the enemy was angry and tried to defile me so I would no longer be clean or counted worthy of God, making me no longer fit for use. So, I believed he attacked me with that dream then woke me on the verge of heightened pleasure to condemn me, but it failed regardless, because when I realized what was happening to me, and believing that demon from hell had done this, before my flesh could fall prey to it, I cried out to God with a loud voice saying, "No! No! No!"

In an instant, God gave me the tools I needed to defeat those demons. [What He actually gave me was *all power* over my flesh.] With power and authority I rebuked those demons and cursed those feelings in the power of Jesus' name. I let them know "This is God's vessel, and you are not welcomed here." I commanded them to loose me, that Satan is a liar. "I am God's child" and they cannot touch me. "Loose me; I belong to God." I bound them in the name of Jesus, that they be cast into the pit of hell from whence they came and be bound in chains till eternity to be cast into the lake of fire and never return to me. All things were commanded with all authority in the power of Jesus' name.

While I rebuked them, the feeling that was a pleasure to my flesh but an offense and a reproach to my mind, my spirit, and, I believed, the presence of God, fled from me without completing its task. I continued to curse them in the name of Jesus, then thanked God with many thanks for rescuing me. The feeling was gone but the memory of the dream was a disdain to me, and my body didn't feel quite right.

I felt filthy, violated, so I prayed for a cleansing and purifying and purging touch from God. "Wash me, sanctify me, keep me worthy that You may use me, Lord, that Your purpose for me may be fulfilled, that Your glory may be seen in me. I thank You for the victory, Lord, I receive it. I love You, Lord. Thank You, for how You love me and for loving me so much. Thank You, for how You care for me. Thank You, for your mercy. Thank You, for your grace. Thank You, for Your kindness. I love You, Lord, I love You. I love You from my soul, from the deepest part of me. I love You, God. I thank You for Jesus (Christ), for loving Your people so much."

I worshiped Him and talked with Him, and the simple truth is, I felt Him hold me. It's a calming feeling, ***totally comforted, totally surrounded by love.*** I'm trying my best to describe it, yet I'm not capturing the essence of the wondrous feeling, just so engulfed in love. *That* is the *exact* feeling: *engulfed in love*. I stopped talking and crying and rested in Him for what seemed like at least two minutes while He spoke to my heart. Never before have I ever experienced this closeness with Him. The height He has counted me worthy to take me to in Him so far is a complete blessing to me, so I prayed to Him a small prayer of thanks and asked Him to keep me humble in all He gives me. I prayed that I will not become proud or puffed up, but to do what He will have me, not of self but in truth to and for Him. I want to receive the Holy Ghost and have God dwell in my soul and to fulfill my purpose that He may be glorified. It feels like He is preparing me for that and much more, and I thank Him. He is worthy, hallelujah. "Keep me in truth to You Lord God."

When I was done praying He gave me a song from the church hymnal at about 3:00 p.m.—"Whispering Hope," another song I had heard in my younger days but didn't really know, but He gave me the tune, and I sang to Him while it also comforted me yet more, as was His purpose and desire of it for me. It brought tears to my eyes as I sang from my heart, then when I was finished, I worshiped Him. *"I love You, Jesus! I love You! I love You! Thank You!"* [What occurred here is, believing I was being attacked made me angry and also afraid, so He made all activity to cease, and comforted me. I was not ready to receive what He was showing me, so He loved on me and let me know that I was OK.]

Written December 26, 2003
On the twenty-first, I believed more enemies were dispatched to visit my dreams, bringing me the same *"filth"* (sexual dream) in a different form (with a man) but still the same crimes against God. The enemy was weakened (I thought), the dream wasn't as powerful as before and did not cause the same reactions to my flesh—God was in control. On waking I realized that I was not as repulsed at that sin (adultery) as I should have been, so I rebuked and bound and cast away the "demons" of that dream in the name of Jesus with all power as given by God. I prayed, asking for and received a cleansing of my mind, body, and spirit as only God can give, and again the enemy was defeated, *hallelujah!* [What occurred here

was, again, He was showing me the things I would encounter, but I wanted to be so pure in Him that I refused to hear it and saw it as an attack.]

On the twenty-second more enemies (I thought) were dispatched in a final attempt to destroy my spirit—again my dreams were visited and contaminated (I believed), but this time in a much lesser, weaker form. The enemy was wounded and unable to touch me with the contents of that dream. God was with me strongly, so my flesh was unaffected; thoughts of God were in my mind. Nevertheless, when I awoke, that enemy was immediately rebuked and bound with the same fate as the others in the mighty name of Jesus. I believe and trust that the tempter and master of those that were sent is totally defeated concerning those things. Glory to God. *"I thank You, Lord!"* [All three dreams were not attacks but were visions of things I would encounter; He trusted to show me these things but I became afraid and annoyed by them and refused to understand. All were fulfilled.]

I had been asking God some serious questions, talking to Him and praying, questions such as why I haven't yet received the Holy Ghost? *"Is it something in me? Am I not ready? Speak to me, Lord, show me, send me a dream, speak to my heart, and please speak so I can understand You clearly that there will be no doubt in me, that I will know. I need You. Lord, You know me better than I know myself. Search my heart and mind and soul. Is there something I am not aware of that's standing in the way? If there is please tell me."*

On the twenty-third He spoke to me as He woke me up. The words were spoken with power, and the voice was so strong as if it would echo within me. The words He spoke were, *"Thou art saved."* With my eyes still closed, I worshiped and thanked Him immediately after He spoke. When I opened my eyes, I repeated the words to myself—thou art saved, then I pondered, what does that *really* mean? I grew up in church so I knew, when you are saved you are forgiven of your past sins and are now doing your best to live for God, but what is the true definition of the word saved? It confused me for a moment, because I had partially received a teaching from someone whom God loves but is misguided concerning the receiving of the Holy Ghost. The person gave the teaching that the moment you are saved, the Holy Ghost is within you; that there is no need to seek or ask for an infilling, and seems ashamed of and dismissive of the evidence of speaking with other tongues as the Spirit gives utterance. I had rejected the teaching, but now it was back to puzzle me.

Is God telling me the Holy Ghost is already in me? "But I don't feel Your presence in me, Lord. The evidence has not manifested itself as it says in Your Word. I know You are with me, I feel You touch me, I feel Your presence about me, I feel Your Spirit upon me but not within me, not in my soul. You come, You perform great works within me and through me but You don't abide. You are with me, but You are not yet in me. *No!* That teaching was not of God. I rebuke that teaching in the name of Jesus."

What does the word saved truly mean? As I pondered to look it up, God spoke to me again saying the words, *"Have ye received the Holy Ghost since ye have been saved?"*

I remembered that the Apostle Paul had written words to that effect in the Bible. I didn't recall the exact words of the scripture, but those were the words that the Spirit of God spoke to me. Paul's words were, "Have ye received the Holy Ghost since ye believed?" (Acts 19:2). "Who, when they were come down, prayed for them, that they might receive the Holy Ghost: For as yet He was fallen upon none of them: only they were baptized in the name of the Lord Jesus. Then laid they their hands on them, and they receive the Holy Ghost" (Acts 8:15–17).

So, now God had spoken, and I knew what I needed to do—seek Him. I was not an offense before Him. I was saved. I can receive Him if I reach out, but did I? *No!* All day and all night a great fear was over me. Where it came from and why it was there, I didn't know, it just was, and instead of immediately turning to God and giving it to Him, I let that fear and trembling rest in me. I said to myself, "You're afraid; why are you afraid? God would never hurt you. This is a blessing, not a punishment. This is your destiny, a promise. Why are you afraid of it?" And, I continued to talk to myself, trying to encourage myself, listening to my music, and listening to Apostle Smith preach and teach on tape, but still that nervousness remained in me.

I then recognized it was another weapon of the enemy to interrupt my progress with God and prevent my blessing. The enemy is terrified of who God has called me to be and is working overtime to prevent it. I called everything by name and rebuked it from me in Jesus' name with all power and authority as given me by God. Now, I will step into my blessing with boldness and faith, knowing that I can only go forward, and God will not only be with me but also in me. I was talking to God, and the clarity of a certain knowledge made me cry to God for the sake of my soul. God is with me, overshadowing me, guiding and leading me like He did the children of Israel.

When that was made clear to me, I cried from deep within, No Lord! I begged Him to abide in me, to lead and guide me from within. I cried, "Please Lord, don't let me be lost," remembering how stiff-necked they were and how they suffered for it. I begged and pleaded with Him, thinking of how the children of Israel had been, though He overshadowed and led them and cared for them, how their hearts were hardened and they repeatedly turned away from Him. I remembered when God had cursed me and what He told me in that curse, and I wept severely, begging Him not to let it be, all along forgetting His recent words to me, that I was saved. I was determined not to end up like that rebellious people, so I decided to seek Him.

On Christmas night at 11:30 p.m., I knelt before God and mostly stayed there till morning, I talked to God and prayed, getting up only to sing the songs He brought to me, then back to my knees and prayed some more, then I was silent, waiting with hope that He would bless me, then I found myself calling on Jesus. He was listening but He never touched me. I tried to be brave, but the fear was still there. I was also fighting against sleep, but in the morning it overtook me there on my knees. I was awakened after about an hour still calling on the name of Jesus. Once awake I then started speaking to God, being disappointed in myself.

[I have to put a break in writing these previously recorded events because God just put a song in my heart that cannot be ignored or left out.

"I'll Fly Away." An answer of reassurance, to such an insecure child as I was and somewhat remain. I am saved, my name is written in the Lamb's book of life. Be patient, only trust Him, only be true, His love and grace is sufficient. He that is with me shall be within me. My home is waiting for me and I shall behold Him face to face and reign with Him, all in due season.

Now, I will continue where I left off before the song. God is not the author of confusion, so I believe all that has been written in this book and the way it has been written will be understood by its readers and those whom God needs to reach, because I only follow as I am led, and He knows what He needs of me, also what you need.]

So, I was disappointed in myself saying, "God it's morning, and I'm still without You on the inside. What is it Lord? Is sleep my enemy?" I continued to speak to God, and in seeking an answer, I opened my Bible, and it opened to Romans 8, and my eyes were drawn only to these verses and in this order:

35. Who shall separate us from the love of Christ? shall tribulation, or distress, or persecution, or famine, or nakedness, or peril, or sword?

25. But if we hope for that we see not, then do we with patience wait for it.

16. The Spirit itself beareth witness with our spirit, that we are the children of God:

17. and if children, then heirs; heirs of God, and joint heirs with Christ; if so be that we suffer with Him, that we may be also glorified together.

18. For I reckon that the sufferings of this present time are not worthy to be compared with the glory which shall be revealed in us.

11. But if the Spirit of Him that raised up Jesus from the dead dwell in you, He that raised up Christ from the dead shall also quicken your mortal bodies by His Spirit that dwelleth in you.

30. Moreover whom He did predestinate, them He also called: and whom He called, them He also justified: and whom He justified, them He

also glorified.

Then, I desired to read the whole chapter and did, but those verses were mine. "I await You Lord. I am available to You. Let Your will and purpose be done in me that You may be glorified. I trust You, Lord, with all that's within me. I trust You and I'm Yours, Your vessel. Use me. I love You. Wherever You send me, I will go. Whatever You say, I will do. There is work for me to do, and I will go. I'm ready, Lord, use this vessel to Your glory. I am not afraid of my destiny, I am not afraid of my purpose, because I know You will be with me, guiding my every step. I know You will put Your words in my mouth, I know You will equip me with the tools and weapons needed and necessary to get the job done. I know You will be with me. Fill me with the Holy Ghost and clothe me with fire (power) as You promised, Lord. I will be patient. I await You with expectancy."

[In trying to remember accurately when God spoke the word that I am saved, I thought I had looked it up, but when I paused from writing and opened up the dictionary, I realized I had not. I had moved on from that thought because He had spoken to me again. Now, that I saw the definition, the full meaning of the word, the full magnitude of what God had done for me, and how He loved me, I could only praise and thank Him between every line I read as I received full understanding and revelation.

This is what God did for me and for all who come to Him in faith and truth: Saved: defended, conserved, kept, maintained, guarded, preserved, protected, safeguarded, rescued, secured, upheld, spared; to make safe and preserve from injury or destruction or evil of any kind; to rescue from danger, to deliver, to rescue from the power and pollution of sin, to preserve from final and everlasting destruction, to rescue from eternal death, to hinder from being lost, to keep clear from; to rescue from the power or influence of; to spare from, to prevent from; to keep (as in kept by God), to render exempt from (as in sin); to husband (as in God/Jesus is our mate, our help, our strength); saved from every kind of evil; spared from those who can, will, or intend to inflict harm or evil; preserve and protect by a special exertion of power to the highest degree.

No weapons that form against me and all who are saved shall prosper.

I am a child of God. I am saved, protected by the Almighty God. I am covered as long as I follow God's lead, stay in the truth, and stay humble. His glory shall be revealed in me, for I am His, and He will know me.]

Over the past three months God took about one hundred pounds off me. How? I could not say, only it wasn't by me or anything I consciously did. God just did it. Over the past couple of days I have had this craving in me; for two days I had just been eating whenever I felt the hunger, but the first day I felt it, in the middle of feeding my flesh, a voice said to me, "This hunger is not physical; it's spiritual." Yet I finished what I was eating. The second day the hunger came, I did the same, and again the voice spoke to me, "This is a spiritual hunger."

So, I stopped myself from feeding my flesh and turned on TBN and watched a couple programs, and one of the speakers spoke a word to me about spiritual hunger, saying something like, "If you feel hungry and you eat and the hunger is still there, try reading your Bible or listening to a preaching tape," and he said a couple other things that I can't presently recall, but these things that he said stuck with me, because it was God confirming the word previously spoken to me, so I will listen.

I will immerse myself in the Word of God because I believe Him, and He is worthy. I will do my part, and God has let me know what is expected of me right now: to read His Word, pray, trust, believe, faith, love, and patience. "I will Lord, I will, I will. All bridges of sin are behind me and are burned. I will only move forward with You by Your grace and mercy and will for me."

God has reminded me of a chorus which I sang to Him; "I say yes Lord yes." He has sealed my vow to Him. "I thank You, Lord God. Glory to Your name. You are worthy. Hallelujah!"

March 26, 2004

While writing and reflecting on what was recorded regarding the word "saved" and what it truly means, the enemy brought temporary confusion to me because of a word God had previously given me on the requirements of entering His Kingdom, so I tried to find my own clarity by trying to find it in the Bible and could not find what was pertaining to my confusion, so I did what I should have done firstly, what I knew to do, what God taught me to do—turn to Him. So, I called Jesus' name for help, and He responded.

This was my confusion: if when you confess and repent of your sins and accept Jesus, you are saved with all its meaning, then doesn't it mean that you will then have eternal life with Him? So, why was the other given to me by Him to write? Which I do know and believe, because that is what He said to me and also said in His Word (the Bible). You must be baptized in the name of Jesus and be filled with the Holy Ghost and living true to Him in all that it means, to spend eternity with him.

And, this was His response in revelation to me: When a person falls in love with someone they believe is their soul mate, given to them by God, and they know in their heart that there is no one else for them, that they want to spend the rest of their life with that person, there are procedures and things that need to be done before this can happen. You love this person; you love God. You want to spend the rest of your life with this person; you want to spend the rest of your life with God. You believe this person is given by God to you; you believe Jesus is given by God to you, so you confess your sins. You accept this person as the gift of God that they are and look for or at no one else; you accept Jesus as your Savior and serve no other god. You are now saved from a life of loneliness; you are now saved from a life of sin. But, this does not give you the authority to just move in with this person; likewise this does not give you authority to enter (move into) the Kingdom of God. There must be an engagement. The moment the person asks you to marry them and you accept, you are engaged, even if the person asks you while standing in front of an officiator and you immediately get married. From the moment you accept the proposal until the moment the last person says "I do," those were the very short minutes of your engagement. You must be engaged. You put on a ring or a promise.

So likewise, Jesus says, "Be mine," and you accept and say "Yes, Lord." You must be baptized in the name of Jesus. In doing so this is your engagement to God; you are putting on His name. You have put on His promise and likewise have promised yourself to Him. This is a commitment that should never be broken. You are to be true and faithful. There must be a marriage. You must marry this person in order to live with them till death do you part (if you are not of the world), and so with God you must be filled with the Holy Ghost with the evidence (proving the presence of God is within you) of speaking in tongues as the Spirit gives utterance. This is your marriage to Him; you are one. You are in Him, and He is in you. You must enter into marriage with God in order to live with Him in eternity in His kingdom.

An engagement is a period of getting to know each other, the learning period. Your engagement to God is the time He teaches you who He is and how you are to be for Him and the time He uses to prove your faithfulness to Him. Sometimes there are cases where you marry first then learn of each other, and sometimes in God, in His foresight and purpose, will first marry you by filling you with the Holy Ghost because He has immediate need of you and has already in His foresight proven you (your brief engagement), then you must be baptized in Jesus' name, putting on His name, His promise to you, and your promise to Him. (He has already given Himself to you by filling you, but where is your promise, your commitment to Him? You must then be baptized in His name.) He will then continue to teach you His will and His way, and what need He has of you: your duties of this marriage.

From the moment you decide Jesus is the one for you, the moment you are saved, He starts caring for you, and grooming you. And, when you become engaged to Him by saying yes and being baptized in the name of Jesus, whether you are a man or woman, God/Jesus is your promised mate and you are His.

What wouldn't He do for you? What wouldn't He do to protect you? What wouldn't He give you? But, you must be faithful. You must keep yourself for Him. You must keep your heart and mind pure. You must now keep your body from sin. You must trust that He is enough mate for you. He is holy. He cannot be one with—marry, pour His spirit into—an impure vessel. This is where familiar spirits seek opportunity and gain access with some, because these spirits are corrupt and *can* dwell in an impure vessel. These spirits have a good knowledge of the ways of God and the things of the church. These spirits are inappropriately intimate concerning all things godly. People having familiar spirits jump, shout, preach, worship, praise, speak in a tongue, quote scriptures, and do *all* as though for and of God, but there is no truth in them, no light in them, and their hearts are far from God.

Impurity does not mean only blatant, outright sins, it is also seeds sown and or fruits borne of the enemy: lack of faith and trust in Him, fear, pride, etc. You must be pure within. When He comes to the altar of your heart to be one with you, to fill your soul, make sure you are ready and settled to be joined in marriage with Him. If you have cold feet, He cannot marry you. You must be very desirous of all of Him as He is desirous of all of you, or the marriage cannot take place, because He will not force Himself on you. He will only search your heart and mind, much like your earthly mate-to-be searches your eyes as you stand before them to be joined. You have to want Him as much as He wants you or the marriage will be postponed, but you don't know how long you have before He is taken away. Because, there will come a day when those who are not yet one with Him, who don't already have Him, will not be able to find Him.

Now, you are married to God/Jesus; you must be faithful to Him. You must not cause Him to be jealous. You must not cheat on Him with things of this world. You must keep Him only. You must not flirt with or have affairs with any other gods or anything that keeps Him from being number one in your life. You must keep yourself a respectable (righteous/upright) mate. You must not deliberately do anything or carry yourself in a manner or speak in a manner that will bring shame to Jesus (your mate), the Kingdom of God (your home), or the angels (your family).

You must be obedient. You must first say, "Will this thing be pleasing to my Jesus?" And, if the answer is no, then you must flee from it. He is faithful to you and cares for you in every way (if you trust Him to), and He expects the same of you. You must do your marital duties—obey

Him, serve Him, love Him, love everyone else, including those the devil is allowed to bring against you as your enemies. You must hate sin and evil (not the people it uses). You must be a witness: tell people what a wonderful mate/God and Savior He is and what He has done for them and what He can do for them: He can save them. You must put Him first; you must make quality time for Him, you must submit to Him, you must be true, etc. *This* is the mate Jesus cherishes, and the mate He wants to spend eternity with. "Thank You, Lord; I love You, Jesus!"

December 29, 2003 – 7:21-10:00p.m.
I felt tired earlier and settled in for a nap. Before I went off to sleep, I prayed, then talked to God concerning a certain man. The last thing I remember asking Him is, "God is there something I need to do, or do I just wait on You? Do I need to do my part; do I need to show my faith with works? I trust You; please tell me what to do." I was then asleep, because I remember nothing more. Then, God gave me a dream.

When I awoke, I did not instantly recall it, then God made me remember within that minute as I lay there: I was standing across a street, and I watched as these two men—it seemed I had sent them—were holding this very large beautiful vase of flowers and were standing at a closed door, as if they could not go in. Then, one of the men got inside somehow as the other stood outside holding the vase—very huge with so many flowers that it covered his face. Then, the one that went in returned and stood beside the one holding the vase, and they both stood waiting. The door opened, and there was another man. This man took the vase inside, and the door closed again behind him, leaving the two men where they stood, and leaving the man from whom the flowers were taken with a puzzled look on his face, then I woke up.

That was not the only part to the dream, it was only the last part, because as I recorded that portion, God brought the rest of the dream back to me. But first, concerning this man, I know God is working on us and I believe God. I know we need to see each other, and it will be so. I know we need to talk, and it will be so. I may need to go to him, but I believe

God will send him to me; whatever is God's will. Any trust issue we have is made void because we both trust God who has made us both whole. A beautiful new beginning. When? I have to wait on God. How? I have to wait on God. What I will say or do, if anything? I have to wait on God to instruct me. God's way. God's time.

Now, concerning the rest of my dream: I cannot recall the order of things, but these are the things that took place. I was before someone as if they were preaching. I cannot say whether my surroundings were inside or outside, but it felt open, and people needed healing. I stood beside this woman who sat or knelt, and I was told by the one in charge of this thing to lay hands on the woman, as if we were going to pray. I stood to her left, and when I laid hands on her, because I was on her left I could lay only my left hand on her stomach. She had stomach cancer.

I had always heard that God had a thing about the *right*, and I held this memory in my dream because I remember thinking that I should be laying my right hand on her stomach. I contemplated going to her other side, but God kept me where I was. I placed my right hand on her upper back, then I started praying, calling on God to heal her. My left hand had remained on her stomach, but my right hand was now lifted up to God, and I felt the presence of God in me, flowing through me, doing the work. I also heard others praying or calling on God or shouting praises, then that part of the dream was over.

Another part of the dream: I was in a church; it was empty except for me and a couple other church ladies. It felt like service was over, and we were those who remained after. I didn't know the church, but it felt like I knew the ladies and felt comfortable and at home, but in thinking now that I'm awake, I cannot put a name to them because it doesn't seem like they are people I know now.

However in the dream, our church was on a hill, and we heard beautiful singing coming from what seemed like the bottom of the hill, from another church. A few members from this church, about three of them, walked up the hill while the singing continued. I was curious to know who they were, and the other ladies said, "Oh! That's Ecclesia." I admired what seemed to be their choir uniform. In the dream it seemed to be their Christmas uniform. The young ladies wore a long burgundy velvet skirt with a pleated burgundy ribbon waist and white blouses. It seemed the most beautiful thing I had seen. Anyway, they walked up the hill, and it seemed straight down the aisle of the church to the doors that we were standing close to. The church building at the other end of the aisle where the pulpit was supposed to be seemed an open path because I could see right down the hill as they came and left. One of the young ladies walked over to the door in which there was a mailbox, and she took something out of it, then they all went back down the hill where there was still singing.

After they left, one of the ladies of my group stated, "I don't know why they continue to get their mail here."

I went over and looked inside the box in the door, and there remained mail that seemed to me like boxes containing checks, so I said to the ladies, "Why didn't they take all the mail?" But, no one answered.

The singing continued; the praises sounded wonderful. It seemed to me that others from this church went to look, though I don't remember seeing anyone else. I was also curious to go, but my feet would not be moved, neither did anything inside me drive me to move, so I stayed where I was, and that part of the dream was over.

Another part of the dream: I was in a house that seemed like my mother's, yet not. I was lying on a bed on my back; two ladies were with me, one on either side of me. Again, I knew them in the dream but not now. I was very comfortable and felt at home with them. We were joyful and discussing something—it seemed like after an event, service, meeting, or something. Then, I got up and said I was hungry, so I found my way to the kitchen. There was food prepared as if my mother had prepared it—I helped myself. As I was doing so, there was a man with me; I didn't know him, but, we talked and laughed, then he left. Before he left, he spoke of something lying on the table, that it was his favorite and he hoped it wasn't something I liked, so, playfully, I said no it wasn't, and we laughed. I decided to store it away for him so others wouldn't touch it, and as I was putting it on a shelf up high, in my hand this thing was like a carton of eggs, and as I placed them on the shelf, the box was opened, and some that fell out onto the shelf and some that remained in the box were broken.

I said to him, "They are all broken."

He said, "They are."

I said, "Yeah, most of them."

After that, he left as I scooped the ones that fell onto the shelf back into the box. They all now seemed broken, and I felt sadness for him, not that it was me who had broken them, for it seemed to me they already were but he didn't know, and I had uncovered this fact. Then, I ate and drank. After I was finished, that part of the dream was over.

God has spoken very significant things to me in this multi-layered, sectioned dream, like answers to quite a few questions or direction to quite a few things. I don't quite understand them all yet, but I was wondering greatly about the part of the dream with the seeming eggs, what it could possibly mean, and I believe God gave me clarity as I wrote the last sentence to that dream. It seems there are some things God needs to uncover and heal—broken things [the things man's hands cannot repair]—while I stay where I am and let Him feed me and give me to drink. The comfort I felt in those places and in these people that were with me is my comfort in God. Always two by my side. I need to wait on Him and be nourished, then all things will be added.

There is more revelation to be had of this dream, but I guess this is the only part I am able to receive right now. He placed those specific words in me to describe this dream, because there was something He needed for me to know: that it wasn't just a foolish part of the dream, that He *was* speaking to me. It had seemed so foolish to me I wasn't going to record it, but I was compelled to record the entire thing, and now though the rest of the dream seems to answer my concerns and the blessings He has in store for me, the part that seemed most foolish and was almost ignored is the part He sent me and used most powerfully and most directly. The other parts are to come, but this part, which seemed most foolish, was the wisest and most profound and something He is doing now. Nothing about God or what He does or says is foolish. If you lean to your own understanding—the natural—all will seem foolish because you have not opened your spiritual eyes. But, God said to anoint our eyes with salve that we may see, which is to put on God that we may be able to see what the Spirit of God sees, wherein is wisdom and knowledge, now apply through Jesus—understanding.

"Thank You, God, for all You have done, are doing, and will do. Thank You, for loving me the way You do, and as much as You do. Thank You, God, for Your grace and mercy toward me. I love You. Please help me to always be true to You. Thank You, for the deep abiding love You have placed in me for You. Thank You, for opening up my heart. Thank You, for the love You gave and continue to have my heart feel for this man. Let Your blessings flow continuously to him. Continue to walk with him, provide and apply to his every need, and keep him close to You. Cover him in all his ways and guide every step he makes; keep him from falling. Fly (nullify) every trap of the enemy and take him by the hand to safety. Cast down every enemy within and without that rises up against him, for it is also against You. Feed him that he may feed Your sheep; restore and strengthen him when he is weak. If he stumbles, pick him up, Lord, for he is Yours, that the enemy rejoice not. Heal his pain and continue to comfort him. Stay with him, Lord. Thank You, God, for Jesus Christ by whom I am saved. Thank You, for the work You have already done in me and for what You have in store for me. Keep me close to You and obedient, that I will not fall short of *any* of my blessings. You are my rock, my strength, my comfort, my friend, my helper, my leader, my guide, my shelter, my shield, my provider in all, and my joy. You are all that I am and ever will be. You are my God, the only one true God Almighty. I adore You. You are worthy to be praised, and I glorify You at all times, no matter what comes. Keep me close to You; keep me true."

11:46 p.m. – A chorus brought to my heart: "By the grace of God that's why I'm saved." The title says it all; truly it is because of great love, mercy, and grace why I have life.

11:50 p. m. – A chorus brought to my heart: "Keep me true." An answer to a great need for power, strength, and endurance to run this race true to the end.

December 2003
During this last week, Christmas week, I had a six-pack of beer in my refrigerator that my neighbor had bought me when I took him to the liquor store on the night they helped me take my things off the moving truck [December 1, 2003]. This same neighbor tried to make me an adulterer or fornicator, but I pleaded the blood of Jesus against him that he would stop making his aggressive advances toward me, and God stopped him. Anyway, in my days of clubbing and parties I could drink a few Heinekens before it affected me, but now I am unable to do that. Since my pregnancy and for years at a time after, I have not socialized in that way, and now, whenever I drink anything at all, I feel it right away. One beer makes my head feel like I have had a few. I don't know if it was my pregnancy or if it is something God did or allowed, but it seems I am now sensitive to alcohol.

So, on this night, I felt like drinking something fizzy and I had no soda, so I took a beer, sat down, and drank it with my dinner. When I was finished eating, I drank the last of it and sat back in the chair to watch TV, and I was feeling tipsy. As I did that, I noticed something going on within me, something very strange—my stomach and inside of me was *very* warm, and there was some action or activity or stirring taking place within me. I wondered for a minute if I was OK, then God gave me knowledge of what was taking place within me, and I sat in amazement as I felt Him working in me. He was consuming all the alcohol out of me, and not just the alcohol portion, but it felt like all the remnants of its liquid was also consumed. As a whole, just like I had poured it in, as a whole He had consumed it from within me. Within a minute or two He was through, and the effects I was feeling from drinking it were totally gone. God didn't want me intoxicated or affected by any substance. He was dealing with me and had been dealing with me and was not through. There was a task He needed of me and was preparing me for and had anointed me for on December 19, 2003.

When the Word of God is in you, and when God has need of you, you are anointed holy unto God and no garbage in *any* form will be tolerated. You are separated unto God. You have to stand on the higher ground which He has placed you. "Follow me," saith the Lord. I realize that I cannot put any alcohol into His vessel until this task is through, and maybe not ever again—maybe because of the effects it has on me or because He just doesn't want it in me.

When He was through cleaning out the mess I had poured into His vessel, He prompted me to get up, so I went as He bid me and said, "Yes Lord!" I took the other beers, opened them all, and poured them down the sink drain, the whole pack, then I thanked Him. I love You, Jesus.

December 31, 2003.

At 5:45 p.m., fifteen minutes into recording the events I will next write about, these words were spoken to me. Because these words are vital to the experience I am about to write, I must tell of them first. These are the words: "Though worms destroy this body, yet shall I see God!" I remembered Job had spoken these words during his suffering, so I looked to God and searched my Bible and found it: "And though after my skin worms destroy this body, yet in my flesh shall I see God: Whom I shall see for myself, and mine eyes shall behold, and not another; though my reins be consumed within me" (Job 19:26–27).

December 31, 2003, 5:30 p.m.

I decided to spend the day doing nothing but read God's Word and pray and just stay in His presence. Sometime after noon, I prayed for heavenly wisdom, knowledge, and understanding; for God to feed me and let me drink of Him, that I may digest and understand the truth of His Word, as given by Him, not by man's translations or what I had been previously taught or heard of others, but that as I read, my eyes and heart would be opened to His truth, and to block the enemy at every turn from intruding or deceiving me otherwise.

After I finished praying, I started reading my Bible. I felt the need to start again from Genesis 1:1. I read to chapter four when I started feeling tired, so I completed reading chapter four, then closed my Bible to take a little nap to rest my mind and body and be refreshed.

Earlier, I had a dream—I thought it concerned my cats. In the dream the significant part was that I was outside on an area of grass, and I picked up one of their litter pans to clean it; when I raised it up off the ground, there was dirt and not grass beneath it, and on top of this area of dirt where the pan had been sitting were worms, just crawling and moving. Though I thought it gross and such things are usually frightening, repulsive, and creepy to me, I wasn't afraid. I just continued to clean the litter, then a loud noise frightened me out of my sleep.

Having lost half of my kittens on the evening of August 30, 2003, that was all that came to my mind in thinking about this dream. I knew it wasn't just a dream. I knew God was speaking to me, because He had also spoken to me that I would lose the ones that are gone, though I never imagined it would be in such a manner. Anyway, as I did then, I did now, asking God to forbid it to happen: "Not another, Lord. No more deaths."

Anyway, after reading Genesis four, I napped, then my son called me to ask something or tell me something, and I awoke; an hour or so had passed. I picked up my Bible again and opened it to pick up where I left off. I read chapters five and six but could barely get through seven and a part of eight. I felt an immense uncomfortable exhaustion upon and through me. I kept falling asleep. I begged God to take it away so I could just read and learn more about Him, but the sleep came. Every time my son called me or came to talk or ask something I would wake up and respond very well, then I would keep trying to read over the verses I had fallen asleep on. This happened five or six or more times, but I could not get through them. The last time I woke up in this manner, I was halfway through chapter eight but decided to go back to chapter seven and read it from the beginning, so there would be nothing I missed in my sleepiness. I started reading and remember nothing else of that because I fell asleep, again.

As my body slept, I had this experience with God. It was not a dream, it was not a vision, it was a true, real, experience with God. First it was like I was someplace else and had to go home to get something for someone. My son was with me, standing outside, and I was about to get into the car to drive home, but these boys that were there with us, about three of them, started to push the car, making it roll away every time I tried to get in. I then started to scold them, telling them that what they were doing was of the devil and that God was not pleased, and as I scolded them, my feet started to rise off the ground. Then, when I focused on putting my feet back on the ground, I went a little bit higher. I saw my son standing there, and I can't remember if he called out to me, but I am feeling like he did. I knew I couldn't let myself go off and leave him there, so I started looking for something to hold on to so I wouldn't float away. I was next to a building so that was my focus. As I reached for this building, my left index finger grabbed hold of something. I immediately recognized what I had held on to. It was a finger, God's finger, and it started to pull me up.

I cried out "No! No!" Thinking, *My son is down there, how can I leave Him? What will happen to him?* Then, I thought almost immediately, *I can't say no to God*, so as quickly as I had said no, I closed my eyes to all that was around me and said, "Yes, Lord! Please take care of him (my son, Sean)."

Then, I started to talk to Him as He pulled me higher. I told Him "I love You," then I took hold of His finger also with my middle finger. I wrapped my two fingers around His finger tightly. I wanted to hold on with my whole hand, but I wasn't sure what would happen if I tried, and I didn't want to lose my grip of Him, so I stayed as I was and held on tightly. It seemed like such a long trip. My eyes remained closed, and I just praised and worshiped Him and just loved Him as He pulled me higher and higher, occasionally increasing in speed.

I wasn't floating—I could feel the movement and speed. I was going home. My Jesus was bringing me home; I knew it, I was ready, and at peace. I was going to be with the One who loved me so, and had been so caring and so good to me: my Father, my friend, lover of my soul, my protector, my provider, and *my all*. I was feeling His physical touch; my body was filled with the warmth of His fire. It was as if I had a fever, just *really* warm on the inside and tingly with His presence all over, and inside me—through me.

I thought about the light that people talked about and thought to myself, *I'll see the light of His presence when I get there.* I looked forward to getting there quickly so I could see and be in that light. I just worshiped Him more. I even felt like I was about to be filled. But, as soon as I started looking forward to being filled, with a sharp quick motion, He took His finger away from mine, and I started gently descending, nothing felt, just floating down. I realized I was going back, and my heart sank with sadness that I would not yet be with Him. Everything in me cried out No! I can't recall if the word came out of my mouth. I felt tears well up within me, then He gave me clarity, that there was still work for me to do.

I guess He wanted to prove me, to see if I would choose Him, to see if He was first with me, and to see how much I *really* loved Him. But, I truly thought time was over for me, and I wanted Him, only Him. I'm glad for my soul's sake that I made the right choice, because even I wasn't sure before this, so I didn't give thought to it.

Yes! I loved Him—said I did, believed I did—but did I really? I was always terrified of death because I knew I wouldn't make it in, but I was mainly terrified because of my son. I couldn't bear the thought of him being in this world without me nor me without him. But, I trust God completely—now—to care for him when I'm gone in the same way as He cares for and protects us now, which is like no other, intensely, and better than I ever could with all the riches in the world. In every sense of the word, He cares for, protects, guides, comforts, and provides. He is, continues to be, and forever will be my all in all, and I don't believe He will care any less for my son when He takes me home. I believe He will only care deeper and protect him more, so yes, I want to have many years with him still, but I am no longer terrified to leave him. The comfort of God has replaced that terror.

So, when God made it clear to me that my purpose on earth was not through (maybe not yet begun), as I descended back to earth still with my eyes closed, I began to thank Him and worship Him, not for sending me back, but for reasons even I was not clear on, but God knew. I asked Him to keep me true to Him that I may fulfill His purpose for me. I raised both hands and arms to Him and worshiped Him as I descended. The trip back was slower than my trip going, but much quicker. Soon, I had descended, not back to the place where I was taken from, but back to where I was lying in my apartment. My eyes were again sealed shut by Him, as they were months ago during my fast when I had asked Him to bless me, and as He did when He anointed me for His purpose.

It took a while for my sight to be released. Again, the thought passed through me that I may be blind, but I trusted God and knew that there was more of His Word to read and learn, and my eyes were opened to the light in my apartment. When I was leaving, I didn't get the feeling like I was leaving my body, but when I descended, it definitely felt like I came back into it. It wasn't like waking from a dream or from sleep. I was fully conscious and the moment my descension was complete, there I was, trying to open my eyes, still talking to God and praising Him. When my eyes were opened, I recognized myself to be fixed in the same position as I was when I was going up, holding on to the finger of God. I realized then that I had truly left my body. [A blessed visit with my Jehovah.]

I lay where I was and worshiped Him, and prayed that He keep me close to Him and help me to do the work He has in store for me in truth and with love. And, to help me do my part in guiding my son in Him that my son's purpose may also be fulfilled, because I believe God wants to use him. I believe God's glory will be seen in him as it will be seen in me if I am obedient. God is doing a work. He has begun a good work in us, and I want us to be and remain faithful and true so God can see His work through. This is my utmost desire, that I do not fail Him, because He has never failed me, and that I may do my part along with Him to help my son be strong and nourished with the truth in God, so neither he nor I will be deceived or fall. My desire is that when we each reach the time that our purpose is fulfilled, and when all our days are done, we each will be taken up into Glory to be with God, the One who loves us most. *Thank You, Lord.*

I continued to lie down in amazement at what had just happened; just loving God, remembering the experience, and feeling so joyful that I made the right choice. I was no longer afraid of death. I was no longer terrified of leaving my son; only grateful, at this time, that my son didn't have to experience the trauma of finding me asleep in God, because He wouldn't have understood this wonderful, glorious thing that God had done for me. He would probably lose sight of God in his pain and fright; but still I had a confidence, that had it not been just a test of my faith or the desire of God to return me, He would have equipped my son for this thing.

Nevertheless, when my son came again to ask something of me as he had been doing before the experience, when he left, my heart felt such love for him, I called him back and gave him a big hug, being grateful that I was allowed more time with him. I wondered if he came to me during my experience and what he had seen, but then thought, God must have kept him away.

Oh! There is work to do. I am still unsure or just not confident of my purpose in God, though He has been speaking to me even more this week than before. One morning this week when I woke up, I don't know what my dream or conversation with God had been, but as I opened my eyes, I found myself smiling and talking to God saying, "OK, so You want me to be Your writer: Yes Lord! I'll be a writer for You." He has been pressing me this week, and giving me His thoughts of what needs to be done. I want to obey, but I feel so weak and inadequate. "Help, Lord! I do love You."

Section IV:
Spirit

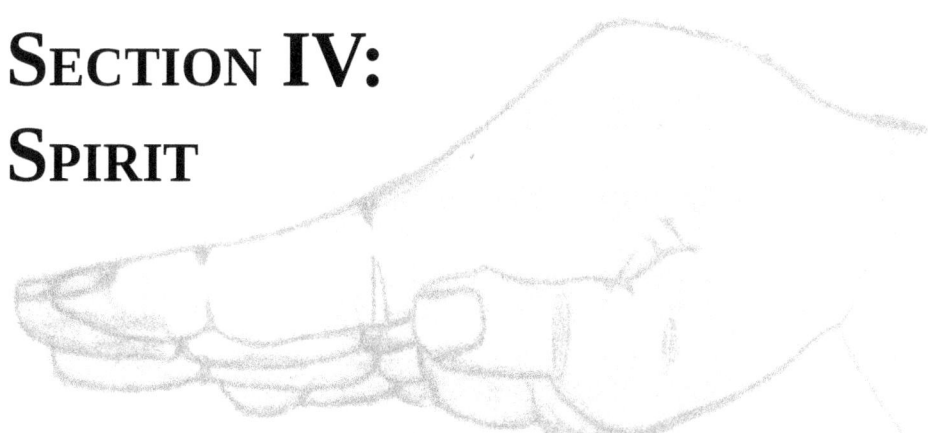

January 5, 2004, 5:00 p.m.
I was tired, so I prayed, then slept. While asleep, I dreamt about a certain man. I was on the second floor of a building, by a large open window with two other young women. We were all looking out the window at him as he walked on the grounds below. It seemed to be like a garden, or some sculpted area with a water fountain, all below this window. Every time he would look up into this window, we all ducked down, so he saw no one in the window. We did this twice.

On the second time, while I was bent beneath the window, I thought, "What am I doing? I can't do this. I have to let him see me. I have to let him know me." So, with boldness I rose up and looked out the window. The windowsill was about the height of my waist. As I was looking out this window at him, he was bent at the water fountain with his back turned to me. Then, still in this bent position, he turned from the waist to the right and looked up at me. He then he gave me the sweetest, most beautiful smile I have ever seen. We both smiled at each other for what seemed like a really long time. Then, he started walking again as if with a few other people.

As he moved out further from this window, it was as if he could see all of me—exposed, and I didn't want that, so we all moved away from the window. Then, he was inside the building, and I was not feeling ready to stand before him.

We all ran; the other two ran ahead of me and found a place to hide, but I was in this long hallway and found no hiding place. Not knowing why I wanted to hide in the first place, knowing it was now or never, the time was here, and I'd better be ready to face him; so, I stopped running and turned back, still nervous, but I did. I went through a couple of doors into and through a few offices in this building.

For some reason I had been crying, and I didn't want him to see me crying; but there, in another hallway, I came face to face with him and a young girl that was traveling by his side. She was no more than ten or twelve years old. They seemed so close, and as if they loved each other so much. To me, she was clearly his daughter, for the love and care I sensed in him for her, and I was filled with joy that he had her. I wondered where her mother was and if her mother was still alive, and if she wasn't, I was glad that they had each other. [Outside of the dream I wondered if her mother was me. But... No. That child is me, and I am without my mother.]

He looked into my eyes and held out his hand, and I put my hand in his. As he held my hand, he smiled at me again. It seemed like we stood that way a while also. He was very friendly, warm, and inviting. Close up he was not handsome, and he had aged, but I felt such love for him.

I wanted so much to hold him in my arms, but I felt the need to restrain myself. He knew me and was comfortable with me, but I never told him my name. I wondered if he recognized I was the one who wounded his heart with my well-meaning words, but I didn't want to spoil this beautiful moment, so I hid the fact that I loved him, but he must have seen it in my eyes.

In this building, it was as if we were both looking for something, trying to get someplace. I left him and the girl and turned back, and they followed behind me. I wanted to be close to and in sight of him, so I didn't move quickly ahead. I followed someone out of the offices through a door, and the door closed behind me. He and the little girl were locked in, so I lingered until the door was opened for them.

Now, we were in a hallway with two sets of big glass doors ahead, and they were locked. It now seemed we were in a train station or a terminal

Spirit

of some kind. The person who had opened the door for the man and the little girl brought me a bunch of keys and told me what to do, then left us.

I moved ahead and opened the first set of big glass doors and they followed behind, then I got to the second and last set of these huge glass doors but could not reach the lock, so this woman, taller than I was, now standing beside me on my left, took the keys, which I freely gave to her, and she reached up and opened the lock to the door, then somehow she knew the directions the guard had given me to return the keys. I was glad because I didn't recall. She put them in a vacuum chute below the keyhole in the wall, and the keys were returned, then we all walked through the double door.

Now, suddenly, we were outside beside this bus. He and the girl got on the bus. When he passed me to get on the bus, he smiled at me again. That was the third time he smiled at me. I believe God has brought peace to him and has turned his anger and hatred from me.

I got on the bus after him, but when I did, the bus was packed, I moved along to the back, looking for a seat and hoping to see where he was and wished there was an empty seat beside him. I never saw him again but felt his presence and knew he was there. I was about to turn back and go to the front when a woman called to me, telling me to "come sit here." But I didn't sit by her. I sat between two sleeping children. The whole time I sat there, though I didn't see him, I felt him there to my right, just watching me, so later when this contentious woman rose up against me for no known reason, I contained myself and quieted her arguing, then the dream was over.

I will treasure the smiles of my dream because as I had told him, I believe his real smile to be most beautiful, and it is, just as his eyes are to me. I think if he were in front of me and it wouldn't make a spectacle of us, that I would muster up the courage and fall into his arms and have him hold me and me hold him for as long as we could, not in a lustful way, because I don't have or entertain such thoughts of him, because God is in control of all things concerning us and has kept me pure concerning him; no filthy sinful thoughts, no dreams, no lust, just love and a clean desire for him, so not in a lustful way for either of us but only in a comforting way. [I await and hope for the full understanding of all the blessed revelations I have been given, not just concerning this man but in all things given that is meant for me to know. Knowing, that not all revelations given are meant to be understood by the person to whom it has been given. Nevertheless, it is a great honor and great privilege, and in all things—to God be the glory.]

My heart loves him much, and I miss him even more, but I trust God to work it out, and I thank Him for the dream. It gave me comfort and screams patience at me. I believe God is telling me that this man's heart has forgiven me and is no longer angry. I believe and trust God for what He is doing concerning us. Whenever I miss him I just give it all to God. I know God allowed me to be cut off from him because there are things God needs of me first. God wants to build me up, make me stronger, teach me patience, and teach me about Him. There is work for me to do, putting myself in a place where God can finish preparing me for His purpose for me, being alone with Him, focusing on Him, and getting deeper in Him.

When my heart felt this love, I was first thankful, then slowly, I became wrapped up in it, laying God and the work He was doing in me aside. My focus was becoming all about this man, but God said, "No! This is not the way. I caused you to feel this love to open the heart I had closed up for your sake. This love is for your healing; he is an added blessing. This love you feel is about Me and you right now, and about what I need of you and will make of you because I love you. It's not about you and him. You need to leave it to Me and have patience. Other things must come before."

God trusted me with that knowledge, but I failed Him, allowing that one blessing of an open heart to love to become my focus. How could He then trust me with bigger things? It was consuming me, turning into something not of Him. I was polluting the work of His hands. I went running in a direction He did not send me and He was not with me. He needed me silent, and I wouldn't be still. I was rebellious, so He set him apart from me because I couldn't handle it and would not keep quiet, but now, God is back in control of all of me, as it should be. All things I gave back unto Him to work it out, to keep blessing, to maintain, to have His way.

This person is just a man, with many imperfections and issues, but whatever they all are, I love him as he is. Whatever problems or disagreements arise, God will walk us through it to victory together, teaching us patience, respect, greater understanding, tolerance, and a deeper love for each other along the way.

I believe God sent this dream to me, at this time, to let me know He already has or is in the process of turning things around. "I thank You, God, and wait for him with faith, trust, and patience. I know You are able to complete this blessing. I receive it in Jesus' name. Keep me humble and filled with strength. I know he is just a portion of what You are pleased to give me, not to be compared to the gifts and works You have in store for me if I stay true to You and am patient as You ask, and even more than him, I await those gifts and works which You will have of me. I love You, Lord. Thank You, for Your patience with me."

January 9, 2004, 4:40 a.m.
One night two months ago, after I knowingly opened my mouth in grave error then went to sleep, God woke me up the next morning giving me Proverbs 25 as a warning, but I did not seek Him to receive the full understanding of it because of ignorance and fear. Now, God gave me the courage to face something concerning this man that my heart loves, it opened my eyes to what He had been telling me which I had refused to hear in its fullness. He cannot give [release] something I never asked for—a message from a program I watched

I never asked for him, so he was not released and could not be received for my husband. I had encroached upon an area I did not yet have access to. What God has not given (released) is empty and without substance (truth) and will fail, my words were empty and without substance and so was I. "Whoso boasteth himself of a false gift is like clouds and wind without rain" (Prov. 25:14), thus saith the Lord, now perfectly understood.

Yes, He opened my heart and planted a great love in me and also caused me to feel true love for this man, but I took that and ran with it without knowing God's full plan. I had found the thing He caused to be in me; true love, and God allowed me contact with him but I messed up, I got carried away, and I crossed the line. "Hast though found honey? eat so much as is sufficient for thee, lest thou be filled therewith, and vomit it" (v. 16), thus saith the Lord.

God was with me in that He defended and comforted me during the times when I was hurt. He picked up whatever pieces fell and molded me back together, making me stronger than before. He encouraged me with love that I may be comforted and trust Him but did not send me to this man to say all I did, and was not leading nor was He with me in going, because I never asked Him. I added to His word, the words I spoke to him were my own words because God did not give me authority to speak those words to him, and without authority my words were lies, and in that I spoke too much. I knew I had messed up the moment the words came out of me, even before God reproved me but I was rebellious and didn't know when to back off. "It is the glory of God to conceal a thing: but the honor of kings is to search out the matter" (v. 2), thus saith the Lord. "Withdraw thy foot from thy neighbor's house; lest he be weary of thee, and so hate thee" (v. 17).

Leave it to Me, He said, stand still and be patient because you don't know what I am doing. "For better it is that it be said unto thee, Come up hither; than that thou shouldest be put lower in the presence of the prince whom thy eyes have seen" (v. 7), saith the Lord. (Don't jump ahead of Me. Let Me call you, bring you, place you where you need to be in this relationship. Don't exalt yourself in this relationship or I will cause you to be abased, to be regarded as evil to this prince that the eyes of your heart have seen.)

"Go not forth hastily to strive" (to try hard or to make great effort), "lest thou know not what to do in the end thereof, when thy neighbour hath put thee to shame" (v. 8), thus saith the Lord. ("When you rush ahead of Me," saith the Lord, "and despite all your efforts everything fails, as it will when I am not in it, and this failure brings you shame, as it will when I am not in it, how will you know what to do or to say lest you let Me lead you and give you what to say or what to do? Stop or you will be rejected and embarrassed. Listen! Listen! Listen!" saith the One who knows best, but I was not obedient. A stiff-necked people I was and somewhat remain.)

"Debate thy cause with thy neighbour himself; and discover not a secret to another: Lest he that heareth it put thee to shame, and thine infamy turn not away" (vv. 9–10), thus saith the Lord. ("Discuss what you said and why you did with no one else but this man only, reveal nothing more, and tell no one else your heart lest you become a public disgrace that time gives no end to," thus saith the Lord).

"By long forbearing is a prince persuaded, and a soft tongue breaketh the bone" (v. 15), thus saith the Lord. ("Though I didn't send you, if you empty your heart to him he will be persuaded, but you will hurt him, you will injure him, because you have gone without Me. Why? You never asked Me, and it is not yet time.")

"Put not forth thyself in the presence of the King, and stand not in the place of great men" (v. 6), thus saith the Lord. ("Do not exalt yourself before Me, you do not have My authority. Do not call My name proclaiming a gift I have not given that it is of Me, it is not so, because you never asked of Me. I did not send you, I am here where you left Me. I love you, I will be there for you and give you what you need when you need it. Just please return to Me, just ask and wait."

"As an earring of gold, and an ornament of fine gold, so is a wise reprover upon an obedient ear" (v. 12), saith the Lord. ("I am speaking to you. When will you listen, when will you bring Me honor and glory by obeying? Things would be so beautiful if you would only listen to Me. It is so much more beautiful here with Me than the way you are going alone.")

"Take away the dross from the silver, and there shall come forth a vessel for the finer" (v. 4), thus saith the Lord. "Take away the wicked from before the King, and His throne shall be established in righteousness" (v. 5), thus saith the Lord. ("Stand still and let Me clean you up inside and out. Let Me refine you. Remove your wickedness [your way]—anything not authorized by Me—and your rebellion from before Me, and allow Me to establish you in righteousness and so shall My throne be established, so shall I be justified.")

"As he that taketh away a garment in cold weather, and as vinegar upon nitre, so is he that singeth songs to an heavy heart" (v. 20), thus saith the Lord. "As cold waters to a thirsty soul, so is good news from a far country" (v. 25), thus saith the Lord. "A righteous man falling down before the wicked is as a troubled fountain, and a corrupt spring" (v. 26), thus saith the Lord. ("What you are doing is wicked and dangerous, he will be made weak and destroyed because I have not authorized this. Your way is no good, your good intentions and expressions of love *will* break his already burdened heart. Please listen and just ask Me, give it to Me, I will work out My plan for you. My way is love, your way is pain. Stop telling him this is of Me, I have not authorized this. He is waiting on Me for this thing, and I am not with you right now. Please stop and come back to Me before you wreck his heart. I have not released you to be husband and wife, do not cause his heart to drink in your good news, you are speaking without authority. Love without Me is not love, only pain. I am waiting. Return to Me, ask and be patient. You are blinded, you are not hearing Me; open your eyes and ears to Me and come back to where you left Me. If he falls to your wickedness, he will not be able to give life to all those I have given to have need of him. He is My fountain, My spring; I need him pure, not broken.")

"It is not good to eat much honey: so for men to search their own glory is not glory" (v. 27), thus saith the Lord. ("Turn around and see that I am not with you; you have run way ahead of Me. I'm still way over here, come back and ask Me and be patient and I will bless you. This love is sweet as honey to you, but it is not good to overindulge in it. Do not seek your own blessing, because what you will find will not be a blessing but disaster and destruction. Ask and I will bless you. All good blessings come

Spirit

from Me, but I cannot release them to you lest you ask in some way or the other, and not until it is time for such blessings.")

"He that hath no rule over his own spirit is like a city that is broken down, and without walls" (v. 28), thus saith the Lord. ("*Stand* and gain some self control. Let it not be that I turn away from you and leave you to your own devices, lest you perish.")

"A man that beareth false witness against his neighbor is a maul, and a sword, and a sharp arrow" (v. 18), thus saith the Lord. ("I have not authorized you to speak of a marriage. To tell this man that a marriage is given of Me is a lie and will be a detrimental wound or death to him. It will tear his heart, and thrust through his soul, and pierce his mind.")

"Confidence in an unfaithful man in time of trouble is like a broken tooth, and a foot out of joint" (v. 19), thus saith the Lord. ("Unless you return to Me, I can have no confidence in you. It would be useless. You are unreliable and useless to Me unless you obey.")

"As the cold of snow in the time of harvest, so is a faithful messenger to them that send him: for he refresheth the soul of his masters" (v. 13), thus saith the Lord, "A word fitly spoken is like apples of gold in pictures of silver" (v. 11), thus saith the Lord. ("Be obedient and let Me refine you. When I send you (give you authority), I will put My Word (truth) in your mouth. Then only, will I delight in you; then only, will you bring Me glory; then only, will you be a blessing to Us (Me)—the Source/the Son/the Spirit. In due season when you speak My Word as I have given it to you, it will be beautiful, it will be as gold and silver to be treasured.")

[The understanding of verses 21-23 was not received by me on the day I recorded the previous things, but now, I hear what God's words were speaking to me. He was saying "though you are shamed and broken do not let anger rest in you, I am the Lord thy God, I will pick up your shattered pieces. Love, pray for, and be kind to them you think are now your enemies and I will bless you." As for verse 24, He brought me back to it again on another occasion when He dealt with the woman and bride He wanted me to be. Telling me once more that anger draws attention, it is loud, it is shameful, it is embarrassing, and it is brawling. No one wants to be around an angry person, it is truly better to retreat to a little corner than to be in a big wide space with an angry person. He was telling me anger did not belong in me, and if I allowed it to rest in me I would not be a fit woman or wife to dwell with, neither by the husband He would give, nor by Him as my God.]

This chapter cuts me to the core, but it was needed and necessary. "Thank You Lord. There is no one like You. I love You."

I had this feeling in me off and on since our last communication on December 8, 2003; lonely, missing him. God has been speaking to me in many ways about many things, but concerning him, I have not always wanted to hear the truth, because I have been afraid that the truth would leave me more brokenhearted and would not be my way, what I wanted, or what I desired.

All along I have been passing over this verse God gave me, knowing it was for me but not wanting to accept it. "Better is the end of a thing than the beginning thereof: and the patient in spirit is better than the proud in spirit" (Ecclesiastes 7:8). All that kept screaming at me every time I passed over it was the word *"end,"* so I didn't want to see any more of the verse. But, God's Word is true. Better it is the end of this thing—this thing *I set in motion*. Better is the end of my way which have quickly led me astray. I will wait on God. I will have patience concerning His whole plan for my life because there is no value or profit in my own way. I finally had the courage to face that verse and see the truth in it just this very moment. Whenever I needed comfort concerning this man, sometimes God would reprove me with such strength and other times He would encourage me so, saying to be patient and how He would bless me.

Last night the feeling wouldn't leave me. Feeling lost and confused, I confronted my feelings, though with much fear. I just talked truthfully to God, telling Him what He already knew of me; that I was afraid to speak to Him lest the answer wasn't what my heart desired. Out of extreme insecurity that I may be wanting too much, and in doubt that this love was made in me, and fear of being outside of God's will, I said, "God, if this (love) is truly not of You, please tell me. I do not want to be disobedient to You. If it is of You, like my heart desires, please tell me, and I will be patient. If it is not of You, then tell me and give me the strength to let go, and please speak to me plainly that I'll understand without a doubt—just this once Lord, and I'll never ask again."

He spoke to me three different times, but because my heart, in fear, was not ready to receive it. I would not hear or understand a single word, for I feared the words were against me. I was most confused and was afraid to ask Him again lest I make Him angry with me, so I just cried and cried.

Lesson learned now in clarity—nothing will be received that you don't truly want to know, no matter how you ask, beg, or plead. Your mouth cannot ask for something that the rest of you doesn't want, is not ready for, or will not receive. When you ask God for something, you have to ask with your whole being. As the words proceed from your mouth, lay your all on the altar of sacrifice slain. Give Him your all, holding nothing back, truly wanting it—not double-minded—with sincere heart and mind; your way must be killed or you will not receive it. He searches you and knows your true wants and desire for knowledge.

After a while of feeling more lost than before I had asked Him to speak to me, and sobbing because I didn't understand what He spoke, and feared to ask again because I gave Him my word that I would only ask once. After a while of this, I just let go and started to worship Him, through my pain, and through my hurt. I just worshiped and sought His face, then I went to sleep. I woke up still with praises in my mouth. Before my eyes were barely opened, I heard my voice calling out with praises to Him. I prayed then got up.

Later, I was feeling broken, not fit for His use, lost, empty, and the list goes on. So, I lay back down to read, but was interrupted because I was listening to some music first, and God spoke a Word to me, that this is only to strengthen me: I just broke down into pure tears, but saying things that I have never said before and never thought I would ever be saying. I was worshiping Him—thanking Him for my pain, thanking Him for all I was feeling. I didn't even recognize myself, but I couldn't stop.

I worshiped Him through thanking Him and asking Him to try me and bring me out pure gold, asking Him to break down all the walls within me, to break down and cast out all within me that stood against Him, to cast down and make level every mountain and every obstacle within me, to cast down every imagination within me that exalts itself against the knowledge of Him; to search, purify, and cleanse me, to make me a vessel fit for use. I prayed fervently.

I wasn't seeking. I was just giving Him my all in prayer, and His spirit came upon me and through me, but He could not abide as was His desire and also mine when I felt Him, because again, as always, the spirit of fear was oppressing me, and I was no longer open to receive of Him. Nothing is received of Him unless you want it with *all* of you, nothing held back. I trust Him with *everything* else, why won't I give Him full control of me? Why won't I allow Him to fill my soul? Why does my heart continue to fear? When I think it's defeated it's back.

He wants to bless me, and God's Word is true. I will be patient as He asked, because He promised to remove the cup of fear and trembling from me. "I await You Lord." Everything else I give to Him freely and willingly, but to allow the Holy Ghost to abide in me, fear defeats me every time and robs me of my breakthrough. I will, through God, overcome. He will give me strength. I have identified the enemy. I have the weapon with which to defeat it—Jesus. Now I need to apply Him till victory is won. Easily said, harder to do on my end? That's just it. There is nothing for me to do but turn it over to God and just keep living for God, keep pressing into Jesus, and through the power of God, in His caring for me, He will remove it. He will defeat it from oppressing me. When I hide in Him He will fight for me.

I took an afternoon nap and woke up calling on and worshiping God. Even before my eyes are opened, the moment I am conscious, I hear myself doing it. I find myself doing that a lot lately, on a daily basis. It's like waking up and catching yourself talking in your sleep, but only I'm worshiping God.

Later this evening I felt the need to just talk to God, and I was missing this man. I decided to do things right this time. I looked at his picture, and I stared into his eyes in this picture and had a conversation with myself first to make sure this was something I really wanted and not just fantasy, the sincere truth of my heart. I faced all his possible faults and imperfections and issues, as there is no one alive without these in them. I accepted with a surety, no double-mindedness, that I wanted this man in my life to be mine and me his, with all his faults, fears, pain, trust issues, and all his baggage.

Then, I turned to God and let it all out of me, at times with tears, all that was in me for this man. Then I asked with all of me for him: that I will love this man like He loves him, and that this man will love me like He loves me, with added desire toward each other. Because that love is true, that love doesn't hurt, that love will not cause pain; that love will last throughout eternity. That love will think of each other first, that love will not cause the other shame, that love will cause us to cover and shelter each other in any situation. I asked that my son will love him as a father and that they will be all a father and son are and should be under God. I asked that his family will find favor in me, and that He prepare me that I will be submitted to him. To be with us in a three-way relationship—me, this man, and God ever present as the head of us. I asked that we will love each other through any argument, that when we cannot agree we will turn it over to Him. To mold us and fit us together as He would have us. To be strength for each other. To love each other through any strife and whatever comes up against us or may try to come between us; to be there and let us love each other through it all and come out stronger and closer. To respect each other always. That I will never repent of asking for him. That I will be his support in all the things He needs of him and not be jealous or selfish with him when he needs to be away or to spend time alone with Him. That we will not just love but also really like each other; that we will be also friends. That we will hold no part of ourselves back from each other.

I just laid it all out and asked that all I said be already in His will and His mercy that I/we should have these things, because God will bless whom He will bless and show mercy to whom He will show mercy. It has to already be in His will, desire, and plan for you to have anything, for you cannot bend God to your will or make Him do anything by your thought.

I then released him into God's hands, along with myself, for this union (relationship and marriage) to be. After our heart-to-heart prayer talk, I found myself thanking Him as though it already were. Again, I was somewhat alarmed to hear myself speaking this way, calling everything by name in thanks to Him. I don't know why; it was just flowing out of me.

When I was through, I felt a burning desire to destroy all evidence of our past encounter, because I had saved everything, including things that were hurtful. Since September 18, 2003, I had been speaking to him. Then I spoke on his heart, and it hurt him deeply and angered him because he thought I was playing a game with his head [as God later revealed to me on February 11, 2004 at 11:45 p.m.]. So he hated me, and severed all contact with me—all things just as God had warned me, but I had not heeded His warning, and so all things were fulfilled, but I trust God to set us back on His path ordained for us.

So, I destroyed everything. This was a new beginning with God. Everything of that past that was not authorized by Him needed to be severed and destroyed without a trace. It was a difficult task to do, but I did it, because with anything, if God isn't in it, I want no part of it. All traces of that lie against God are eliminated. Again, I reaffirmed the release of us both into the hand of God.

After this, Satan tried to deceive me with pure lies. He cast such a feeling of doom over me. I felt utterly useless, void, desolate, a vessel not fit for use, empty, lost, nowhere to turn, so confused, doubtful, and weak; saying to God, "Where do I go from here? I need you. How can I trust anything in me now? I need the Holy Ghost within to lead me. Without Him I'm lost (which is true, but the enemy meant it for my disposal and destruction). I thought You were leading me before, and I was so wrong. How will I know when it's You that's speaking to me? I don't want to mess up again in anything. Everything else I thought You told me, did You? I

Spirit

don't know anymore. I can't move without You. I need You."

I felt so totally and utterly lost. I lay down to talk to God, and I couldn't. The enemy had robbed that from me, so I turned on some music, and God sent me the Word to be strong and stand in Him, and I cried for a while. Then I felt the need to write what I was feeling, so I set the music on repeat and picked up my pen and book and started writing. The last thing that happened came out first as God gave me such clarity on what He had been telling me all along, and as I wrote, the obedience I felt to Him strengthened me.

[Now, God gave me a word when I inquired of Him deceitfully, pretending I wanted the truth—for my mind wanted to know, but my heart was deceitful, not wanting to accept it. I had to revise my writing concerning these three verses, because not until the first week of March did I realize the true meaning of His words to me. I thought it was in answer to what I had asked Him, but it was not. With Proverbs 25 and others, and the dreams He had given me, He had told me quite a bit about that relationship—all I needed to know and all He would say for the moment—and had now moved on to what He needed of me. The rebelliousness He spoke of was because I was stuck on that situation to which He had already answered me quite plainly. He wanted me to stop being so insecure and trust Him, trust in His Word and all I had received of Him concerning this man. He was saying, heed Me; follow Me over here now and let Me do this thing which I have need of—"I want My book."

I knew concerning that other situation, the verses didn't make total sense to me, but I knew God knew best. I knew He wanted to feed me and give me what to say, but I wouldn't allow my eyes or ears to be opened concerning the purpose. I had no faith that I was who God said I was. I was looking for outside affirmation concerning my purpose and calling. I wished and wondered if He would send someone to prophesy to me, because though He was speaking to me mightily, I didn't believe in myself, but there was no one but God—as it should be, and as He had made it and preferred it, that no one could rob His glory. But I wasn't yet fully receiving into my spirit the true purpose—what He was feeding me for—

but nevertheless I was being obedient.

During the first week of March, I was in the shower, not thinking about anything specific, when I heard a voice. God was speaking to me, and as He spoke, the power of His voice echoed and vibrated in my mind and within me, saying, "Eat this roll that I give thee!" Immediately, I remembered the verses He had given me, and in this moment understood the meaning of those Words He spoke and the verses that contained them. "Yes, Lord! Yes, Lord! Yes!"

Conviction was now within me. For the next couple of days, His voice would not leave me, so I opened my Bible and read the verses again and received His counsel and direction. Then I was led to read the whole Scripture and was in awe as He unveiled all to me, not only what He would do but what to expect and how to handle it, and I am not afraid, because He is with me. Now I'm full of conviction and committed, unshakable in God concerning this, no more creeping issues with myself, God is enough, His Word is enough. *I am who God says I am*, so the enemy better watch out.

He had spoken to me otherwise concerning what He needs, but this affirmation I had received stripped away the lingering doubts that the enemy brought against me to impede his defeat and my faithfulness and obedience to God in this thing He wants of me. Since the Christmas and New Year holiday, He put a true conviction in my spirit to do this, and I got serious, and started, but before then, I just found myself recording things here and there, for what purpose I wasn't sure or was too afraid to face.

It's been quite a process. I wanted to go visit my mom over the holidays, but on the morning I was to leave God kept me home by presenting a problem with driving the car for that great distance, and I recognized that it was His will and spoke in that manner to my son and told God that His will be done and that I loved Him, and He dealt with me as He had never done before. I was a quarter of the way through my task, and during the second week of March, He used me day and night, at times no sleep, working straight, and in seven days, He had three quarters of it done.

The scripture He gave me was Isaiah 8:11. I refused to understand, so He led me to Ezekiel 2:8. My ears were still closed, so He lead me to Ezekiel 3:3, then during the first week of March, He pressed me to read Ezekiel chapters two and three. He was saying to me, "*Listen! Listen! Listen!* I have been there for you. I am teaching you for a purpose. I have called you for a purpose. I will bless you with blessings, but other things need be first. You need to focus on Me, on nothing or no one else; this is your first duty to Me. I have need of you; be obedient. Sit a while, let Me feed you. I have something to say; let Me give it to you, let Me use you, let Me fulfill a portion of your destiny."

I want to do my part, no matter what it costs me, because I love Him and I don't want Him to raise someone else up in my stead. It is my deepest desire more than *anything* else to serve Him and be pleasing to Him in everything that I do. I will sit at His feet, I will listen, I will be obedient, I will learn of Him, I will receive of Him as He feeds me. Oh! What a choice place to be, at the feet of my Savior! I got here kicking and screaming and resisting, but He loved and guided me to Him with a mighty yet gentle hand. Oh! What mercy, and now such peace and comfort and joy! God's way is always best. Thank You, Jesus. Please keep me humble. You are worthy. I love You Lord.]

January 10, 2004
Since early yesterday morning, God has placed the gift of greater joy, much joy, deep within me, even to my soul. I have been praising Him in song most of the day, also thanksgiving in prayer.

My mom called today. It was a blessing to hear her voice. I appreciate her so much, just because she *is*. We spoke for many hours, possibly four. She told me about a phone plan she now has with free long distance. God is good; now she can call me freely. She told me to inquire about it for myself, and it is available for me, and I trust and believe God for it. Soon I will be in touch with those in my life freely, as God allows.

Anyway when I hung up from her, I was pleased and grateful for the time spent with her, but I was drained and tired in my flesh, so I lay down to take a nap. I prayed and put on my headphones, listening to my gospel music while I fell asleep. My spirit was lively within me, and I praised God in song while I lay. As my body got more sleepy, twice or three times I felt God touch me; working in my flesh. It felt like someone tugging at me in my back, waking me each time, and each time I woke up praising and worshiping Him.

Then I eventually fell asleep, and God gave me dreams, prophetic dreams, concerning servants of God, but I must not be ready to receive them because when I woke up later, the memory of them was not clear to me, then they faded away before I could grasp them. I woke up worshiping Him again. I got up and did a little work around the apartment while I praised Him in song. Later I prayed and listened to my music while I read His Word until deep into the morning after 4:00 a.m. I took the headphones off and turned off the music. I needed silence. I wanted to be focused on God, to hear Him if He needed to speak to me. I read some more, then fell asleep after 5:00 a.m.

I was given a dream. Let me first say since a few days ago, maybe the seventh or eighth, each time I prayed, I found myself not just praying for others in general but calling all names with specific purposes. No matter what was going on with me, this is the way I found myself praying.

Concerning my third brother, praying for healing to him and to be called of God and answer yes, for right now he is most lost by indecisiveness, stating that he is not sure if God even exists. Once God is revealed to him through Jesus Christ, I see him being a mighty warrior for God, and I believe God for all concerning him.

Praying for my mother, that God draws her even closer to Him, that she may be all He wants her to be. For He already knows her by name, she is already His, so my prayer for her is only that He heal her within and without and work in her life to bring her closer to Him. And for Him to walk with her daily and that my brother who is with her be not a snare or hindrance to her and what He wants of her.

Also, Big Sis, whom I had been praying for specifically before (God answered yes), along with my mom's prayers for her, has set in motion a mighty blessing concerning her which He has witnessed to me, and I believe Him for it. So I keep her in my prayer for God to block the enemy from coming against her blessing and to bring it through speedily as only He can, all things being perfect concerning Him.

Praying for my cousin that I love, to be delivered from a thing which God gave me a dream about. My dream concerning my cousin was this: My son and I were out somewhere, and the enemy was after me and chased me through the streets, then through a half-built construction site (my cousin's profession). When I came out on the other side of the site, there were people who intended to stop and detain me for the enemy, asking "Aren't you the one they are looking for?" Then they suddenly allowed me to pass through them, and my son and I got in a car and escaped the enemy.

Then the dream changed; my two brothers (the first/eldest and the third) and my cousin and I were all sitting in a living room on the sofas, and my cousin was sitting beside me. It was a dream inside of a dream, because I was now in this part of my dream telling my brothers and my cousin of the dream I had of being chased. In telling them, it was as if I was speaking of someone else being chased, and I described the color shirt the person being chased was wearing. We all at that time looked down at what we had on, even me, and all said, "It's not me." Then I looked at my cousin's shirt and the front of it was black but the back of it was brown, the same brown color of the clothing of the person being chased, so I said to my cousin, "It's you." Then we all looked at him, and I woke up. I rebuked the enemy and prayed for my cousin that God deliver him from this enemy and have maintained him in my prayer.

Praying for Sis and her family, to be rescued back to His presence from a way they are going. My eldest brother and his concerns, and others I prayed for that I cannot discuss, for it is their situation for God to apply to their needs and His purpose.

Anyway, concerning my mom, it seems God has responded; it was in His will for her. She told me in our phone conversation the dream God sent her: A woman was in need of healing, and the woman was brought to her, and she laid hands on her. I believe she said she laid her left hand on the woman's back and her right hand on her head, and she was calling on God for this woman, and she woke up worshiping God and rebuking in the name of Jesus. When she was done, she thanked God for restoring the gift of healing to her—*Glory to God!* "Use her, Lord; I thank You."

Now, this is the dream I had on this day: I was standing in a room beside a bed. I wasn't alone in the room, but I cannot now identify who was with me. It seemed my brother who is afflicted was lying in the bed, and I was standing by the side of the bed, and the door was on the other side of the bed a small distance away. I was praying and rebuking the enemy out of him, then as I called on God for him, he was no longer in the bed. But there lying in the bed in front of me was the spirit of infirmity; its likeness was like unto a woman. I rebuked it and chased it with all power given to me by God in the name of Jesus, and it slowly and reluctantly dragged itself out of the bed and along the ground on its arms. It never stood up. I walked behind it calling on Jesus' name and rebuking it continuously as I watched it seeking another part of the house to escape to when we got outside the bedroom door.

While outside the bedroom door, it was evident to me that I was inside my mom's new house. I continued to rebuke this demon out of the house as I walked behind it to the front door, never taking my eyes off it. I opened the front door as I continued to rebuke it out the door. It was very reluctant to leave from the doorway, and I called on Jesus and rebuked it the more, and it vanished from before my eyes as it very slowly crawled over the threshold. I never saw it again, but I sensed it as if walking down the street to my right behind some trees.

As I was closing the door, my cat Precious (the sick one) ran pass me to outside and stood in front of the doorway on his rear legs with his two front legs and paws up on the side wall to my right. I was concerned to get him inside lest the demon return and enter into him, so I got him inside and closed the door. For a bit of a time the door was too narrow and would not meet the door posts to close properly. I called on Jesus then the door became of proper size and I was able to bolt it securely. When I did that and turned around, I saw a man in a gray sweat pants and like a white tee shirt walk by me to the kitchen counter as if preparing something there. His back was turned to me; it was my brother. He was whole, completely healed. My heart rejoiced and I thanked God. As I did that he went and sat on the sofa, and I went and sat down on the end of the sofa right beside him. Smiling and prepared to minister God through Jesus Christ to him, I showed him or was giving him a tee shirt with something pertaining to Jesus, and that part of the dream was over.

Now I was in another house, and there was a gathering of some kind with food and drink and activity. I was with Big Sis and other family, then we were in another place where there was an activity and a fee was needed to join. I didn't have the fee so I asked of Big Sis and also Sis who was now with us. They both searched themselves, but Sis got to her money first, and she pulled it out and placed what I believe to be seven dollars in my hand (a five and two ones) to pay this fee.

Then we were not there anymore; now we were on what seemed to be the top floor of a building. Now it was just Big Sis and me. We were hurrying down flights of stairs, as if trying to escape from something or someone. Big Sis was ahead of me. As we hurried down the stairs we came to this area that seemed like a huge maze-like slide, so we started sliding down, Big Sis still ahead of me, still trying to escape something. Now I stood at the bottom and it was like a field, and I saw Big Sis running back and forth and around, so I called out to her, but she wouldn't come to me. She just kept running, and as she ran with her back to me, I saw as it were a small stream of smoke (deception) coming from a wound in the middle of her back.

Then I looked over to the right and saw a woman with a gun pointed right at her, so I called out to Big Sis saying, "You have a bullet in your back." I called her to come to me so I could help her, but she just kept running around and would not come. So my focus was now to capture this one who was after her. This woman came close to Big Sis, still pointing the gun at her. Now, Big Sis stood facing her as she spouted words to what Big Sis had done to her and taken from her, and Big Sis responded to the woman that it was not so.

As they spoke, I found myself standing behind the woman a little distance away with a long thick branch: its bark stripped off to reveal the smooth, brown wood and with curvature and bumps and thinner at the other end. This was in my left hand, and a large stone was in my right hand. Sis and her mate stood to my right with the same posture as mine, with the same items in the same hands, left and right, and as it were a large group—which I now believe to be God's army—standing behind me with the same posture as mine (standing straight up, arms at my side with the items in them, feet slightly apart), holding the branch, smaller end out and away from us in the left hand, and the stone in the right.

Now, I found myself directly behind the woman, who I now recognized as an old friend of mine and Big Sis (only, she was and is not a true friend of mine). In an instant I was upon her as the army remained behind me, and she was disarmed; I never saw the gun again. Now, the woman was face down on the ground with her face in the dirt, and my left foot was in her back as the army stood close behind me. The woman raised up her head to speak, and her face had dirt all over it. She seemed to be a spiritual enemy because I found myself pressing her with my foot as if to grind her into the ground, all the while rebuking her while doing this.

Then I woke up, and I began to call on Jesus, rebuking these enemies I had seen in my dreams; calling on Him for deliverance concerning my brother, Big Sis, and my animal. Then, I began to thank Him for their deliverance: for the healing in my brother and the saving of his soul, for Big Sis concerning His defense and protection of her from the enemy trying to block/rob her blessing and about all I had seen, and for the healing and protection of my sick animal. Again, I found myself calling out every name to God; family, friends, the church, and people I know. Calling out their circumstances and their need, for God to cover, pull down, destroy, loose, bind, cast out, protect, reveal Himself to, pour out blessings, and to apply to every need. I thanked Him and worshiped Him, then my prayer ended. I am still filled with joy in my soul and renewed strength to my inner and outer being.

Spirit

I got up a little after 8:00 a.m. and went to wash my face and brush my teeth. While in my dressing room, my eyes caught my reflection in the mirror. I marveled for a moment at the person looking back at me. When a person is obedient to God, His glory shines through them; it's all beauty. I saw a bright, rosy, beautiful face looking back at me. It is a most wondrous thing, a beautiful thing inside and out to sit at the feet of Jesus. "I love You Lord. Nurture me, feed me, give me to drink, nourish me, strengthen me, and keep me close to You daily. I adore You. Please keep me humble in You and focused on You. Thank You, Lord."

January 25, 2004, 2:24 a.m.
[This is a letter I wrote on this date at this time to God while in my frustration of literally not being able to pray or read the Bible, I needed to communicate with Him so I felt the need to write to Him.]

Jesus: My God, my friend, I know You are with me, but I feel so far from You, and I miss You dearly. I feel so lonely for You, I don't quite understand it. I feel the need to pray, yet I cannot, so I just talk to You when it overwhelms me. I try daily to read Your word, yet each time, no matter what or when, I feel fine till I open Your book, then the enemy of sleep snatches my time away from You. No matter what I try to avoid this thing, the moment I open Your book, I can't read but two verses before this thing comes. I used to read many chapters, even books at a time, yet now I can't even read a verse, and in that, I understand nothing.

What is it, Lord? Is it You, Lord? Have You taken Your Word from me? Have I done something? Have You taken Yourself away from me? Or is it the enemy blocking me? I need You, Lord. I didn't keep track of the corners I turned to get here, but I desperately need You to help me get back. I was at Your feet filled with joy only three weeks ago. I afflicted my soul unto the door of death, and while at death's door I cried out to You, and You delivered me. I thank You, and I'm grateful for my life that Your purpose may be fulfilled in me, that I have another chance to make my soul ready to be with You in eternity and not be lost. It's been difficult for me, fighting my way back, and I thank You for how You have restored my body.

Since the day You kept my spirit within me till now, I feel the distance growing, and it is as if I am helpless to stop it. I need You. The enemy is against me. I know it, I feel it. Please don't allow it to continue. I need You, I miss You, I love You, I want You with me. I am still Your vessel. Make me fit for use and dwell in me. I want to know You more than I ever did. I want to hear You when You speak to me. I want to know Your voice distinctly. Speak to me as You spoke to Your people in times past that I may hear You and say, "Here am I, Lord."

Tell me where to go and where not to go, what to do and what not to do, what to say and when to say it. Tell me what time is best for such and such, in everything no matter how small, speak to me Lord. Instruct me in *all things* and in *all my ways*. And in all Your speaking, that I so desperately desire to hear, speak so I will not be afraid. I need You to bring me into a place where we can talk together, You and me, always in Your presence, always pleasing to You, always obedient. Show me how to walk with You, Lord God. Let it be already in Your mercy that this thing should be—close, intimate, real—for You will only bless whom You will bless and have mercy on whom You will have mercy.

Teach me balance—how to live and walk in the Spirit—that I will ever be with You and You with me, yet how to be present, doing what needs to be done for You, for my family, and other things down here that needs be. This is what I hunger for. I don't know how to, and I cannot. Only You can bring me to this place and teach me how to stay there.

You already are my everything, but I feel the need to ask You, God, please be my best friend and find favor in me that I may be Your friend. I know You love me without measure, but I want to be Your friend, a true friend, one You can count on, one You can trust, faithful. Let me find grace in Your sight that this thing should be. Also, continue to nurture my love for You till it's like unto Yours for me, truly unconditional and faithful unto death. Help me to give You my all without fear. Remove fear and trembling from me, for it is a hindrance between my soul and You, and I want nothing between—nothing.

My thoughts now draw me back to moments where You physically held my spirit within me, keeping it from rejecting this flesh, and I know You didn't keep me on earth for the enemy to rejoice over my soul by gaining victory. Thank You, Lord, for restoring my mind. My eyes are still dim, and other parts of this vessel are still afflicted, but I know You are working on me, so I thank You now for my full restoration in body. I thank You for restoring and strengthening my spirit within me.

I feel the oppression of the enemy against my soul, trying to devour me, and he's pressing hard and seems to be gaining, but I cannot and will not lose, for I have come too far with You, farther than I have ever been in all my years. Fight for me, Lord God, my Sword, my Shield; cover me, fight for me and lift me up in victory. Remember this day Your promises to me, Lord God, fight for me, Jesus, I need You. Stay with me, Lord.

I also have another burden Lord, take control of what and how much I put into Your vessel concerning food, for since You have delivered me from death, I seem to have either lost control to the spirit of gluttony, or I have the desperate need to restore this vessel myself. I impatiently consume things prepared in front of me and drink until I'm bursting, yet my body desires more when there is no room. I have never in all my years felt such lack of control. It's like I have returned to this vessel a different spirit, with the same gluttony I had during my affliction in the experience which You fed me. Take control and remove it from me, oh God, for nothing I can do will restore me as I should be. Only You know the way. I give it to You right now, because my way will only destroy me.

I trust You, Lord, please take full control. Build a fence of protection around me, Lord, and fight for me, every single battle great and small. Let all that come against me be totally defeated while You heal and restore me, mind, body, and spirit and draw me closer to You. Into Your hands completely, I remain Yours. I love You, Lord.

March 21, 2004

Now that the letter has become a part of this book, I feel driven now to tell of the experiences I had. So, about my experiences during my affliction:

1) Drink of Me.

I was at the site of an old building, and outside this building was a well that was covered up with a heavy piece of stone, like concrete, and a young girl was standing by it and could not lift the stone. I was thirsty so I walked up to it. The well stood to the height of my hips. I removed the stone, and pure, crystal-clear water started shooting straight up before me in a stream like that of a water cooler but with a thicker stream of twice or three times the width around. The height of the stream shot up to my shoulders, flowing back down within the same stream continuously. The girl allowed me to drink, and it was very good, then I stepped aside. It seemed so real, I was afraid that I had sinned, so I repented of drinking it and wished it out of me. Then the experience was over and I prayed for forgiveness because I realized that it was God caring for me, blessing me, and I had rejected Him.

2) Eat of Me.

I was in a house with my eldest brother and my sister-in-law and her family. I had three tomatoes in a bowl and one in my right hand, and all my desire was to wash this tomato and eat it, but my sister-in-law and her mom and her sisters were all over the kitchen, just busy cooking. In the sink and in the hallway, they had all kinds of meats they were cutting up and preparing to be cooked, but all I desperately wanted was this tomato in my hand, so I squeezed and bored, and pressed through them and got to the sink and washed it, then squeezed, and bored, and pressed my way back out of the kitchen.

When I got out, I realized the tomato in my hand had been squeezed, and the flesh on top was broken open revealing the little fleshy seeds inside, and a part of the flesh or skin was hanging against my thumb, and that part against my thumb was purple like a plum. Still my utmost desire was to eat this tomato, so I went through the hallway, stepping over all the meats they had laid out, trying not to step on them. I got to a living-room like area where my brother was sitting with the men, and I also sat, and immediately, my brother asked me to go get something for him that would cause me to have to go back down the hall through the obstacles. I wasn't pleased to have to go through them again, but I got up, and while going, I put the whole tomato in my mouth. Now the size seemed to have gotten smaller.

When I got to the cabinet at the end of the hallway where this thing my brother wanted was, I stood and started to chew this tomato. But in my mouth it was no longer a tomato, it was not a plum, it was like nothing I had ever tasted. It was a fruit but the most absolutely delicious thing I ever ate. It made me groan with delight. There was nothing common about it. I knew right then, while still in the experience, that it was given of God. But I was greedy because my mind went back to the other three tomatoes that I had in the bowl, and in hoping that they would taste the same I said to myself, "I have to have another." And immediately God brought me out of that experience, and I asked Him to forgive me for my gluttony.

3) I Will Feed You, But Be Satisfied with What I Give, When I Give It. I Know What to Give, When to Give It, and How Much to Give You. I Am Enough!

I was in this outdoor place lying on my back and looking up. I seemed to be in a gigantic globe, and the walls of this round globe were formed by tall trees with beautifully colored leaves like autumn. The rounded walls reached up to the sky and at the very top was an opening where the sky was blue with white fluffy clouds, and the sunlight shone in with beautiful rays of light against the colored leaves. It was to me not of this world but heavenly. I lay there admiring its beauty.

Then I was somewhere else. Over my head was a large grape arbor as far as the eyes could see. There was no way out from under it, like it was enclosed in a gigantic one-room building. Under my feet were planks of wood laid down for paths over the lake of water, under this grape arbor. There was a man, seeming like he was keeper of this vineyard, walking on the planks with a very tall stick with a hook on the end of it, and he walked around picking these grapes and putting them into little barrel-like containers about the height of one's knee.

I desired some, and suddenly in my hand I had a long stick just like the keeper's, but mine had no hook on the end. I started walking behind him without his knowledge (I thought), moving when he moved and stopping when he stopped. When I came to a certain part, I poked at a bunch of grapes I desired, and not through my clumsy efforts but by God, a small bunch of red grapes fell right onto my left chest, and I caught them from falling. I ate of them and they were so delicious. I gobbled them up and wanted more, so I followed the man again and at another point again I poked clumsily at another bunch I desired, and God made a small bunch of green grapes fall to me, landing on me just as before, and I gobbled up those also. Yet it wasn't enough for me, I still wanted more, but now suddenly my stick fell into the water—as if snatched from my hand—and I could no longer pick at them, so I desired in my heart to go steal some from the keeper's barrel.

I continued to walk behind the keeper, no longer protected by God, no longer an apprentice but an enemy because now I had done/thought evil in His sight. As I crept behind him, he turned around and saw me, but instead of just running away, I still had this gluttony within me, so I did run but with the intention of grabbing a bunch of grapes on my way out. I ran and he chased me, and when I was near to a barrel and reaching for it, I fell into the water which had eel-like monsters in it, and the keeper seemed to have control over them and set them after me.

I struggled for a while, but I was able to rise out of the water away from them because I realized that the water only came up to my waist. Still going after the barrel of grapes, I intended to steal some before I escaped. I got onto the planks again, and now I was in a church just off the planks where more barrels of grapes were, and the keeper had entered also in his attempt to catch me. Now, it seemed to me the keeper was a demon, for I could see great anger in his eyes and hear it when he spoke as he proclaimed how he was going to get me, and said something else "in the name of...." I feared greatly because I believed this was a demon

Spirit

speaking to me. Then, he said "Jesus." I said, "Oh, Jesus!" while laughing out of relief, for nothing to do with Jesus would cause me harm. But, it was as if I didn't regard my Jesus, as if this thing or this one held more power than my Savior does. Then, God brought me out of it. I knew instantly it was a test that I failed. Again, I asked for His forgiveness for my gluttony and that I had failed Him so miserably, not being satisfied to the point of stealing.

In the midst of writing this third experience, God opened my mind to many things. He has been feeding me in the presence of my enemy and giving me to drink, but I have been wanting too much too soon. God has His perfect plan for me, giving me a portion at a time, only what I was ready for and could handle, refining me, building me as He saw fit. He had given me to drink of that wondrous well of water springing up into an everlasting fountain, living water, *His Spirit*, and I rejected Him because of fear. He was feeding me His Word a little at a time, but I wanted too much at once, and when I didn't get it, I didn't trust Him enough to supply my needs, so I went my own way, and the moment I sought my own way, that was a rebellious and evil thing, stealing from Him the honor and glory of caring for me, to clothe me in righteousness, and in the end showed little regard for His holy name and His great power, fearing who I thought to be a demon instead of Him, so He punished me by taking away access to the grapes; sustenance, life, the Word, and forbade communion with Him, thus I was tormented, blocking and preventing me from being able to pray, because in His sight I was filthy, very rebellious, stiff-necked, and vain within.

He must have been gravely wroth with me to do such a thing, because if I were allowed to pray, He would hear me, and His heart would allow Him to forgive me. He did not want to hear me because He was gravely angry. His wrath was great against me, maybe even making Him repent of His promises to me, so I needed to be punished if only for a moment.

The more I write, the more He presently reveals as I go, and as I read the words He gave me to write, I'm shocked at the way I treated Him and hurt Him and angered Him. I am blessed and grateful that He gave me a way out through my letter, an opportunity to return to Him. He was telling me what would be, but I never see till it's too late. What do I need to do?—*Receive perfected knowledge,* be patient, obey, listen, hear, and see; receive direction and counsel, be attentive to Him, be sensitive to Him and the things of Him and the things He forewarns me of, that I don't fall into it.

There are three main things He has told me He wants within me: heavenly wisdom, understanding, and knowledge; and three things He wants out of me: rebelliousness, foolishness, and anger/quick temper. [**Understanding** drives away anger/quick temper; **Wisdom** drives away foolishness; **Knowledge** drives away rebelliousness.] I chose Him, so He is working on me. My anger is not one harboring violence—now. God has done a wonderful work in me; now there is almost nothing that ignite me and if anything is a bother or is offensive to me I give it all to God as He has instructed me to do at all times. "If there is anything at all, tell Me" was His spoken instruction to me, and I rest in that command. When evil comes at me, I see through to the root of people's words, behavior, and deeds—and through other people's anger so they don't get a rise out of me, and at times I am able to pacify their anger. Only still, within me, is just this grave intolerance of things I consider foolishness from those closest to me, making me shut them out till I can, through God, find a better way to deal with them, while allowing God to deal with me. God is not through with me, so I expect the day when that wrong way will be plucked out of me and discarded.

"Jesus, I'm sorry that I failed You then and so many other times, even those two other times consecutively during my affliction when You allowed me to be tested with the same exact sin and circumstance, and I failed You both times so miserably. Keep my heart and mind open to You that I will understand when You impart things to me, and that I will not fall into a way or a thing that You have given me foreknowledge and warning of, because my aim is to please You in everything that I do and with every breath I breathe. Uphold me, Lord, please continue to order my every step and keep putting Your words into my mouth, and in all this keep me true to You. *I love You, Jesus."*

January 25, 2004 – 10:50 a.m.
To my Friend,
I thank You for another beautiful day—beautiful because You made it. I thank You for the breath I breathe in this day. I thank You for the peace my soul feels right now, and thank You for the sleep I had early this morning; it was more restful and comfortable than I have ever felt. I can't quite describe it right now, but it was most different and *quiet*. I thank You.

I still want You in control, Lord. Teach me how to care for this vessel, what to put in it, what to put on it, how to present it, all in a manner acceptable to You. Teach me how to care for Your vessel: spiritually, emotionally, physically, in every way. I feel a difference in my will, my patience, that spirit of gluttony or the need to restore my own body. I feel a difference, and I thank You. Please keep working on that for me. Teach me how to rule over my own spirit in all ways, and cover and keep me till I learn. Teach me the sound of Your voice, Lord. Just as I know the earthly voices of those people I know and love, teach me to know the sound of Your voice better than I know those. Touch my ears, heart, soul, mind, and spirit and cause me to hear You intimately every time You call me, every time You speak to me, and in every way You speak to me, never missing a sound or a word, never mistaking my own thoughts for Yours, never mistaking my own voice or that of the enemy for Yours. Let me know Your voice better than I know my own, better than I know *anything* else. I understand that when You speak, it is never without direction and purpose, so in showing me enough grace to allow me to personally hear You, I pray also that You equip me with boldness and the tools needed to be always obedient to Your direction and purpose, to bring You always honor and glory.

I just want You, and I realized that more than ever during my affliction when I was at death's door. All I wanted was You, all I could cling to was You, all I could stand was You. I had use for nothing else save You. You were my only peace, You were my only comfort, You were my center, You were my breath. I thought of saving myself and when it would be over, but You showed me only You could save me, and I thank You for keeping me obedient through my suffering and for delivering me. I thank You for how You spoke to me with a strong hand about obedience when I thought of rebelling and tried to bargain with You, and with a gentle, merciful hand when You bid me "give it to Me and see what I will do."

I thought of saving my own life and almost lost it, but when I surrendered it to You, You restored it with such love and care. *I really, really love You.* My heart is so filled with You right now, I can't find words for it, but I know You know and feel what my words cannot express. You really cared for me in a personal, close way last week, and I just want You to know right now, I truly appreciate You in a way I can never repay or even begin to express. I adore You right now; You are more than worthy of any praise I could ever give. Keep me wrapped in You that I will never look back or turn back, that I will worship and praise You for the rest of my life; yet my praises will never be enough. Only let me love You deeper each day and continue to be Your friend and do daily as You will have me. Not my will, only Yours, always Your will Lord. Amen.

February 2, 2004
I had a sexual dream of a male, and woke up affected in my flesh, still not being properly awake. Nevertheless, I immediately turned it over to God in prayer. I asked Him to forgive me for what I dreamed and experienced, and I asked Him to take my sexuality and cleanse it, wash it, purge it, purify it, of all filthiness and all things not of Him, and return it to me as He would have it. I said, "You made it Lord, You know how it should be. I don't like what keeps happening to me. Fix it, Lord, make it (my sexuality) acceptable to You, keep those things from me. I have no use for such dreams, not even in marriage, so please remove it from me, never to return to me in any form. I trust You Lord, I know You are able. I love You Jesus. Please help me, I need You."

Then, I rolled over and went back to sleep. I realized my error in dealing with this perverse thing. I was cleansed of each episode but not covered. I dealt with it the wrong way. I sought God after the thing had already happened, but it should have never been allowed to happen because it was a known enemy. It wasn't a new thing; I needed to intercede with God that He may intercept it before it took place, deal with it as a whole, not by individual episodes; find its core, pluck it up from the root, and cast the source of it into the pit of hell till eternity where it will be cast into that lake of fire. And through God and by God, this has truly, finally, and eternally been accomplished.

Since this day I have felt the difference in me—just clean and pure. I can't describe it, I just feel changed, different in a good way. My sexuality is not gone—it's in me—I just feel such a sense of control. This is a new thing for me. God has been doing a few new things with me. It feels good; I like it, I love it, and I have no more sinful dreams and as long as I stay in God they will not enter, access to me will be denied. *"Thank You, Jesus. I love You."*

March 16, 2004, 10:00 a.m.

When I was called and told I was to start on this day, I rejoiced in God, then prayed His blessing and favor toward me on this job. I have stepped into the job God prepared for me. It is part time but will enable me to stand and maintain. On February 28, 2004, I received my temporary Alabama nursing license, and on March 1, 2004, I called the nursing home that hired me back in September of last year. They told me to come in.

When I did, I went through the hiring process over again with the woman from last year, and she administered another drug test right then at the facility. When I passed the drug test she seemed to express joy or surprise as she called out to someone "she passed!" which took me back to a place of feeling offended, and wondered again about their previous motives, but I again gave it to God. They told me that they first needed to check my three references and that I could start orientation as soon as the next two days. My references were my two last jobs in New Jersey and this new pastor. God delayed my start date for exactly two weeks instead of two days by putting the pastor and my last job (the one I quit when I came to Alabama) out of reach that whole time, which seems next to impossible, because all I usually had to do is pick up the phone and reach them in one phone call. But it was God because He needed to use me and did so greatly over that time period. When God had accomplished what was enough for that time, He allowed the nursing home access to my old boss and the pastor (they spoke to his wife). All three had given really good references. So now, I have stepped into God's preparation for me, and it is good, as all gifts from Him are. *"Thank You, Lord. I love You, Jesus."*

March 22, 2004

Beginning the sixteenth I had three days orientation to the facility, off one day, then four days orientation to the units on which I would be working. This day was my third day of unit orientation. About 4:30 p.m. my supervisor (the woman that hired me; the same that had offended me last September with her comment about my pain medication) came to me while on a short break and asked me if I would be interested in working with the psychiatric patients. I thought about it for a second then told her, "Yes, I don't see why not."

She said she wanted to know because they were going to build that kind of wing onto the facility, and in case a class came up concerning that, I could take it. I told her how blessed I have been in the past to have those patients listen and behave with me most of the time—even when they would try to tear another person to bits, they were most times sweet to me. It's only God.

So I told her yes, I definitely didn't see why I couldn't work with them. I then told her I had called the instructor for the training center that belongs to their company and left messages but that she hadn't called me back, so my supervisor said she would get in touch with the instructor and find out for me. When I got my temporary license, the State gave me three months to get twenty-four hours of continuing education credits as is their requirement by law. When these are gotten, then I will receive the permanent license. These credits can sometimes take months to achieve and cost quite a bit of money, but if I can get it from this center, it will be free because I work for their company now. *"Thank You, Jesus. I love You."*

March 23, 2004
God showed me great favor. About 6:30 p.m. I got a phone call at work. I was concerned because I thought it was about my son, but it was my supervisor. She told me she got in touch with the instructor, and the instructor told her that I was already signed up for *all* the classes. I started to question her how it could be, then before I finished what I was saying, I stopped myself in mid sentence and told her I won't question it, I'll just count it a blessing, and she agreed with me.

She said they are going to work with me until I get all my credits. In getting those credits, I will be gaining much-needed education and also certifications which I never had and one that I had years ago but expired. The charge nurse giving me orientation called me aside at the beginning of our shift and placed a twenty-dollar bill in my hand. She said because she knows how it is, that it was to hold me over until I got my first check. I received it because I knew God had touched her to do it, and I thanked her and God. I am still thinking about the possibility of working with the psych patients, and it is appealing to me. I am beginning to desire it. *"Thank You, Jesus. I love You, Lord."*

March 24, 2004, 7:00 p.m.–8:00 p.m.
I received one continuing education credit (CE credit). *"Thank You, Jesus."*

March 25, 2004, 8:00 a.m.–10:00 a.m.
This class was supposed to be from 8:00 a.m. to 12:00 noon, but the other half could not be completed because I noted and made it known to the instructor that the second instruction tape was the same as the first. The State had made an error and mailed the department two like copies, so we were not able to get the four CE credits for this day. The instructor

said when the other tape comes in we can view and discuss it after another class, and then we will receive the credits. But God has a purpose in all things. *"Thank You, Jesus."*

March 29, 2004, 8:00 a.m.–12:00 noon
At the end of this CPR class and its tests, I received 3.6 CE credits. *"Thank You, Jesus."*

March 29, 2004, 3:00 p.m.
Received God's first fruit. I smiled when I saw how much it was because of His way and purpose with numbers. *"You are worthy, Jesus. I love You."*

March 30, 2004
The evil one tried to rob me today. I was supposed to be in class at 8:00 a.m., but I did not jump up until 8:30 a.m., unsure what to do because I did not have access to a phone to call but knew in my spirit that I could not just sit and let time keep on going by. I couldn't just not show up. God prompted me so I got dressed quickly and rushed over. It was 9:00 a.m. when I walked in the door to the classroom. I quickly explained to the instructor that I overslept and told her I would leave if it was not OK with her, and she told me to sit down. The class had just finished watching a video tape concerning this First Aid class and were about to take a test. I sat quickly and she placed the test in front of me, and I pled the name of Jesus over it, and when it was over, I had gotten *all* the answers correct.

The class proceeded till 12:00 noon and I got 4.6 CE credits. When the class was over I realized that the video tape we were waiting on and needed on March 25 had come, and this was the day she intended to complete those credits. We viewed the tape and reviewed it orally and at minutes after 2:00 p.m. it was over, and I got 4 CE credits. Satan tried to rob me of 8.6 credits in one day. This was over one-third of the credits needed for my license, which would have been grueling to regain because the calendar for next month's (April's) classes were out, and not one class I could take was on it. They were all nurses' aide classes, and I need these credits by mid May or I will not get my permanent license and cannot continue to work until I do. Satan you *are* defeated in the name of Jesus. *"I love You, Lord. Thank You, Jesus"*

March 31, 2004, 8:00 a.m.–2:00 p.m.
LPN IV Therapy class was a blessing. At the end of it God enabled me to pass the test with a mark of one-hundred percent and receive 7.6 CE credits. All 20.8 CE credits were received in five days with no cost to me—something which takes some others months and costs them hundreds of dollars. There are still 3.2 credits for me to get, but I have home-study packets for 2 credits each, and doing two of those will bring me to 24.8 credits which is more than I need, so God willing I will have my permanent nursing license in my hands by the end of April. *"Thank You, Jesus for caring for me the way You do. I love You, I adore You, and again thank You."*

April 5, 2004
After a weekend with God, on Monday morning I received a note on my door. My other supervisor had dropped by because they were not able to call me. The note told me to call him, so I did, and he delivered the good news. He asked me if I wanted full time, and I said yes, and he told me the days and times I would be working, and it's perfect. It fits all needs, and I am off every weekend, which means all my Sundays are available to God, and the position is with the psych residents. I am to start tomorrow and orient to that unit for three days, then start. God is truly amazing. He also provided minutes to my cell phone through my mom who bought the coupon and applied it to my phone without it being asked of her, enabling me to make that phone call. After I hung up from my supervisor I called my mom, thanked her, and told her everything. *"I love You, Jesus."*

May 11, 2004

God gave me Proverbs 23 and 24. I read them and know God needs to let me know something, but I am not yet receiving that understanding.

May 12, 2004

I see that the proverbs have started to unfold themselves since last night at work. I have been reading them over and will do so daily with prayer.

May 14, 2004

I received a message early this morning that my mom had left on my service on the evening of May 12 saying that they were coming to see me today. I called her and it was confirmed that they all were coming. When I hung up, I took a nap, then cleaned up and went on a small shopping errand concerning them. They called at 6:00 p.m. (Central) and said they were on their way. They went in the opposite direction and had to turn back, so they did not reach my town till 1:00 a.m. They could not find my street so they called and I went out to meet them and brought them home. It's like a dream. I can't believe they are here. I'm nervous that I may not be able to show them a good time, but I prayed, so I know it's covered.

May 15, 2004

My family arrived at about 1:00 a.m. I was filled with joy to see them, but I was nervous and had prayed to God that they would feel at home and be pleased with their stay and have a good time because I am mostly quiet and am not the life of any party, but I guess they already know that about me.

My mom was supposed to bring her sleeping bags but she forgot, and there would have been no room in the vehicle for them had she remembered. I was looking around my apartment for sleeping accommodations as my room was not accessible to company. It's the only room left in my apartment that still has boxes and bags and things still unpacked from storage. I had found one air mattress but could not locate the other and the air pump, then God put a wise thought into my son, who asked if I could take one of the mattresses off my bed and give it to someone, so I took them both off and everyone had comfortable sleeping arrangements. I offered my son's bed to the driver, but he had made himself comfortable on the sofa, so my two nieces and my nephew joined my son in his room, Sis slept on one mattress, and my mom slept on the other mattress. My brother decided not to sleep that night, as he does sometimes, so since I hadn't seen him in a while and don't know when we will meet again, I decided to stay up with him (we are both night owls anyway), so we sat at the table and talked till morning light, about 6:30 a.m. Then, Sis and her mate (the driver) had to leave for another town, so I made breakfast for them and they both left.

The children all wanted to stay with their cousin (my son, Sean), and that was fine by me because I love them, and my son missed them immeasurably. The children weren't ready for breakfast, so I told them whenever they were to let me know. I drove in front taking Sis and her mate back to where I had met them and they left. I showed my mom and brother, who were with me, a couple of supermarkets because they needed to buy a few things, then we came back home. The kids still were not hungry, but a couple of them had eaten cereal, then they fell asleep. Because they were excited to be together and the boys had not seen each other in one whole year, they had stayed up playing video games, and I allowed them because I understood their longing for each other that was now being filled.

While the children slept, as usual my brother brought God and things of God into our conversation, and as usual the things he said were not things pleasing to God, because he doesn't believe, but I trust God concerning him and await the day when he will receive the truth within him. So, we had a very strong dialog, but I knew he wouldn't believe, because God had given me forewarning of him by Scripture. Nevertheless, I continued with him. Then, the children started waking up about 11:30 a.m. so my mom suggested and I decided to just make the children hamburgers. My brother and I continued; I made cheeseburgers and fries for everyone except my brother because he doesn't eat those things. He ate fish, and they all ate.

My brother likes to talk and likes to convince people of his beliefs and his way, and he seems to like dialog with me because I believe he finds me a challenge because I am firm in my belief concerning God and the things of Him. As I was cooking, my brother was trying to tell me certain history of Christianity, to which my mom was agreeing, but I refused to be attentive to another thing he had to say, and I told him that I have a very large problem listening to someone who doesn't believe in my God, telling me anything about Him, and that until he believes and accepts the truth of God, I will not hear him (I can be stubborn sometimes).

But he continued to try to make his point as he usually does, so I told him I was warned of him, and I stopped all my speaking, as much as I did. As I sat and ate, he said something I had heard him say before on other occasions, and I had to stop him, so I did, and God allowed me to let him know the truth and proved it to him in Scripture, as he requested. He believed that after Moses, out of anger at the children of Israel, broke the tablets of stone containing the commandments God had written, that it was Moses and not God who rewrote them on the second set of tablets; but it was God who wrote them at the first and God who rewrote all He had written at the first. So now that truth is within my brother, for he accepted the Word of God concerning that. After this, my mom gave up on us, as she can only take so much of my brother's *philosophy*.

As I was eating, he said something false, and in response I spoke a word that God had given me and to write. When I was finished eating, my body was exhausted and aching, so I went and lay on one of the sofas, and the word I had spoken to him stuck with him, because right then he challenged me on it with a question, and I responded. My answer shocked him, and he did not believe, so he told me I better be careful of what I say, and in that moment I doubted and thought to go back and change what had been written; what God had given me. In my own mind I wanted to clarify what had been written so it wouldn't be received by others the way my brother had received it, but this was a deception of the devil that I didn't yet see.

So I lay there in my doubting, yet speaking boldly to my brother the things of God that were within me. As I lay, I felt God working in me, dealing with me—a touch, and I thanked Him. Then, I became troubled within, so I was no longer attentive to my brother as I had began talking to God, asking Him to forgive me for anything I said that was not of Him; to wash me and cleanse me, to forgive me for any lies against Him that came out of me, to help me to be true to Him in all my ways and in all I say, to keep me—that I speak nothing of myself but only His truth.

As I started speaking these things to God silently within, and as my brother continued talking, not being aware that my attention was now with God, as I began to speak to God, I heard a voice speak to me. The voice was very clear, interrupting what I was saying to God. The voice said, "Touch his leg."

Immediately I received and understood it was said concerning my brother's healing. After the voice spoke I continued to ask for my forgiveness in case I had sinned, then I returned to what the voice had spoken. I started to think of ways to touch his legs without having to explain, for I could not tell him. I did also consider telling him the truth, but if I did, he would not believe and would also be extremely hurt and angry and probably feel mocked. So I thought of ways to do it, for I had to be obedient to God, but all the ways I thought of seemed and were very deceptive, and I knew those ways could not be of God, so I prayed.

I said, "God, if the voice was not of you, please remove it and such things from me. If the voice was yours, Lord, then please tell me and show me what to do. I trust you Lord." I finished praying then fell asleep.

While I slept, my brother cooked dinner, and my mom called and spoke with Big Sis. When I woke up I started to pray, but my mom saw me turn so she came and sat on the sofa chair that was beside me and started talking because she wasn't aware I was praying, so I said a quick prayer and then listened to her.

It was my smallest goddaughter's birthday and her mom was keeping a party for her, so Big Sis bought her some gifts for me (for which she refused to let me know the bill so I couldn't pay her back; she is kind hearted that way). Afterward, when the party was breaking up, Big Sis called me and let me speak to my god-children's mom and another old friend. They are all doing well, and God is nurturing the baby. She is holding on and taking steps and meeting milestones that other preemies born at that time have not yet met, surprising the doctors, but I am not surprised, only joyful because I know of a surety that God is able of *all* things.

I told Big Sis to hold her for me. My heart was touched when I think how she is growing and will not know me. I long for her, but I am strengthened because God must come first and His will and purpose *must* be accomplished. I will see her again and she will know me, all in God's time.

I dished everyone's dinner, and we all ate, then I cleaned up. I had promised my son cookies, so I mixed up some batter and baked cookies, then went and tempted them with one of them saying how warm and yummy it was, so they all ran out of the room and attacked the cookies, then went back into the room after thanking me.

I felt the need to work on this book and have some time with God, so I told my brother I wouldn't stay up with him this night. I talked to him and my mom a little, then spent a few minutes with the kids in my son's room, then went to take a shower.

As I showered I remembered the words of God, and again ways not of God began to enter my mind, so I spoke to God out loud saying, "God I give it to You. I know what has to be done, because You said it, but how and when I await You, Lord. May You be glorified." And so I spoke to Him, and I thanked Him.

I went out to say goodnight, but both my brother and my mom were already asleep. I said goodnight to the kids then went into my room and made a place to lie down. After settling in, I just talked to God and prayed more of what I said in the shower, then I spoke to Him concerning myself, because I was still troubled. I read over the scriptures God had given to me as a forewarning, trying to see if I had fallen in anything He had said, and though I was encouraged, one verse troubled me for I wasn't receiving its meaning, its truth; then the meaning was given to me, and I was comforted, and I fell asleep.

May 16, 2004
I woke up early and got up to the bathroom but still felt tired so I went back to bed and fell asleep, then I woke up again. Something in the air smelled very good. My mom was cooking dinner as she does every Sunday morning as a habit and a necessity since I was a child, so that when we all got home from church, no one had to wait for dinner, because the churches of our faith go on for quite a while. Then we would return to night service, but it was all joyous. I miss that kind of worship/ fellowship, yet I regret nothing, because the closeness He has now allowed me and brought me to in Him, to it *nothing* can be compared. I just want more of Him.

Anyway, I lay and prayed. As I prayed I was interrupted. My mom came needing something from me that she needed for cooking. I waved to her but she didn't understand, so I told her I would get up in a little while. I started again to pray and asked God to use me today that He may be glorified. I thanked Him for another beautiful day and thanked Him for bringing my family here, and so I prayed, then I got up.

The kids brushed their teeth as I made breakfast with the works: pancakes, eggs, bacon, hot chocolate with marshmallows and whip cream. We all ate. My brother ate fish again, because that's what he likes. I cleaned up as the kids got dressed, then we all went out. I drove them around, showing my mom and brother what I knew of the town, the places where I stayed before I got my apartment, all the parks I knew and the spot where I tented (first time back), the movie theaters, the stores and plazas, the dam, and a beautiful park near home that I found last week.

This park was our last stop, so we all came out and stayed a while. We rode a very short trip on the tour bus, then took a trip around the park in the train they had. The kids went on the shaking bridge and rode my son's scooters around, they also played on the playground, and climbed the hill beside the waterfall. My brother brought his camera and asked me to take his picture by the waterfall, then the kids wanted theirs, too, so I took their pictures. Then my brother wanted me to take his picture by the fountain, but to get where he wanted, he had to climb down some steps, five high ones and two lesser ones, but I don't think he considered how he would get back up. He was a bit fussy about how and where he wanted these pictures taken and this frustrated me a little but I didn't allow my frustration to get the best of me. God kept me.

I took the pictures he wanted, then we walked to the steps, and he said, "This seems like quite a challenge, doesn't it?" And he snickered then began to climb them.

I walked beside him on his left, he climbed the first one, and I feared he would fall, so I said, "Why don't you give me that one [pointing to the cane in his right hand] and hold on to the wall." (The steps had short walls on the sides of them.)

He gave me the cane and climbed another step, then he sat down, so I sat down in front of him on the opposite wall, and we sat a few minutes and talked as I held the cane in my hands, then he lifted his right leg unto a higher step. I expected him to do the same with his other leg, but he didn't. He got up, then I made mention that he could climb all the steps this way by sitting and putting his legs on higher steps till he was at the top, but once he got up, he braved it and climbed them all without ceasing.

When we were on the fifth and last high step, I placed the cane back into his right hand so he could climb the lesser and final step, and he did, then we stepped up onto the sidewalk and went to the car. I had sent the kids on ahead to play and ride the train one last time, and they did, then we went home.

I sent the kids to take their showers, then gave them ice cream and re-warmed the rest of the cookies that I made last night, and they ate while I finished the dinner my mom had started. When it was finished, we adults ate. The girls had already eaten, and the boys said they were not hungry only because they were running out of time to play, and I allowed them that pleasure.

By the time the adults were finished eating, Sis and her mate were back. I dished dinner for them in a container and wrapped my nephew's dinner, which he ate in the car on the way home. Everyone gathered their things and put them into the vehicle, then my son and I gave and received hugs from everyone, and they got into the vehicle. I came back to my mom who was sitting in the front seat and opened her door and gave her another hug and kiss and thanked her for coming.

As I did that, seeing my brother in the back seat behind my mom, I remembered the words God spoke and thought, *Oh no! I didn't touch his legs!* Again a deceptive thought not of God ran through me to open his door and do it, but immediately I gave it to God and said to Him, "It's in Your hands, Lord. I trust You, I know You are able, I know You will make the way. I believe You, I thank You."

Then they drove away and I came to the balcony and waved back at my nephew who was waving through the window, then he stuck himself through the window and yelled for his cousin and they stopped suddenly. I thought they wanted my son so I told him, and he ran to the vehicle, but they didn't. They had stopped so my mom could pray a safe journey. They left about 6:00 p.m.

My son came inside and went to bed and right to sleep because he was lonely for his cousins. I became exhausted while clearing my cell phone messages, so I also went right to bed. The thing I had said was back to haunt me, and again it troubled me that I may have failed God, but as soon as I lay down, God interrupted my thought process and allowed me to receive the knowledge that His Word was accomplished, that I had touched his *leg* as God had commanded, for the cane/brace *was* his *leg*. Therefore my brother's healing was released and is already done as He showed me in the dream; the Word was spoken by God and His Spirit performed it by the anointing touch. I await with expectancy the manifestation of my brother's wholeness in his body.

I marveled at the way God moves and works. I told Him how amazing He was, that I loved Him and thanked Him for His love, and mercy, and grace toward my brother, then I prayed a short prayer and for a safe trip for them, then I fell asleep.

May 17, 2004
I awoke at 12:30 a.m. and waited for my mom to call me, because this is about the time I expected them to get home. As I waited, I read the scripture again, and this verse troubled me greatly, which God had already answered and comforted me on the night of the fifteenth, but the fear had returned. I was burdened because my greatest fear is to displease God and be out of His grace even for one moment. The verse says, "The morsel which thou hast eaten shalt thou vomit up, and lose thy sweet words" (Proverbs 23:8).

I thought back to the touch God gave me and how He was working in me, and I wondered with sorrow. I started to speak to God; "Lord that touch You gave me, was it a blessing or was it to my hurt? Were You removing Your Word from me? Were You taking Your anointing from me? If that is what You did, how will I write that book? I cannot do it without You, for it would be a lie. God have mercy on me, cleanse me of all the wrong I have done, redeem me, make me fit for use, and give me a fresh anointing that I may do Your work, that I may finish this for You. I cannot be without You, Lord. Please speak to me that I may receive it and understand these words You have spoken to me."

I was greatly distressed and felt wounded and alone. I opened up my Bible, and God gave me Isaiah 48 which He had given me before on other occasions to scold me nevertheless to bless me. It is a chapter of scripture He uses to let me know that though He could not look upon me and smile, I am a child of His purpose. Telling me He has much invested in me, that for His name's sake only, He would withhold His wrath from me; therein lies my blessing. I immediately knew He was very displeased, and this made me cry. I cried tears of sorrow through reading the chapter. I read the last verse and lay there with my Bible open in a state of sorrow and peace mixed within me—sorrow because God was displeased with me, and some peace because He was still with me and would still use me. His Word would go forth, His book would be accomplished.

My heart was aching for the sorrow I felt, then He led me to lift up my Bible, and He showed me chapter forty-nine and said *"Read!"* So I read and cried tears of joy and worshiped Him as I read, and the pain within me was removed. Then as I read the last verse of chapter forty-nine, He gave me understanding of the verse in Proverbs that troubled me. Proverbs 23:8 was received by me with perfect knowledge: *sweet* wine—*new* wine; *sweet* words—*new* words. The new words of clarification I thought to add to God's words was the morsel (lie) I had eaten that would be vomited up/ejected/discarded. Those new words were not of or from God. They were lies that God saw in me before they were manifested and He vowed to cast them out of me. The morsel (truth) God was feeding me that I believed He had removed in His touch was never in question. My anointing was not removed, God was still feeding me His truth. It was only my new words (my lies that I told myself) and my stubbornness in not recognizing and heeding His voice that angered Him. Not letting His words of comfort to me on the night of the fifteenth be enough, causing Him to speak again and again before I would receive and hold understanding is why God was so very displeased with me. I prayed and thanked Him for the knowledge and all else He had done, and the joy and peace in my soul was greatly increased.

I also received the knowledge that the touch He gave me and the work He was doing in me at that moment was an anointing to accomplish what He had commanded of me, anointing me to *touch his leg*.

It was now 2:30 a.m. (3:30 a.m. mom's time), and I hadn't heard from my mom, so I picked up the phone to call her and heard the interrupted dial tone, so I collected my messages, and my mom had gotten home and called at 11:20 p.m. (12:20 a.m. her time), so I listened to the message then went back to sleep.

I woke up later that morning and prayed and read my Bible again. Later that afternoon, after 2:00 p.m., I called my mom, and she told me of the trap the devil laid in their path. A whole tire just lay in the road which had a median to separate the traffic of opposite direction and prevented them from driving around it that way, with no just cause of how the tire could have gotten there, but God covered them and the vehicle.

May 24, 2004

One day over the last two weeks I came to the realization of a certain thing, and it amazed me. Whenever I would dream, in *all* my dreams I was never able to speak clearly, if I could speak at all. My mouth was always stuffed with something—at times food, other times just some unrecognizable gunk/garbage. I would try to clear my mouth so I could speak, but the stuff coming out was never ending. The more I spit out, the more was there. All my words were muffled and unclear.

On that day within the last two weeks, I realized that my mouth has been opened in my dreams and has been for a while. I have been trying to remember when I was set free, and I can't at the moment. When I had the dream about the broken eggs, my mouth was open. When I had the dream about the woman I laid hands on, my mouth was open. When I had the dream about Big Sis being shot in the back (being deceived), my mouth was open. When I had the experience of being lifted up by God, my mouth was open. I was not attentive to when it happened, but I know it was within the past few months since God has been dealing with me. I thought that this thing was just foolishness in a dream as many things can be, but it seems it was of much significance with me. It seems to have been an oppression of the enemy against me. I am even more sure of this, because the moment God made this freedom clear to me and had me jot it down to write it in this book, the liar oppressed me that very night with such a dream, trying to make a liar out of me and God. When I awoke, I cursed and rebuked him for the liar he is, and no longer is my mouth stopped, for that oppression has been lifted and removed eternally by God.

May 2004

I am resting in the love of God and am filled with the joy and peace He has given to me, and I am aware that He has only just begun with me, and whatever He wills, my soul says *yes!* With His commands of me comes much support from Him, supplying all that is needed to complete the task. "I am Your vessel, Lord. May You be glorified. May Your people hear and honor You, and may Your enemies be ashamed and tremble. Please keep me wrapped in You, Lord. Let it be in Your will that I remain true and faithful. Thank You for making me whole; refined not as silver but as pure gold. *I love You, Jesus. Abide with me.*"

Section V: Revelation

April 17, 2004, 5:00 a.m.

The First and the Last – The Beginning and the End

Father: [God; Godhead, Source], [sent His Son in His name; Jesus].
Son: [God; God's Word, God manifested in flesh, birthed/came out from the Father—Christ], [came in His Father's name; Jesus].
Holy Ghost: [God; God's Spirit], [Comforter, Spirit of Truth. Spirit of the Word (Jesus Christ), was sent from the Father in the Son's name; Jesus].

  The Word is Truth and Truth is the Word; birthed out of Christ, from the Father; of Jesus, by Jesus, and He is Jesus.
  The job of the Holy Ghost is to comfort, help, and support the Christian. He is sent from the Source (Father), by the Son, and in His name; therefore, the Holy Ghost must be called by His name, *Jesus*, to be sent to your aid. When someone loves you, and you call their name, you get their immediate attention. If you don't call their name, how can they come to your rescue without delay? Throughout your life, when you have had those near misses, accidents, danger, or trouble—whenever you were in need —and you found yourself automatically calling out or whispering the name *Jesus,* or pleading **the blood of Jesus**, that was the Holy Ghost you called or whispered for; even though you may not have known the specifics of this call. So, when you called, He had to perform His job (set

by the Source as a gift of help to you), and He did His job. That's why you were able to walk away, that's why you are still alive, and that's why things worked out because He got there in time and covered you. It was in the Father's will and mercy that you be covered, and you were.

All are of One, and is One, who is God, and His name is Jesus.

The only true God.

The only living God.

Female is who I am, woman is who I am, child of the King is who I am, and my *name* is Andrea. And so, with God: God is who He is, Omnipotent is who He is, Great is who He is, Wonderful is who He is, Savior is who He is, Lord is who He is, Everlasting is who He is, Righteousness is who He is, Truth is who He is, Love is who He is, Peace is who He is, and His *name* is Jesus.

So, as this may not yet be evident to all, this is what Jesus has placed in me to be revealed: One God called by two chief names. The whole world knows Him to be God and calls Him that, but the believers, those that are His, know His name of a certainty, and it is Jesus. I have the name I was born with that the world knows me by; and, I have another name, that only my family and close friends, which are those whom I love and that love me, have the privilege of calling me; just as I have the privilege of calling them by their other name. When I am called by that name, immediately, I recognize that it's someone that I love, and that loves me. They know me, and I know them, so I respond quickly.

So it is with God. When you call Him by His name *Jesus*, He knows you are a believer: one of His; so, He responds attentively: ready to move on your behalf. "Whatever you ask in My name—*Jesus*, will be given to you of My Father—the Source." "No one comes to the Father (Source) but by Me (Jesus)."

There is no access to *God,* the Source, but by believing on His name and calling it—*Jesus*. For if you accept Christ, the person, then you accept His name: Jesus.

God: Source of gifts: gift of the Holy Ghost (Jesus), the nine gifts of the Holy Ghost, salvation, grace, blessings, protection, joy, peace, righteousness, mercy, comfort, miracles, healing, etc. He is the Source of all the needs of His creation. When you call His name, He says, "Here am I," but only if you are one of His.

If I am out somewhere, and someone learns and yells out my other name, I will be alerted, yes, because I hear my name called. But, if I don't recognize the voice calling my name, I will know it is not a loved one or a friend and will ignore it thinking the call is not to me, or I will look around to see who else has the name. I won't know they are calling to me or have need of me until they approach me face to face; then, I would wonder why they were calling me because I don't know them.

And so, if you are of the world and you learn His name, but you hate Him, and you call, you cannot fool God. If you know of Him, yet you remain in the world, then you hate Him, for if you loved Him, you would serve Him. When you are truly His (loving, serving, and believing Him), He knows the sound of your voice, and also discerns your heart and mind, and He knows if you are true and sincere. (Matthew 7:21 "Not every one that saith unto Me, Lord, Lord, shall enter into the Kingdom of Heaven; but he that doeth the will of My Father [the Source] which is in Heaven.")

(Deuteronomy 5:11 "Thou shalt not take the name of the Lord thy God in vain: for the Lord will not hold him [you] guiltless [innocent] that taketh His name in vain [as though useless or meaningless].") If you are walking in truth and light with Him, don't call His name (Jesus) in vain, don't call Him without purpose, don't call Him when you are not in need (asking of Him or giving to Him), don't call His name in passing, don't call His name while playing around, and don't call His name in swearing (unacceptable if you are saved anyway). Because, when you call the name Jesus, it alerts the Source to you, and the Holy Ghost is activated for deliverance or help on your behalf: if it be the Father's will. The Holy Ghost is not to be played with: this is wickedness. He is blessed and holy, and loves you. He is to be respected. [It must be said, not everything you ask of the Father is good or right for you, or is the plan He has for your life; sometimes your answer will be no, or not yet. In those times it may seem like you are alone, but you are not, His Spirit was sent: to keep you still, or to strengthen you to endure whatever is being allowed, and to pick up the pieces after the thing is done. The children of light are never alone. Never curse God, He knows the good end He desires to give you. Whatever is allowed in your life just hold on to Jesus, and trust Him; He loves you, and it will be well with your soul. Whatever door a person is kept from, or allowed to walk through, does not indicate that they are loved and cared for any less or any more than another: because all are loved with a great eternal love. Every experience allowed to a person is only Jesus' testimony in them. Only He knows why the innocent are made to suffer, and He will bring wholeness to them that lay themselves in His hands, and glory to them that allow Him to use them as He will.]

Jesus (Christ the Son), though still magnificent in power, is the part of God (the Source) that we can handle—our portion—for the Source (Father) is too great and powerful for us to handle in all His glory. He would cause us to be afraid and tremble because of His terrible power and great glory: just as the children of Israel did experience when He came to them. He was too much for them to handle in their state (a rebellious people). Even Moses, after God had molded him and brought him to that higher level in Him: behind the veil: thought to thought, and spirit to Spirit, when he was on the mount, did experience the pure presence and glory of the Source (Father), and was affected and changed because the Source's power was so great and glorious.

Jesus (Christ) is the only way; there is no bypass around Him. He is our portion from the Source; fit for us to handle in our state (a rebellious people: Israel and spiritual Israel). If you cast Him away or don't believe on Him, then you have nothing—no life, no truth—and can have nothing. He (the Son) is the only portion of Himself (the Father/Source) that can be shared/given; He is the first part, the only part, that you can handle and have while you are yet in sin. He calls you out of sin, having been sacrificed for you and given to you. He is salvation, life, and freedom from sin.

A simple prayer: that sinner's prayer, doesn't give you access to the Kingdom and eternity with God, but it *is* a vital beginning. Salvation is a gift freely given, and when you pray that confessing prayer, earnestly, from your heart, repenting of your sins, saying yes to Jesus, receiving your portion sent to you, and believing on Him, yes, salvation will be given, but it does not give you access to the Kingdom. You must now live: walking in the example Jesus Christ set for you and teaches through His gospel (the first works) in order to be in eternity with Him. Jesus will teach and change you to be more like Him. Though God will do what He will do, when and how He desires, He has plainly marked the way.

Once you claim Him as your Savior, you *must* be baptized: being immersed/buried in water in the *name* of *Jesus*. For what is the name of the Father? Jesus. What is the name of the Son? Jesus. And what is the name of the Holy Ghost? Jesus. [All three are one: one name, one God. Poured out for us because of His great love for us. God is father of all, Jesus Christ was poured out from God to redeem us, and the Holy Ghost/Holy Spirit was poured out from God to comfort, guide and keep us. The name "Jesus" is the full embodiment of God and who He is: Father and Source of all life and their needs; Christ and who He is: Savior and Redeemer: that He was sent from and by the Father and did accomplish all He was sent to do, and ascended back to the Father; The Holy Ghost and who He is: Comforter and Helper: that He was sent from the Father by the Son and performs all things spoken by Them. When you call *"the name"* it acknowledges, honors, and gives justification (does justice) to all three persons of the Trinity: who is God, and "the name" is His—"Jesus."] You must therefore call His name; claim Him and His Salvation by His name. [Acts 4:12 "Neither is there salvation in any other: for There is none other name under Heaven given among men, whereby we must be saved."]
In water baptism, you are buried in Him and rise with newness; dead to sin and alive to God/Jesus and the things of Him. You are putting on His name, becoming one of His. Now, because you love Him you live (serving Him, going to church, walking in Him, being faithful, living as He taught, loving as He loves, etc.). The Father smiles on you because He loves you, and He sees by the content and intent of your heart and mind that you love His son, so He sends you a gift. He gives you more of Himself—His

Spirit (the Holy Ghost). He is now not only with you, but has poured of Himself into you; He has sealed you with His Spirit, you are His bride/mate. Receive Him.

You have *repented of all your sins*; no longer sinning deliberately, and repenting if you fall or stumble. You have been *baptized in Jesus' name* (Jesus, the name of all three persons of the Trinity): putting on His name, coming into the fold as one of His. You Have been *baptized of the Holy Ghost*. You are *loving and serving God* with all your heart and all your soul; resisting sin in every form, walking in truth with God, being obedient, spreading His gospel, testifying of Him, *having and giving charity* (*love*; the love of God). *Now*, you are equipped for the Kingdom and will reign with Him in eternity as promised, and He is a God of kept promises. His word *must* be fulfilled.

You may say, this is too much; you may say, to live for Him is too hard, but how hard is it to love. When you are in love with Him, you want to please Him, which will cause you to live the way He desires. He does all for us because He loves us; why can't we do the same for Him? Fall in love with Jesus; being in love with Him will cause you to live right, and if you stumble, your love for Him will cause you to turn quickly back to Him. You'll know you are in love with Him when you will do *everything* for Him; when you desire Him and His ways desperately; when He is *always* number one in your life and thought; when you dislike and resist *all* sin great and small; when you love others like He loves you; etc. If you can go one whole day without giving Him consideration, then He is of no importance to you: you are not in love. If you don't have this kind of love for Jesus, then seek Him with all your heart and He will plant this awesome love in you. You are never too old, you are never too young, and you are never too sinful; His love will cleanse and change you. If you are in church (leader or member), even for many years, and don't know this love, it's not too late for you—He is waiting.

When you have salvation and the Holy Ghost, don't sit back and relax with those portions of Him. He wants to give you more. Wrap yourself in Him. The deeper in Him you go, the higher He will bring you, sharing more of Himself with you (i.e., the nine gifts of the Holy Ghost: *wisdom, knowledge, faith, healing, working of miracles, prophecy, discerning of spirits, divers kinds of tongues, interpretation of tongues*: your portion selected and given according to the use He has of you); allowing Him to perform, through you, mighty works and miracles, for and upon His people, to His Glory.

When you go deeper yet still, the Father (Source) will keep refining you, drawing you closer, equipping you to handle more and more of Him. He will share more and more of Himself with you, until you are able to handle perfect knowledge of Him—behind the veil: His thoughts directly to yours: a direct link to the Source; no intercessions, and nothing between. His secrets revealed to you because He has now molded you to that higher plane, where you can stand in the glory of Him and not perish—spirit to Spirit—the devil will want to touch you but cannot.

You are clothed: wrapped completely in God. He is within you and has fully armored you with Christ on the outside. You are cloaked in Him; cloaked in His glory and power. When you enter a room, the presence of God is felt. The devil/evil will fear and tremble at your presence: the pure presence of God the Source within you and on you; just as the children of Israel feared and trembled at the sight of Moses after he went behind the veil with God on the mount: being exposed to the raw presence and pure glory of the Source/Father/God.

It would please God for us all to be perfected to this place, but only a few will attain this level in God because there is still some form of corruption in us: compromising with and conforming to the world in order to be accepted or followed; making some things not of God acceptable for the sake of peace; still full of secrets and lies, knowing God sees us, "But no one else knows, so I'm safe." We don't trust and believe God to do this for us. We still listen to the devil's view of us; but, who does God say you are?

We have put limits on Him. We don't believe anymore in His true greatness and power, and we don't trust ourselves with that responsibility or feel that we are worthy of this. But, we are worthy: worthy because He loves us, worthy because He is merciful toward us, worthy because of grace, worthy because He desires us to be this close to Him, worthy because we are faithful to Him and He to us, worthy because we trust and believe Him, worthy because He is our Father, and worthy because we belong to Him. We need to put ourselves in God's hands, and trust Him to elevate us by believing in ourselves and in Him. He is a God of His Word and of kept promises. He is still able, and I want Him to bring me to this place in Him. I want Him to keep preparing me, bringing me to and maintaining me at this level, where I can stand in this glory and not perish. There is great work to be done for Him, and He wants it done now. He wants His people (holy, righteous, true, faithful); He wants His church; He wants His sheep; He wants His true shepherds; He wants to return. It's closing time.

Father: *God/Jesus* – "I am come in my Father's name, and ye receive Me not: if another shall come in his own name, him ye will receive" (John 5:43).
Son (Christ): *God/Jesus* – "And she shall bring forth a Son, and thou shalt call His name Jesus: for He shall save His people from their sins" (Matthew 1:21).
Holy Ghost (Comforter): *God/Jesus* – "But the Comforter, which is the Holy Ghost, whom the Father will send in My name, He shall teach you all things, and bring all things to your remembrance, whatsoever I have said unto you" (John 14:26).
"But when the Comforter is come, whom I will send unto you from the Father, even the Spirit of truth, which proceedeth from the Father, He shall testify of Me" (John 15:26).

December 2003
The revelation of God to me, for growth, knowledge, and His purpose.
Revelation 1–3.

What the Lord [Jesus] saith to the seven churches and the seven angels for the seven churches: The seven parts of the body of Christ, and their seven spirits (their center/life/breath: the core of who they are).

   A) **Ephesus** – My beloved.
   B) **Smyrna** – My anchor.
   C) **Pergamos** – Followers of worldly things.
   D) **Thyatira** – Pretenders.
   E) **Sardis** – Backsliders.
   F) **Philadelphia** – My perfect ones, My children of Light.
   G) **Laodicea** – My absent ones.

   A. Revelation 2:1–7 expounded
   1. Unto **Ephesus**; These things saith He that holds the seven stars (angels, messengers, witnesses of God) in His right hand [in His power], who walks in the midst of [who is the center, stability, strength of, and head of] the seven golden candlesticks (churches, the body of Christ);
   2. I know what you are, and your struggle, and your patience and belief in Me, and how you can't tolerate them that are evil: and you have tested and proved them which say they are Apostles [sent of Me], and are not, and have found them to be liars:
   3. You have suffered, and have endured with faith, and for My name's sake you have toiled to weariness, and have not given up or grown feeble.
   4. Nevertheless I am very displeased with something about you, because you have abandoned Me (your first love).
   5. Remember Me therefore from Whom you fell [Whom you forsook], and repent, and live as I lived, live as I taught, and love as I loved (the first works); or else I will come to you quickly, and will remove you, cut you off, and discard you from My body, except you repent.
   6. But this is good about you, that you hate the deeds of the Nicolaitanes (those believing, living, and teaching that the scriptures are half fact and half myths, fables, and false accounts), which I also hate.
   7. All people, may you have perception, may you hear and heed what the Holy Ghost is saying to the churches (you, My beloved; you, belong-

ing to the body of Christ); To them that overcome I will give everlasting eternal life (Me), which is in the midst of My Kingdom and in the presence of God.

Heed God! Repent! Love God! (Don't just carry on for My name's sake but live for Me and in Me, love Me, be one with Me; regain the intimate relationship with Me, or I will reject you, I will cut you off from before Me). Do His will! Be faithful!

B. Revelation 2:8–11 expounded

8. Unto **Smyrna**; These things saith the first and the last, which was dead, and is alive [Jesus Christ];

9. I know what you are, and your great trial, struggle, distress and great lack/pressing need, (but you are rich [in Me]) and I know the blasphemy of them who say they are Jews [of Me], and are not, but are the synagogue [vessel and the servant] of Satan.

10. Fear none of those things that you will suffer: behold, the devil will cast some of you into prison, bondage, temptation; under great burden, great anguish, turmoil; that you may be tried, tested, proven of God; and you will have tribulation, great anguish ten days [a season]: be you faithful unto death, and I will give you a crown of life, eternal life, Me; I will crown you with My glory.

11. All people, may you have perception, hear, and heed what the Holy Ghost is saying to you, My anchor; you, belonging to the body of Christ; He that overcometh—holds on to Me, stays true to Me—shall not be hurt of the second death [shall not lose their life to eternal damnation; you will be spared, you will reign with Me]. Hold on in faith! Do not fear when tribulation and trouble come! Be faithful!

C. Revelation 2:12–17 expounded

3. Unto **Pergamos**; These things saith He who has the sharp sword with two edges [He Who has the power to cut you off from Him with one swift move of the sword/word of His mouth by saying, "I know you not" and the power to cut you out of the death of sin and give you eternal life

with one swift move of the sword/word of His mouth by saying "enter into My rest;" He Who has the power to punish you and the power to forgive you, the power to allow sickness and the power to heal; He Who has the power over death and the power over life, He to Whom all power is given];

13. I know what you are, and where you dwell, where you are; you are even where Satan's seat is [Satan's place of power, you're in the furnace of affliction], even in the midst of your enemies, even where Satan's center of activity is: and you hold on tightly, securely to My name [Me] and have not denied My faith, even in the days when Antipas was My faithful martyr who was slain among you, where Satan abides [and have not refused to acknowledge trust in God, even during times as when Antipas remained My committed witness and sacrifice, who mocked and was amused/deceived in the company of you, in a purpose that Satan leads astray].

14. But I am very displeased with a few things about you, because you have among you them that hold and believe the doctrine of Balaam which he taught Balac; a doctrine and things not of Me, the doctrine and teaching that is a stumbling block in the way of My people, a teaching that it is OK to partake of, to be a part of things not of Me—things of the world—and to commit fornication, to do things not of Me, to do things of the world.

15. You also have among you them that hold the doctrine of the Nicolaitanes (believing, living, and teaching that the scriptures are half fact and half myths, fables, and false accounts), which thing which I hate.

16. Repent; or else I will come to you quickly, and will fight against them, cut them to pieces, and destroy them with the sword of My mouth.

17. All people, may you have perception, hear, and heed what the Holy Ghost is saying to you, followers of worldly things; you, belonging to the body of Christ; To him that overcomes I will feed things hidden of the Spirit, I will reveal and share with him things shared with My angels, I will feed him spiritually with things no one else yet knows, and will give him a white stone, and in the stone a new name written, which no man

knows but him that receives it [and will give him eternal life with Me, and in this eternal life a new name recorded (My new name)], which no one will know or recognize except him who receives it of Me. Repent! Don't partake in or be of things of the world! Don't love or do things of the world! Be faithful!

D. Revelation 2:18–29 expounded

18. Unto **Thyatira**; These things saith the Son of God, who has His eyes like unto a flame of fire, and His feet like fine brass [Whose eyes are full of light for there is no darkness found in Him—all seeing, all knowing, searching the hearts and minds of men, trying all men, able to consume all things worthy of fire and refine all things worthy of Him, and Whose feet are perfected, refined, pure, holy, excellent, accomplished, beautiful, admirable, praiseworthy, the End—will bring the ceasing of all things];

19. I know what you are; I know you love as I love, and your place in Me, your assistance to Me, your benefit to Me, and your faith [trust] in Me, and your patience, commitment, and the things you do unto Me and for Me, and your uplifting and support to each other without giving thought to yourself or your position.

20. Notwithstanding I am disappointed in a few things about you, because you tolerate that woman Jezebel (person with an impudent, daring, vicious, evil spirit—traits as are the nature of a woman outside of God; a seducer, and a great pretender) that calls herself a prophetess to oppress and teach and mislead and entice My servants (My people living for Me) to commit shameless immoral acts against Me, and to partake in things of the world, in things the world does, and to put other things before Me.

21. And I gave this person space to repent of the acts against Me and forsaking Me; but they repented not.

22. Behold, I will slay this evil one, and them that were unfaithful to Me, that were lewd, that forsook Me with this false prophetess (vicious spirit) will I cast into great anguish, except they repent of their deeds.

23. And I will kill her children with death (of all birthed from this

false doctrine and this false way will I make an end, so that they are no more); and [then] all the churches [all people] will know that I am He who searches the will, minds, and hearts: and I will give to everyone of you according to your deeds.

24. But unto you I say, and unto the rest in this church—this part of My body—as many of you that do not have or partake of this doctrine, and who have not known the depths of Satan, who have not been possessed with these things of the devil, who are not false, as they speak (as they utter this evil doctrine/teaching); I will protect you, I will shield you, I will cover you, I will fit you with the truth, I will put upon you none other burden, stress, hardship, or trouble.

25. But what you have already (which is My doctrine, My faith, My gospel, My truth) hold on to it tightly, with all strength—securely anchored—hold fast till I come.

26. And he that overcomes, and does My deeds unto the end, to him will I give power over the nations (I will anoint him with all power):

27. And he will rule them with great strength (he will move and operate in great spiritual strength and power); as the vessels of a potter will they be broken to shivers (as the vessels of a potter will all not of Me—not in line with Me—be broken into shivers by his anointing): even as I received of My Father (even as My Father anointed Me, will you be also).

28. And I will give him Me, I will be his and he will be Mine, I will apply Myself to him, I will abide with him and in him, I will give him eternal life.

29. All people, may you have perception, hear, and heed what the Holy Ghost is saying to you, pretenders; you, belonging to the body of Christ. Keep your heart pure and true to God! Do not want after things of this world! Inwardly (heart, mind, and spirit) do not partake of the world! Do not love things of the world! Do not consider things of the world! Be faithful!

E. Revelation 3:1–6 expounded
1. Unto **Sardis**; These things saith He that has the seven Spirits of

God, and the seven stars; I know what you are, that you have a name by which you live, and are spiritually dead.

2. Be watchful (seek for Me, maintain interest in Me), and strengthen/grow in the things that you still have (that you are able to receive of Me), that are about to die (fade away, before there will be no more time): for I have not found your deeds perfect before God.

3. Remember therefore how you have received and heard of Me—the truth—hold on tightly, anchored, secure with all your heart, mind, and soul, and repent! If therefore you do not seek Me and the things of Me and maintain interest in Me, I will come upon you quietly and quickly to destroy you and your evil deeds, and you will not know the hour I will come upon you.

4. You have a few names/people even among you who have not been unfaithful to Me, who are still pure in spirit; and they will walk with Me in white/righteousness: for they are worthy.

5. He that overcomes, the same will be clothed in white raiment (in My glory); the same will be full of light; and I will not blot out his name out of the book of life, I will not remove him from My Kingdom promise, I will not refuse him eternal life, but I will confess his name, how he has lived, who he is and what he has done for Me before My Father and before His angels (I will not deny him, because he has not denied Me).

6. All people, may you have perception, hear, and heed what the Holy Ghost is saying to you, backsliders; you, belonging to the body of Christ. Repent! Be mindful and pray and hold on to God! Remember what Jesus has done for you and the things He has said! Live by His example! Stay in God! Be faithful!

F. Revelation 3:7–11 expounded

7. Unto **Philadelphia**; These things saith He that is holy, He that is true, He that has the key of David, He that opens and no man shuts; and shuts, and no man opens;

8. I know what you are: behold I have set before you an open door—behold I have given you all power—and no man can shut it [and no man

can take away from you what has been given you by Me]: for you had a little strength, and have kept My Word, you have been faithful and have not denied My name and have lived in truth to Me.

9. Behold I will make them which are of the synagogue of Satan, who are the vessels of Satan, who have been unfaithful to Me, who have lived as the world lives, who say they are of Me, and are not, but do lie; behold I will make them to come and worship before thy feet, I will cause them to come worship Me in your presence, and to know that I have loved you, and open their eyes and ears to see and hear that in you is where I am—My truth, My faith, My doctrine, My gospel.

10. Because you have kept/lived the word/truth of My patience as I have lived, I also will keep and protect you from the hour of temptation, trouble, and evil that will come upon all the world, to try, test, and prove them that dwell upon the earth.

11. Behold, I come quickly: hold on very securely to what you have in Me. Be anchored in Me, that no man take your crown, that no one or no thing in or under earth causes you to lose your eternal life in My Kingdom, your righteousness, light, joy, peace, or gifts that I give. Hold on tightly to Me and don't let go, that no man be raised up in your stead and receive your glory.

12. He that overcomes will I make a pillar in the temple of My God, and he will go no more out (him will I make of great spiritual strength and power, chief in the body of Christ, in Me, and he will be secure in Me and abide in Me and with Me eternally): and I will write upon Him the name of My God, and the name of the city of My God, which is new Jerusalem, which cometh down out of heaven from My God: and I will write upon him My new name (I will choose him to reign with Me in My Kingdom and will reveal to him My new name, all of Me, and Who I am).

13. All people, may you have perception, hear, and heed what the Holy Ghost is saying to you, My children of Light; you, belonging to the body of Christ. Stay in the will of God! Keep doing God's will, and He will make His path straight before your face. He will bless you and keep your strength. Keep God's Word, and He will keep you from the tempta-

tion and trouble of these last days to try and prove those that dwell upon this earth. Confess the name of Jesus, do not deny Him, and He will exalt you and show all that He loves you. Hold on to God so you won't be lost. You are on the path of truth; renew your faith, wrap yourself in Him, be faithful!

G. Revelation 3:14–22 expounded

14. Unto **Laodicea**; These things saith the Amen, the End, the faithful and true witness, the beginning of the creation of God;

15. I know what you are, that you are neither cold (unbelieving of Me) nor hot (believing of Me): I would that you were cold or hot (I want you to believe in something; I want you to choose).

16. So then because you are lukewarm, and neither cold nor hot, I will spue/vomit you out of My mouth (because you don't believe in Me, and are neither against Me nor with Me, because you have not chosen, I will cut you off and cast you away, eject you from before Me; I will deny you because you have denied Me, I will say "I know you not" because you have not known Me, I will give no thought to you because you have given no thought to Me).

17. Because you say, I am rich and increased with goods and have need for nothing; and know not that you are wretched, and miserable, and poor, and blind, and naked (because you say, I am well, I have everything I need, I am all I need, there is no one or nothing above or below, I provide for myself, I make my own destiny, there is no heaven or hell—there is no life after this one so I will just live, making my own way till I die—and you don't know that you are full of sin and iniquity and have no joy, you are without My promises and eternal life and unable to see the truth that faces you daily, and without My protection, glory, righteousness, and care):

18. I counsel you to buy of Me gold tried in the fire, that you may be rich (I counsel you to seek and receive of Me salvation made sure by Me through My blood by My suffering and sacrifice, come to Me that you may gain My promises and eternal life); and white raiment (and righteousness,

light, purity, and truth), that you may be clothed (that I may clothe/cover you), and that the shame of your nakedness does not appear (that the shame of your old sinful self is not revealed, does not rise up and cause you to fall). [When you are covered by Me, I strip away shame and disgrace from you, I maketh not ashamed all who are mine]; and anoint your eyes with salve, that you may see (desire the truth that you may see Me that I Am, that I may reveal myself to you).

19. As many as I love, I rebuke and chasten: be zealous therefore, and repent (I love you, and all who I love, I tell them when they are not walking right, I scold them and punish them that they may obey Me: so gain and show great interest in Me, believe in Me, be eager in turning to Me, and surrender your life to Me).

20. Behold I stand at the door, and knock: if any man hear My voice, and open the door, I will come in to him, and will sup with him, and he with Me (behold I am come to you, I am calling you: if you hear Me, feel Me, and let Me in, I will abide in you, and will partake with you; I will share myself with you, and receive you unto Myself).

21. To him that overcomes will I grant to sit with Me in My throne, even as I also overcame and am set down with My Father in His throne (he that remains true will I anoint to reign with Me in My power, even as I [Christ] also remained true, and was anointed and now reign with My Father [My Source] in His power.)

22. All people, may you have perception, hear, and heed what the Holy Ghost is saying to you, My absent ones; you, belonging to the body of Christ. Repent! Believe in God! Be on fire for God! Say not that there is no God and no devil; don't stand in the gap or gulf neither believing nor unbelieving or you will be rejected of God. Don't you know you are lost? Seek God; you need God, so turn to Him. Seek salvation, and He will meet all your needs. Seek purification and He will clothe you in righteousness. Seek Him in Spirit and He will show you the way, reveal Himself to you, and guide you. He's calling; let Him in, let Him dwell in you, let Him be one with you and you with Him; be a vessel for Jesus, serve Him, let Him care for you. Be faithful!

Jesus loves you all (the whole body of Christ). Love Him, serve Him in truth, hold fast to His doctrine, hold fast to His faith. To the five parts/branches of this body that are maimed or lifeless, remove your foot from the world lest you be slain, cut off from God, removed from before Him, plucked up from your root, pruned away, and cast off as bramble to be burned in the eternal fire of God; hewn down as a tree that is withered. Be nourished, be fruitful, be healed, be whole, stand firm with both feet on the rock which is Christ Jesus; live in truth and not falsehood. Repent! Repent! Repent! Be faithful! Each faithfulness has its own just reward, thus saith the Lord God Almighty.

A chorus brought to my heart and memory: "Keep me true." Jesus, please give us all strength, power, wisdom, knowledge, and understanding. Please make all people/nations your children of Light, as is the desire of your heart, and fit us all with the tools and weapons needed to win this war / this race. May Hell be empty, save (except), the devil and his angels. May we all endure every second, every minute, every hour, every day, Lord Jesus, and may we all overcome. Please keep us true.

Jesus is walking in the midst of the churches, calling them to Himself, calling them to be of Him, calling them to be healed, to be whole, to be one in Him—the one in the midst of them. Heed the Lord! Heed the Lord! Heed the Lord! You must stand apart from the world (sin, children yet in darkness) in all things; there must be seen a difference in you (your heart, mind, and soul must be separated unto God and the things of Him). Christ *must* be seen in you. You must not look (act) like the world or speak as the world speaks; you must be holy. Yes, associate yourselves and be friends with the children (people) who are not yet in the Light as we are; just as Christ did; but, do not desire, partake of, or lust after the things of them. Be the light to them Christ called you to be, that they will be drawn to Jesus. We are not better than they are, for we were one with them. Only now, we are separated into light because of Christ's love; so, love them with the love of God, that they may come into the light in their due season. If they see not the difference of Christ in you, how will they be drawn? What need will they feel for change? If you profess to love Jesus, and have or show no respect or dedication to Him, why will any associate or friend do so? Therefore, let Jesus be seen in you, that all may desire after Him, and be one with Him. Jesus is calling for holiness. You must be one with Christ: whole, pure, the perfected church, the perfect body of Christ, without spot or wrinkle. Time is *very* short. *Hear* what the Lord God Almighty is saying to you, and *obey!*

December 20, 2003
The revelation of God to me, for growth, knowledge, and His purpose.

Revelation 6–7

Jesus (Christ) opens the seven seals.
God's seal placed on the 12,000 of each twelve tribes of His people Israel.
The faithful (spiritual Israel) raptured/gathered and stand before Him.

Revelation 6:1–17 expounded
1. First Seal Opened.
2. White horse (purity, righteousness released). He that sat on him had a bow (hope, promise); and a crown (power) was given to Him: and He went forth conquering (taking control) and to conquer (gain victory).
3. Second Seal Opened.
4. Red horse (vengeance released). Authority was given to Him that sat thereon to take peace from the earth (church), and that they should kill one another (they being without peace, spiritually—tearing each other down, cutting/slaying each other with the tongue, robbing the truth/Word of God from them that are weak in God and giving them falsehoods): and there was given to Him a great sword (great word, of great

power, cutting asunder those of falsehood: deceivers, liars, pretenders).

5. Third Seal Opened: Black horse (judgment released). He that sat on him had a pair of balances in His hand (to weigh and measure the church).

6. A voice in the midst of the four beasts said, "A measure of wheat for a penny, and three measures of barley for a penny" (church being measured for worthiness, numerous souls found to be of little worth; found wanting); "and see thou hurt not the oil and the wine" (and ensure that the children of light are not hindered but secured).

7. Fourth Seal Opened.

8. Pale horse (destruction and extinguishment released). And His name that sat on him was Death (the End), and Hell (evil and great suffering) followed with Him. And power was given unto them (evil and great suffering; the evil one and his workers of iniquity) over the fourth part of the earth (church), to kill with sword (words; lies, falsehoods), and with hunger (hunger because of a lack of the Word of God, the truth which will not be found; only falsehoods—no nourishment, no substance, dying of spiritual malnutrition/spiritual starvation), and with death (spiritual), and with beasts of the earth (with things not of God—evil, vicious, false doctrines, familiar things, great lies of the church).

9. Fifth Seal Opened: Under the altar the souls of them that were slain for the Word of God (the faithful in Christ, those that suffered spiritually and naturally for the gospel), and for the testimony (witness) which they held:

10. And they cried with a loud voice, saying, "How long, O Lord, holy and true, dost thou not judge and avenge our blood on them that dwell on the earth? (How long before You come Lord? How long before all is ended? Do You not punish the wicked that are against us / against You? Is not all performed?)"

11. And white robes (glory, honor, righteousness) were given unto every one of them; and it was said unto them, that they should rest (wait in God, be comforted) yet a little season, until their fellow servants also and their brethren (those called of God and the other chosen ones), that

should be killed as they were, should be fulfilled.

12. Sixth Seal Opened: And, lo, there was a great earthquake (churches shaken: a great disruption, breaking apart of the churches); and the sun (the light, the truth, the Word) became black as sackcloth of hair (became completely obscure, was covered, refused to have dealings with unfaithful hearts), and the moon (the prophets and the preachers and teachers of the true word) became as blood (an offence);

13. And the stars of heaven fell unto the earth (sheep falling away from God, losing their source of life), even as a fig tree casteth her untimely figs (even as the unfit ones are cast away from Me), when she is shaken of a mighty wind (when shaken by My Spirit: the unfaithful/impure being sifted out, being tested and proven unworthy and cast away from the body of Christ).

14. And the heaven departed as a scroll when it is rolled together (and the great power, glory and presence of God was hidden, removed; was shut up; was separated from us, a boundary was formed); and every mountain (every exalted thing) and every island (every thing detached from Me, not of My body) were moved out of their places (were caused to yield, surrender).

15. And the kings of the earth, and the great men, and the rich men, and the chief captains, and the mighty men, and every bondman (sinner, captive of the devil), and every free man (believer), hid themselves in (gave themselves to, joined themselves unto) the dens (places of hidden sins, places of evil doers) and in the rocks of the mountains (and strongholds of high places, things against Me);

16. And said to the mountains and rocks, "Fall on us (take us), and hide us from (cover us against) the face of Him that sitteth on the throne (and prevent us from facing God), and from the wrath of the Lamb (Christ):

17. For the great day of His wrath is come; and who shall be able to stand? (And will any be found worthy?)"

Revelation 7:1–4, 9–17 Expounded

1. And after these things four angels standing on the four corners of the earth, holding the four winds of the earth, that the wind should not blow on the earth, nor on the sea, nor on any tree.

2. Another angel ascending from the east, having the seal of the living God: and he cried with a loud voice to the four angels, to whom it was given to hurt the earth and the sea,

3. Saying, Hurt not the earth (church), neither the sea (world), nor the trees (shepherds), till we have sealed the servants of our God in their foreheads (till we have confirmed the servants of our God, strengthening their minds).

4. And there were sealed an hundred and forty and four thousand of all the tribes of the children of Israel (the chosen)—12,000 of each tribe (Juda, Reuben, Gad, Aser, Nepthalim, Manasses, Simeon, Levi, Issachar, Zabulon, Joseph, Benjamin).

9. And after this, lo, a great multitude, which no man could number, of all nations, and kindreds, and people, and tongues (the rapture of a multitude of the called, and of the chosen; the faithful believers of Christ, those who lived true to Jesus), stood before the throne, and before the Lamb (Christ), clothed with white robes (righteousness, purity), and palms (victory) in their hands (their possession);

10. [They worshiped God and the Lamb (Christ).

11. Then all the angels stood around the throne and the elders and the four beasts, and fell on their faces and worshiped God before His throne].

12. Saying, "Amen (Truly/so be it): Blessing, and glory, and wisdom, and thanksgiving, and honor, and power, and might, be unto our God for ever and ever. Amen (Truly/so be it)."

13. What are these which are arrayed in white robes? and whence came they?

14. These are they which came of great tribulation, and have washed their robes, and have made them white in the blood of the Lamb (these are they who had great trials but believed, were tested and proven faithful/

worthy, and have repented of their sins, and have lived and accepted and confessed God and Christ Jesus, the cleansed, the redeemed, they which are clothed in righteousness).

15. Therefore they are before the throne of God (they are in the presence and glory of God), and serve Him day and night in His temple (and worship and honor Him at all times in His holy dwelling, His sanctuary): and He that sitteth on the throne (God/Jesus) shall dwell among (in the midst of; within) them.

16. They shall hunger no more, neither thirst anymore; neither shall the sun light on them, nor any heat (He will forever be within them, He will be their God and they will be His people. They shall be fitted with the Truth (bread) forevermore; His Spirit (living water) will abound within them forevermore. He will be their light, their way, no trouble or harm shall befall them forevermore, they shall have perfect peace and joy unspeakable).

17. For the Lamb (Christ) which is in the midst of the throne (which stands in power, which reigneth) shall feed them, and shall lead them unto living fountains of waters: and God shall wipe away all tears from their eyes. Glory to God, hallelujah!

December 19, 2003
The revelation of God to me, for growth, knowledge, and His purpose.

Revelation 8–10 expounded
Seventh Seal, Seven Angels, Seven Churches

The third part of each church lost for every trumpet their angel sounded, which is six, the things concerning the seventh remains sealed, hidden. When the seventh angel begins to sound, then woe to us all because time shall be no more. It will not be a pleasant day; there shall be weeping and gnashing of teeth.

The Churches Are Shaken
Revelation 8:1–2, 7–13 expounded
Seventh Seal Opened
1. Silence in heaven, about half an hour.
2. The seven angels/witnesses for the seven churches stand before God and are given seven trumpets.

The First Angel Sounded—concerning **Smyrna/***My Anchor*
7. Hail and fire (God's wrath) mingled with blood (the blood of Jesus that was shed) cast upon the earth (church held accountable), and the third part of the trees (shepherds) and all the green grass (sheep) were burnt up (consumed, cut off from God).

The Second Angel Sounded—concerning **Sardis/***Backsliders*
8. Like a great mountain burning with fire (God's great exceeding wrath) cast into the sea (world): and a third part of the sea (world; the ungodly and the things of them) became blood (was an offense to God, was condemned);
9. And the third part of the creatures (ungodly) which were in the sea (world), and had life (once had Jesus/the truth), died (completely lost to darkness); and the third part of the ships (leaders and teachers of things ungodly) were destroyed (consumed, cut off from God).

The Third Angel Sounded—concerning **Pergamos/***Followers Of Worldly Things*
10. A great star (deceiver) fell from heaven, burning as it were a lamp (seeming as though it were good light, holy, of God, shining as though it were the way, as though it were the truth), and it fell upon the third part of the rivers (missionaries), and upon the third part of the fountains (pastors/ministers/teachers) of waters (churches belonging to the ways of the world, the churches with one foot in the world);
11. And the name of the star was called wormwood (Lucifer, Satan): and the third part of the waters (churches belonging to the ways of the world) became wormwood (evil, bitter, lost full sight of God, doing more so as the world does, forsook God, became completely unfaithful to God); and many men died (were consumed by darkness/evil, cut off from God)

of the waters (wayward churches and their doctrines) because they were made bitter (not of God, they were made corrupt by the devil, their doctrines were made fully polluted with lies and things of the world).

The Fourth Angel Sounded—concerning **Philadelphia/My Perfect Ones, My Children Of Light**

12. The third part of the sun (church that holds the truth, light) was smitten (attacked, shaken, hit hard), and the third part of the moon (prophets, preachers and teachers of the Word), and the third part of the stars (sheep); so that the third part of them was darkened (lost the truth, doctrines were corrupted, lost the things and ways of God which they had, became spiritually mislead), and the day shone not for a third part of it, (a third of the church in darkness, without the truth, without the Word, without the Light of God, spiritually sick and malnourished, receiving no nourishment or care, receiving of and partaking in things not of God) and the night likewise (a third part of the prophets, preachers, and teachers likewise lost sight of God, were spiritually malnourished for lack of being fed by God, separated from God, no light in them, no truth, possessing and giving things of the world, things not of God to be partaken of, not able to receive and reflect the light of God to His people).

13. Behold, An angel flying through the midst of heaven heard saying with a loud voice, Woe, woe, woe, to the inhabiters of the earth by reason of the other voices of the trumpet of the three angels, which are yet to sound!

[The revelation of this chapter nine is not yet fully received by me. I thought of leaving it out but God wants it here, and I am obedient, for His will and His purpose must be fulfilled.]

Revelation 9:1–21 expounded
Fifth Angel Sounded—concerning **Ephesus/My Beloved**

1. A star (the angel of God) fell from heaven unto the earth (church): and to Him was given the key of the bottomless pit (hell),

2. And He opened the bottomless pit (hell); and smoke arose out of the pit, as the smoke of a great furnace (great evil, great suffering) and the sun (the Light/Jesus, the Word, the Way) and the air (the Life/Jesus, the Word) were darkened (were removed, made obscure, were hid) by reason (for it was time) of the smoke (great evil) of the pit.

3. And out of the smoke (evil/deception) came locusts (an army, demons from hell, trouble, destruction, things and ways that devour) upon the earth: and unto them was given power, as the scorpions (demons, things and ways that poison and corrupt) of the earth (church) have power (for these demons, familiar spirits of the church, already have great power of falsehood, lies, deception and destruction).

4. And it was commanded of them not to hurt the grass (God's sheep) of the earth (His church, the body of Christ), neither any green thing (all that are His, anyone that loves Him in truth; green, not withered, bearing or capable of bearing fruit, nourished by God) neither any tree (God's shepherds); but only those men which have not the seal of God in their foreheads (only those who have not been confirmed by the Spirit of God and given strength in their minds).

5. And to them (demons) it was given that they should not kill them (those not in line with God, those that forsook Him), but that they should be tormented five months: and their torment was as the torment of a scorpion, when he striketh a man (sudden and unexpected, aggressive and malicious, injecting poison, causing bitterness and deep anguish to that which was stricken).

6. And in those days men shall seek death (Christ; the daily dying, death unto sin, life unto God; daily sacrifice that Daniel the prophet spoke of), and not find it; and shall desire to die (shall desire to lay themselves on the altar of sacrifice slain, shall desire Christ), and death shall flee from them (Christ shall not be found; He shall be removed, He shall be hid. Truth shall not be found, known, or understood and power shall be given to the evil one [the chief prince of darkness]. Life unto God shall not be found, death unto sin shall flee from all who are not yet His. "Heed the word," saith the Lord God!).

[The Abomination of Desolation (profound disgust and hatred that maketh desolate, empty, abandoned, alone, causing the forsaking of God; now set up), spoken of by Daniel the prophet, and affirmed by Jesus to His disciples; now to all, "Stand in the holy place!" Thus saith the Lord God. (Stand with God.) "Hold fast that which thou hast—My doctrine, My faith" saith the Lord God Almighty, the Beginning and the End. "Blessed is he that waiteth."]

7. The shapes of the demons were like horses prepared unto battle (powers, once a portion of the strength of heaven filled with light but since cast out, now the powers of darkness); and on their heads (leading them) were as it were crowns like gold (principalities, once a portion of the princes of heaven filled with glory and light but since cast out, now the princes of darkness, of earthly power, in high places, given to rule men), and their faces (outward appearance) were as the faces of men (working in men).
8. And they had hair (covering) as the hair of women (disguised in sincerity and beauty; admired, things sincere, things of beauty, things admired), and their teeth (concentrated force of destruction) were as the teeth of lions (were ravenous, vicious, deadly, crushing, devouring).
9. And they had breastplates like iron (had great strength and dominion); and the sound of their wings was as the sound of chariots of many horses running in battle (great and mighty force/army fiercely attacking).
10. And they had tails like unto scorpions (they spoke things familiar), and there were stings in their tails (there was corruption, poison and death in their tongues): and their power was to hurt men five months (to corrupt, distress, confuse, deceive, cause discomfort and pain within and without).
11. And they had a king over them, which is the angel of the bottomless pit (once a prince in heaven filled with glory and light but since cast out, now the chief prince of darkness and their king Satan; come to steal the Word of God from them in whom it is not firmly planted; come

to kill the people of God spiritually with lies, falsehood, and things familiar; come to destroy the receipt of the promises of God to His people; the destroyer of souls, disrupting peace and joy as he is allowed, causing the forsaking of God), whose name in Hebrew tongue is abad'don but in the Greek tongue has a name apol'lyon.

12. One woe is past; and, behold, there come two more woes hereafter.

Sixth Angel Sounded—concerning **Laodicea/My Absent Ones**

13. A voice from the four horns of the golden alter which is before God,

14. Saying to the sixth angel which had the trumpet, loose the four angels which are bound in the great river Euphrates.

15. And the four angels were loosed, which were prepared for an hour, and a day, and a month, and a year for to slay the third part of men.

16. And the number of the army of the horsemen were two hundred thousand:

17. Those that sat on the horses had breastplates of fire (armored with destruction) and of jacinth (armored with deception) and brimstone (armored with death): and the heads of the horses (vessels) were as (disguised as) the heads of lions (respected, regarded, admired); and out of their mouths (the vessels) issued fire and smoke and brimstone.

18. By these three was the third part of men [spiritually] killed (consumed, possessed, destroyed by the falsehoods, cut off from God), by the fire (false doctrines, backbiting, and other evil, causing the destruction of the receipt of your promise and your soul), and by the smoke (deception: robbing that which you have lest you hold fast to it), and by the brimstone (death by lies and blasphemy: causing eternal death by the enemy when you believe his lie), which issued out of their mouths (vessels).

19. For their power (authority, control, and strength) is in their mouth (vessels), and in their tails (tongues): for their tails were like unto serpents (vicious, poisonous, untrustworthy, deceptive, lying, evil), and had heads (control, direction, purpose), and with them they do hurt (destroying, scattering, robbing, doing all manner of evil to all people—hold

fast to that which ye have already!).

20. And the rest of the men which were not killed by these plagues yet repented not of the works of their hands, that they should not worship devils (any but God Almighty, the only true, only living God, Jesus is His name, Christ Jesus is His Son, the portion of Himself He gave for our deliverance), and idols of gold, and silver, and brass, and stone, and of wood, (jewelry, gems, paintings, houses, and money, things held as valuable in this world instead of God): which neither can see, nor hear, nor walk, (as the living God Jesus does):

21. Neither repented they of their murders, nor of their sorceries, nor of their fornication, nor of their thefts.

Revelation Ch.10 expounded: Jesus Christ appearing, and cried with a loud voice, as when a lion roareth: and when He had cried, seven thunders uttered their voices [to the 7 churches]. The things which the seven thunders uttered were sealed up, and not written. Time shall be no more (There will be no more time to choose, Laodicea).

Seventh Angel—concerning **Thyatira/*Pretenders***
When the seventh angel begins to sound the mystery of God will be finished—What shall become of you, Oh ye pretenders? *There shall be weeping and gnashing of teeth.*

Christ is the End, but He is speaking through His prophets while there is still time: calling to His people for righteousness and obedience to them that are not in line with Him, and, for strength, faith, and perseverance to them that are in line with Him because His desire is that *none* should be lost.

There are still more mysteries to be revealed, but God showed me and authorized me to receive only what was needed to be known now, and what I could handle now. Thank You, God. May we all hear.

I love You, Jesus. Amen.

A chorus brought to my heart and memory: "Closer than a brother." Truly, there is none like Jesus. Let Him be the closest to you, let Him be your all.

"I Feel Like Going On"
Every time I turn around I meet Satan face to face.
Every path I take gets harder every step.
The wrong way is an easy road but when evil appears in Jesus I'll stand.
I feel like going on.

"Eternally Grateful"
All the way with Jesus I will go,
   Never again to roam.
Following Him through death's dark valley
   To get to my beautiful home.
Thank You, dear Savior and loving Friend,
   For You were there through times of doubt,
You shone Your light into my dark soul
   And gave me victory over Satan's deceptive power.
My love for Him grows stronger each day,
   Just get to know Him, you'll feel the same way.
It's not easy to go the rough journey but keep pressing on,
   Your home (Heaven) and family (angels) awaits...
Eternally grateful to Him who loves me,
   Eternally grateful to Him who died,
Eternally grateful to my Redeemer,
   His name is Jesus, He'll save your soul.

Awake
Awake – to rouse or emerge from sleep or from inactivity; to be watchful or alert; to stir up.
"Awake to righteousness, and sin not; for some have not the knowl-

edge of God: I speak this to your shame" (1 Corinthians 15:34).

"Wherefore He saith, Awake thou that sleepest, and arise from the dead, and Christ shall give thee light" (Ephesians 5:14).

"Love worketh no ill to his neighbor: therefore love is the fulfilling of the law. And that, knowing the time, that now it is high time to Awake out of sleep: for now is our salvation nearer than when we believed. The night is far spent, the day is at hand: let us therefore cast off the works of darkness, and let us put on the Armor of Light" (Romans 13:10–12).

Awake—I will be aware of the laws of God and walk uprightly.

When I am in sin, I am asleep or inactive; I am spiritually numb to what God wants for me and wants me to do. But, when I am awake, God's Spirit causes me to be aroused and excited, and I will take interest and become active in the things of God.

When I am unsaved, I am dead or asleep to Christ in sin.

When I meet and accept God, it is my awakening. I am now alive in Christ from sin. When I receive that message or word that makes me want to give my life to God, I am awake to the fact that God is real.

When I become fully immersed into the water being baptized in the name of Jesus Christ, as I rise, I am awake to the fact that I am now a new person walking in Christ—all sins washed away.

When God sends the Holy Ghost through Jesus Christ to me, filling my soul, I am awake to the fact that God/the Spirit of truth now dwells in me. Every time I sing to God, pray to God, praise, worship, thank God, read, study God's Word, and call on Jesus, I am awake and wise to the fact that Christ is real, that He died for me and was risen/awakened from the dead, and ascended back to the Father in heaven and lives forevermore.

I am now walking in light, walking in righteousness, walking in truth, walking in love, walking in peace, walking in protection, walking in deliverance, and fully awake: wherein lies heavenly wisdom, knowledge and understanding.

In the last days, so also shall they that are dead/asleep in Christ be awakened, as Christ awoke; and, those that are alive/awake in Christ, shall be caught up with Him. May God help us all. Please remain awake!

Comforter
The first Comforter was Christ, Who was with us.
The last Comforter is the Holy Ghost, Who is with us, forever; and also in us.
All this is the Holy Ghost:
Comforter – One that comforts; a friend, a supporter, and a provider.
Comfort – To soothe one in distress, sorrow, grief, or fear; to console; a state of ease, well-being, and quiet enjoyment; to help, relieve, or assist someone; to give new strength, to give renewed strength, to cheer, or to uphold; security from want; above want.

When the Holy Ghost, which is the Spirit of Truth, is come upon me, He will testify of Jesus. He will teach me all about Himself, and the ways of God that I am to live—only as long as I seek to know more. When I need a friend, when I need advice, when I am sick, when I am weak, when I am hurt, when I am in pain, when I am lonely, when I cry, when I am afraid, when I am sad, when I need more strength, when I am hungry (spiritually and naturally), when I am thirsty (spiritually and naturally), when death is upon me (spiritual and natural), when I need deliverance, when I need love, when I am confused, when I need to talk, when I am in doubt, when I am lost, when I am undeserving but need you still, when I need to come home, when I need to go on, when I can't pray, when I don't know what to say or do, when I have no peace, when I need courage, when I need to be held, and when I just need You—whatever I need, whenever I need it—I will look to Jesus, because by Him only, does the Comforter come from God. He is there to bring me through.

When I believe on Jesus and call His name, God's Spirit will be with me. If I am faithful to God, at times even before I call, He will send help because He knows my heart and all my needs, and how best to care for me; so, help will come and let me know He's already with me, and I will know of His response through the peace I feel.

In order to be saved, and have eternal life, and live in peace and comfort, I must believe on and love Jesus Christ. He is the only way: the way to God, the way to the Holy Ghost, the way to Heaven, the way to eternal life, the way to peace and joy, the way to righteousness, the way to salvation, the way to all help, and the way to comfort (living above want, spiritual and natural). He is comfort. He is the Comforter.

Holy Ghost, Holy Spirit, Spirit of God, Spirit of Truth: all names are the same Blessed One: the Comforter.

"But when the Comforter is come, whom I will send unto you from the Father, even the Spirit of Truth, which proceedeth from the Father, He shall testify of Me" (John 15:26).

"If ye love Me, keep My commandments. And I will pray the Father, and He shall give you **another** Comforter, that He may abide with you forever; Even the Spirit of Truth; whom the world cannot receive, because it seeth Him not, neither knoweth Him: but ye know Him; for He dwelleth with you, and shall be in you" (John 14:15–17).

Bread/Water
Bread – sustenance; the necessity of life; the root of; maintenance; food in general; nourishment.
Water – essential for most life.
Jesus/Christ – Bread of life, spiritual meat.
(Truth, the Word: necessary, vital, and essential for all spiritual life.)
Jesus/Christ – living water, spiritual drink.
(Holy Ghost: necessary, vital, and essential for all spiritual life.)

Jesus is the necessity of my life. If I believe on Him, He will sustain me. When I hunger, He will feed me. When I thirst, He will give me an everlasting fountain of water within. Without natural bread or water I cannot physically live, and without spiritual bread and water, my soul cannot live, and if my soul dies (in sin), my body will be affected.

I use money to buy natural bread, and good pure natural water costs. To get that spiritual bread and water, which is Jesus Christ, I need—faith, believing on Him, loving Him, serving Him, knowing He is able of all things at all times, hunger and thirst for knowledge of Him, desire for

Him, etc. Also, knowing that He came down from God and by God and is God, walked the earth, died for me, was risen and is alive, ascended to heaven, and will return for me soon.

If all I can afford is just some or one of these, I will start with that, giving myself to Him, and He will be with me and build me and strengthen me until I am rich in all these things and more and able to give it all to Him. Then, He will maintain me in a life of comfort, above want: I will never again hunger, and I will never again thirst.

"And Jesus said unto them, I am the bread of life: he that cometh to Me shall never hunger; and he that believeth on Me shall never thirst" (John 6:35).

"And did all eat the same spiritual meat; And did all drink the same spiritual drink: for they drank of that spiritual Rock that followed them: and that Rock was Christ" (1 Corinthians 10:3–4).

"They shall hunger no more, neither thirst anymore; neither shall the sun light on them, nor any heat. For the Lamb which is in the midst of the throne shall feed them, and shall lead them unto living fountains of waters: and God shall wipe away all tears from their eyes" (Revelation 7:16–17).

Ambassador/Ambassadress for Christ

The highest ranking diplomatic representative that one sovereign power (Jesus Christ) or State (Kingdom of God) sends officially to another (the world). He (we) represents his (our) sovereign (Jesus) personally as well as the State (Kingdom of God). One of dignity (righteousness), privilege (salvation), and etiquette (morality and uprightness). Next to royal blood (next to Jesus/God), may (we may) ask audience (hearing and attention) at any time of the chief (Jesus/God) of the State (Heaven) to which he is (we are) accredited (authorized).

He/she (we) and his/her (our) household are exempt (not obligated) from local jurisdiction (to the world and are free from worldly bonds and bondage by the enemy), and from imposts and duties (sinning and serving the devil).

[We ***don't*** have to live in sin, we ***don't*** have to serve the devil. ***Jesus already made the way***, the devil ***can*** be resisted; Just say yes to Jesus. The enemy has no power, except we give in to him, or if God allows him the power to affect us, in order to prove and build us. In this case, he can harm but not completely destroy us because God won't allow more than He sees we can bear. In essence a Job-like experience, where there are limits set that the enemy ***cannot*** pass.]

He/she enjoys (we enjoy) immunity (resistance) of person/prison (self or things or addictions that would keep us from being all He wants us to be) and freedom of religious worship (rest from our enemies that we may worship Him with all our heart and all our soul).

"Therefore if any man be in Christ, he is a new creature: old things are passed away; behold, all things are become new. And all things are of God, who hath reconciled us to Himself by Jesus Christ, and hath given to us the ministry of reconciliation; To wit, that God was in Christ, reconciling the world unto Himself, not imputing their trespasses unto them; and hath committed unto us the Word of reconciliation. Now then we are ambassadors for Christ, as though God did beseech you by us: we pray you in Christ's stead, be ye reconciled to God. For He hath made Him to be sin for us, who knew no sin; that we might be made the righteousness of God in Him" (2 Corinthians 5:17–21).

The meaning of ambassador (male) and ambassadress (female or wife of ambassador) for Christ is an official messenger with a special mission authorized and certified by the Kingdom of God as a representative for Christ to the world.

Now then, we are representatives for Christ with the special mission to witness of Him (Jesus) and spread God's Word through speaking, telling, doing, and living God's will. It is telling someone that is in doubt or sorrow that God cares, and giving comfort to them. It is telling someone who's troubled that God understands and will help—and helping them to turn it over to Jesus. It is helping a person in need by showing kindness and giving love. It is going to church and applying ourselves to listening to the Word of God. It is to worship Him in fullness and truth, allowing

God to uplift and restore us spiritually. It is sharing our testimony—proving that God is real, living, and able of all things; for the world needs proof, lest they believe not on Jesus, for they have not faith. It is telling a friend or someone you just met the Word of God and entreating/encouraging them to accept God through Jesus Christ (not forcing or badgering them, for that's not how God called us), and encouraging them to read His Word that they may have the courage to love Him and serve Him and come into His house to worship Him.

We need to stay wrapped up in Jesus; so, God (our Source), can fill our mouths with His words, that there will be no falseness or deceit against God or others when we speak—only truth. Wait on Him, that we may not go where He did not send us, for only then will He be with us and go with us. It is a terrible, rebellious, and stiff-necked thing to go anywhere without God. It is going against His Kingdom and His purpose, against our duty to Him, and if we do, no little disaster awaits us—certainly spiritually, but maybe naturally also.

If our actions are consistent and deliberate against Him, we have abandoned our post and duty, we are none of His, and He will cut us off without remedy; leaving us to our own (the devil's) devices and destruction; because if we *truly* love Him, we *will* be obedient to Him. Only when He discerns a true need for change in our heart, will He hear us and receive us back to Himself, and restore us to our official post and duty as representatives of Jesus Christ.

All these things are a part of our duty as His representatives: We are to always live holy and talk holy; live in love and talk with love; clothe ourselves in righteousness, even when we are alone (or think we are alone, but are not, because God is ever watching, ever listening, and ever discerning and judging our hearts).

Do not deliberately sin, no matter how small or insignificant we allow the devil to convince us it is, or because he convinces us that no one is watching and we won't be caught. He is a liar and there is *always* a consequence, even if only our guilt. If we get weak, and fall, or unknowingly/inattentively fall into anything not of God (sin), or fall into anything displeasing to God (likely a prelude to sin), as soon as knowledge of the thing or sin is within us, let us not play those deadly games with God by pretending and denying and fooling ourselves. We will only be further destroying our own life and soul. Let us not wait; let us look up without hesitation, and not wait for what we think is a better time, because to our damnation, that better time may *never* come because the next minute isn't promised to us. Besides, what if when we needed Him, He said, "not now"? Where would we have been? How much would we have suffered? So, let us look to Him, right then, and cry out to Him in true repentance, whether silently within (that's if we can contain it), or from our mouth and lips. He will hear, and respond mercifully to us, and bring us to Him or back to Him.

God has great things in store, and wants to increase us beyond our greatest dreams concerning everything, if we just love Him, serve Him, and believe. He loves us all so much, there is nothing good He wouldn't do for us or give us, if we just turn to Him and believe. He is not just a God of years gone by, He is *still* a Mighty, Wondrous, God. He is still the same. He is still able to tell the winds to "Be still" and they must obey. He is still able to hold back the waters. He is still able to make a way out of no way. He is still able to talk with us. He is still able to move our enemies (those that hate us and would do us harm). He is still able to do *all* miracles. He is still our God and we His people. He is still able to do what He will, when He will. We have not seen great things from Him because we don't believe Him, we don't trust Him, we have no faith in Him, we are not obedient to Him, we have given up on Him, we have turned to other devices, and we have not known Him. For if we did know Him, we would believe. He is waiting on us: Believe, trust, and know. He is still able! He is still able! He is still able! He is still God.

Let us put on Jesus and walk in righteousness, salvation, uprightness, morality, faith, faithfulness, trust, belief, kindness, love, wholeness, peace, joy, truth, and mercy, having resistance to the devil. Believe of him (the devil) that he is a liar and a deceiver. Be true representatives of the kingdom of God and Jesus Christ, that God may use us mightily to His glory, so that the unsaved and young people of the world will be drawn to God. They will be drawn and kept by His Spirit, not by trappings.

If we are faithful, real, and standing in truth before Him, we will see an amazing side of Him we never knew. But, if we are putting on a show and living a lie before Him, no matter how we convince ourselves to believe it, God abhors (despises) liars and deceivers/pretenders. So, if we continue on that path and refuse to seek truth and live it, He has no use for us, and will cut us off and raise up someone else in our place, because He *will* receive that which belongs to Him—honor and glory. It is not a wise thing to fool with God (Jesus Christ). He wants His sheep—His people—gathered unto Him, for He is the true Shepherd, Lord, Master, and King. If we are frauds, professing His name while only standing in His way, causing His sheep to be scattered, He will make no hesitation to pluck us up from before Him and cast us off to be burned: For we (frauds/pretenders) have remained a stench in His nostrils and He can no longer look upon us, for we are as waste and filth in His sight. And, what a terrible thing—so many miles behind us, so many wasted years "serving fraudulently" only to lose. If we hate Him, and mock Him, with the games we play, He can be to us a mighty and terrible God: giving to us all the rewards of our evil heart. But oh, if we love Him, He would literally move mountains for us.

[I have been made aware the previous paragraph seems "harsh" and is, so, I have sought God concerning that and He has given me a Word for His people: Ezekiel 33:10-11. "Therefore, O thou Son of man, speak unto the house of Israel; Thus ye speak, saying, If our transgressions and our sins be upon us (be many and continuous in us), and we pine away in them (we have weakness for and hunger after them and suffer in them), how should we then live? (what likelihood is there that we will be and will remain saved?) Say unto them, As I live, saith the Lord God, I have no pleasure in the death of the wicked; but that the wicked turn from his way and live: turn ye, turn ye from your evil ways; for why will ye die, O house of Israel?" (Spiritual and natural Israel, all people of God.)]

My heart aches for the multitudes that refuse to believe Him. His arms are open and waiting, yet they won't obey and come. Those that are ashamed to serve Him openly—if you are ashamed of Him, He will be ashamed of you also. I know of the great difficulty in breaking free of the world and sin. I was not too long ago in it. There are habits, and addictions, and pleasures (false pleasures, trappings), but all are lies.

Happiness is also a trapping of the world, and a lie that is temporary; this is why, when you are of the world, one moment you are up and the next you are down. There is no stability in happiness because it goes hand in hand with sadness, and they are both of the world and terrible trappings. You can't have both happiness and sadness together inside you; it *must* be one or the other. When one comes the other *will* leave. That's why when sadness comes, you feel like locking yourself away; there is nothing to balance it. That's why some people don't make it out, because sadness has friends it calls to, that joins it within you; friends like depression, hopelessness, misery, suicide, shame, anger, rage, etc. Through all these things, where is happiness? Can you feel it anywhere inside you? No! It does not resist sadness, it flees; it's off trapping someone else until it's time to fool you again—if you survived that last round with sadness.

But, joy is always maintained. Sometimes it's very little, sometimes it's very great, but it is always within you, keeping you through whatever else comes at you, as long as you stay with God. When you are in Jesus, and not just playing games but true to Him, He releases joy within you; it is a feeling like you have never had, and it never leaves you, unless you leave Him. There will come difficult times; for some, even extreme hardships, because once you accept Him and put yourself in His hands, your testing, proving, and refining begins. The world and those you thought were your friends—the enemy—they all now hate you because you are no longer of them. They will seek to destroy you and to rob your joy, but if you stay true to God and believe Him, He will fight all your battles and remove them or give you relief from them; all the while, maintaining your joy because it is a stable blessed thing.

Once joy is given to you, no one or nothing can take it away, except the One who gave it to you, which is God. He will remove it from you only if you are unfaithful by walking or looking away: whether physically by going back into the world to your old ways and things you did, or within by allowing your heart and your trust to leave Him, or having the heart and mind of the world though you still claim Christianity. These people have no joy or peace but are good at pretending, but when they are locked away by themselves, they are in misery. Do you know someone, or are you someone, who claims Christianity, yet, are no different from people you know in the world—still angry, sad, in misery, full of complaints, etc.? This is because they have no joy, they are not right with God—trusting Him, believing Him, loving Him, and serving Him. He doesn't have their heart. Then joy has to be removed from you because joy is found only in Him, so you have to stay with Him, being true to keep it.

Joy has many friends/companions that it goes hand in hand with—peace, comfort, guidance, security, compassion, love, a way out, understanding, wisdom, knowledge (of what needs to be done if it is a job you can handle—if not, God handles it for you), hope, more faith, more trust, freedom, life—all good things. And, when anything comes against you to destroy you emotionally or physically, joy and its companions never flee. They stand firm and protect your heart, mind, and soul from being devoured or destroyed by resisting and overcoming the attacker; so you are still able to smile, sing, praise Him, get out of bed, go about your day with purpose, help others, love yourself and others, be kind, speak kindly, etc. He will give you joy and its companions, and it's like nothing you have ever felt.

You will have disappointments, hardships, pain, and the usual things that come up against you, but through it all, now that you are no longer of the world, the peace and joy that are maintained in you will carry you through it, and it will not destroy you or wreck you but only bring or increase strength (another companion of joy and peace). Give it all to God and trust Him, and He *will* handle it, I promise you.

He has done amazing things for me and concerning me so far. The fact that I am writing this book is one proof, and He will do the same for you: caring for you in whatever ways you need, because He loves us all the same—greatly. He keeps His promises and His Word. There will be a difference in you, and things that once affected you negatively will no longer do so; now you are covered. You will know that your troubles will be fixed because of the joy and peace now within you. So, through it all, you will find yourself praising God, and because of your faithfulness and belief, He will give you the knowledge of what to do. Then, He will open doors to your help and close doors to you from harm or further difficulty. And, the more faithful you are, and consistent in your belief in Him, as you love Him and serve Him, the more He will bless you and will increase your joy and peace within.

Through pain, there is joy, peace, and comfort. Through grief, there is joy, peace and comfort. Through suffering, there is joy, peace, comfort, strength, and guidance. Through times that would be stressful, there is joy, peace, and guidance. Through sorrow, there is joy, peace, and comfort. There is no depression with joy. Joy defeats it and keeps it from finding rest in you. Through death of a loved one, there is joy, peace, and much comfort. Through your own death, there is joy, comfort, and much peace to the end. Through sickness and disease, there is joy, peace, much comfort, strength, hope, more faith, more trust, healing, and miracles.

Joy, peace, and their many companions are given to you according to your need, and the strength of them according to the degree of your need, as God sees fit. Trust Him. Why does joy remain? It is a blessed gift from the Lord, an assurance from Him within you. You know of a surety that He will bring you through, up, over, under, around, or by whatever means necessary, but you know He will bring you out, and He does, because you believed and trusted Him. That's all He needs to move for those that truthfully love Him.

There are gifts and benefits from Him. He cares well for His people that love, trust, and believe on Him and in Him. You may look at some Christian people that you know their life or situation; you just know they are worse off than you are. They are barely making it. You think they are so messed up; you don't know how they do it. You wonder how they make it, how they survive, and how they live. You know if it were you,

you would just lie down and die. Yet, they never complain; they are still going to church, still praising God, still smiling and you know that smile is real, so you wonder, what do they have to be happy about? They are not happy; they have joy, peace, and their companions. God is providing, and making ways for them that you don't see, except in the manifested joy in them and about them. They trust and believe Him, and He rewards them. They feel joyful because God woke them up that morning, and allowed them full use of their bodies, and kept them through the day. Seems simple, but in the world, daily, there's at the very least one person, from babies to adults, sick to healthy, that goes to sleep and never wakes up, or wakes up but cannot function like they did before they slept, or have accidents that others would walk away from, but they don't; so this, life and health, is enough to be joyful for.

But, God doesn't stop there. He keeps rewarding them with a paid bill, the next meal, keeping their home when they almost lost it, a healing to their body, healing their aches and pains, a good health report that was against all odds from the doctor, brought through a scary situation without incident, literally saving their life, letting some trouble great or small pass, and gave them strength to deal with some difficult person. Whatever it is that a person goes through: physically, emotionally, spiritually, within you, or from the outside against you, all the issues of life and in this world, if you are in God and true, He is always doing something for you, because those who love Him are special to Him. He delights in doing good things for you, so there is always a reason to smile from the heart.

Some Christians may live all their lives and go to sleep in God without ever having received earthly riches, but they lived in comfort with joy and peace. So, help and pray for people, but don't pity or scorn them, because if they are in God they have something we want and need. So, go to Jesus and get yours. When you are fully cared for and loved by Him, it is a wondrous and indescribable feeling of love, joy, peace, safety, and just covered.

If this feeling and state of being could be bottled and put on a department store shelf, the whole world would buy of it. If it could be seen or touched, the whole world would seek after it, or if they gained courage to come to Him and truly feel and experience it, they would never leave Him. But because it takes faith, belief, and trust in order to come taste of it, they cast Him aside because they are afraid; they don't know how to truly love or what true and complete love feels like, so they don't trust to give their hearts and souls and lives to Him. But, who better to give all yourself to and trust all yourself to than the One who made you, the One who knows you already, the One who has your best and greatest interests at His heart, and the One who loves you unconditionally. He already knows *all* your secrets and faults, and all those things you hide from others—those that only you know or do, He knows them all already, and *still* greatly loves you. He only wants you to acknowledge Him.

If you don't come to Him, there is not much He will do, except wait on you, and maybe keep you from a few things for His purpose that only He sees and knows, because His Word *must* be fulfilled. But, He loves *you*, He wants *you*, He is watching *you*, and His heart is breaking. If you are not in Him, I pray you come know Him like I know Him, and better. He is so beautiful and loving all by Himself, without all the works and deeds—just in loving me—but I do still need His works and deeds in my life.

Growing up in church, I always said I loved Jesus/God and did, I guess, but I have never felt this before, and never thought or knew I could. I am *truly* in love with Him. At times my heart feels so full toward Him it overwhelms me.

Once, I prayed earnestly, asking Him to allow me to feel the love He feels for His people, in order that if He sent me somewhere I would have His heart toward them. This, is why I say we should all be *very* careful what we say to God. As I lay talking to Him, after I had prayed, He responded to me, and it was a *very* wonderful and *very* terrible experience, and something I will never ask in that way again. It was very wonderful because He showed me He loved me so much as to do this for me, yet it was a very terrible thing because the love He feels is so extremely great, my heart couldn't contain it. To me, it was like a terrible, gripping heartbreak. My heart truly ached, and because it was brought on so suddenly, it was unbearable to me. The pain filled my chest, worst than any heartache I had ever felt with any past love. That moment when I was feeling that pain, I bore it for a few minutes as I talked to Him, thanking Him for allowing me to feel it and that I loved Him. Then I cried, telling Him I was so sorry that this was the way we caused Him to feel, and I kept talking to Him a bit. Then, the pain/heartache was too great, so I begged Him to take it away from me, and within a few minutes, He took me to sleep. Then, about two hours later, He woke me up and had healed me. The pain/heartache was gone, but the love remained with a portion fit for me, and I thanked Him. I am not sure when He gave me conviction of it, but I now know that because the love He feels is too great for me to handle, that's why I felt pain: the capacity of His love, actually *broke* my heart.

I know that at times we grieve His heart with our rebelliousness, but I am rejoicing that I was never foolish enough to ask Him for the experience of His pain, because if His love was so extremely great as to break my heart, how much greater is the pain we cause Him because He loves us so magnificently? He still allows me to feel for people and situations, but not to the magnitude as to be unbearable for me. I am seeking to, and desire to know so much more about Him. He is still working on me, and as He puts the Word in my mouth and brings it out of me, it's not only going out to prayerfully heal you, but has also returned to me to heal me and increase and build me. I desire to be and remain a bold ambassadress for my Jesus, and I pray you choose Him, too. Say yes to Him this moment.

"Touching Jesus." A chorus placed in my heart and memory. Call on Jesus and believe, and He will be your God, mighty and true. He will change your life and change your way, making you to be all He called you forth from your mother's womb to be, and making you all you are in Him. However you were caused to come forth, and however you are now, you are a wonderful creation and plan of God. Jesus knows your beginning, knows you now, and sees your end, and knows the good His heart desires for you; give Him full control of all of you, love Him and follow Him as He guides you to that good end He desires.

Post-word

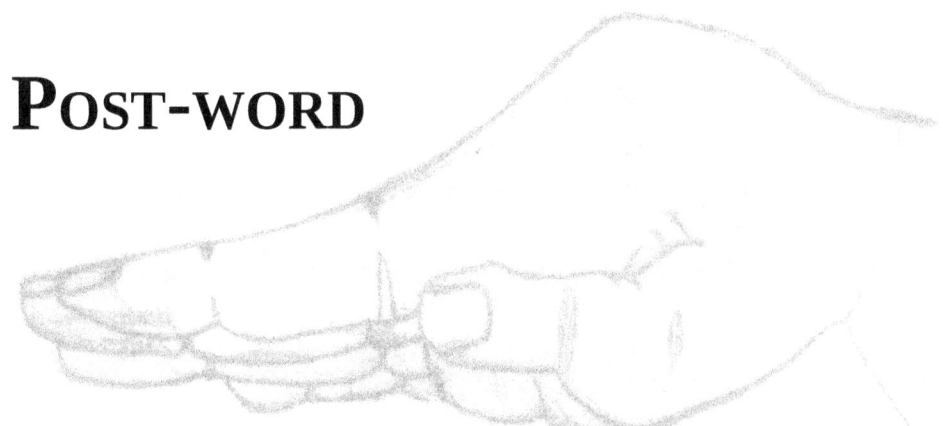

I, *us*, and *we* were used in the exhortations, so whoever reads and needs the healing and restoration it contains, as they read, they will speak the Word into themselves and receive the blessing God seeks to give.

Again, I must thank God: I was previously hurting for the lost, but God wrote me through it with the previous few pages, and has now eased my pain so greatly, it's very barely there.

The fullness of where God is taking me, or what tests and things I will have to persevere to get there, may not be completely known, but I trust Him completely. Whenever fear and doubt in myself, or whatever else the enemy throws at me comes to me, I don't allow it to rest with me, not even for a moment. I, immediately, give it to Jesus. I thank Him, for that **mustard seed faith** He has taught me about: though I be small upon this earth, if I contain and possess that *potency*—that *pungent potent faith,* to prick/affect His heart, He will move mountains out of my way as I bid. **Faith knowing**: knowing the *all* mighty, *all* powerful, omnipotent God I serve, that *He is able of all things*. There may be things that outside of God would be unbearable and shameful, but, I *know*, He will not make me ashamed, for He has proven that He is leading me and *is* with me.

I made a grave error before, thinking Jesus was leading me, but He wasn't: not to the extent that I went. I was out there blowing in the wind because I let myself be swept away in the devil's way of pleasure and impatience, which did cause me to be ashamed, and that's what happens when you are not obedient and God is not with you. Your best intentions and loving heart can wreck someone or yourself, if God doesn't say, "Go!" And you go. God was calling me back, but I wouldn't listen, until it was too late. Then, I returned to Him and repented, and He forgave me for my rebelliousness in going without Him.

He, then, showed me some of what He wanted to do, which I didn't understand all at the time. Even recently, a part of what He showed me, that day of my error, was finally made clear to me: the veil was just suddenly taken away, revealing it while I was thinking about something else. But, I put all, completely, in His hand, sat at His feet, and I am being obedient, trusting, believing, and patient, concerning His whole plan for my life, while He feeds me. So now, I wait and pray and make *very* sure, that whatever it is I feel prompted to do or say is coming from God, and not my old enemy, trying to rob me of what is possible, through God, for me to have. Jesus has shown me that He will bless me with all the desires of my heart and all the desires of His heart for me, but *all* in His time and His purpose. He desires so much more for me than my heart can fathom, so, all His desires aren't yet mine because they are not known to me; I only know that all my heart's desires are one with His; because, I want only what He wants for me—nothing more and nothing less. Forevermore, as He reveals more of His heart for me, those become my desires also. I am in His hand, that He may do with me as pleases Him, and for me, that is enough. I can do nothing of myself, *I must obey*, so I seek Him at every opportunity, to make sure that I am. Whatever I find in me that is not of Him, and whatever comes against me, I give them all to Him, to remove, wash, and cleanse away because they are not wanted and have no right there. I don't prefer what He allows/permits: because, if I don't hear, He may *allow* me to indulge in and reap the consequences of the wrong ways I have chosen. I prefer only what He gives and authorizes: that His will and desire for the plan of my life be done. Nevertheless, He will do what He will do, and I accept that. I love Him so.

In the beginning, God made it very clear to the point of reproving me, that there are things that ***must*** come first, this book being one of them. So, I held on faithfully and patiently: because, I did also pray such a prayer;

Post-word

telling Him I wanted Him first, and to use me for His glory. And, that is not a prayer in error, that is what I want, and as it should be. I trust and know that *all* His promises to me concerning *all* things, and His plan for my life *will* be so.

God is first, above everything else, and I wouldn't want it any other way. He is head of my life, and I aim to keep it that way. Everything, and everyone else, comes after. He is teaching me the order of things, and molding me into the kind of woman He wants me to be, also, the bride He wants me to be—first to Him, then to my promised mate, if we remain true to Him.

Now, Jesus is head of my life, and all of me is in His hands. He is preparing me to receive all He has promised, and all He desires to give me, great and small, so in the end, I will know what to do and how to be, when I have those blessings. When He is through preparing me, I will not bring shame to my mate, home, and family, which He will entrust to bless me with—both heavenly and earthly. Though I don't yet feel ready because there is a lot I desire between God and myself first, Jesus is my strength and my all, so I lean on Him and am obedient to His every direction and leading. While He is working on me for His full purpose, I feel Him preparing the way to other blessings, setting all things in order, and I trust Him.

ENCOURAGEMENT

Scripture:
Romans 1, 6, and 8
Matthew 24
John 3:3–5
1 Corinthians 13

Songs from the Pentecostal Hymnal:
"Hide You In The Blood"   #84
"The Ninety And Nine"   #61
"Jesus Opened Up The Way" #137
"Fill Me Now"   #226
"Speak To My Soul"   #232

    A chorus brought in memory to my heart on April 12, 2004 at 1:20 a.m.: "We shall have a grand time up in Heaven." *Victory*. After all trials, tribulation, shaking, purging, purification, and after *all* God has purposed to be is done, we will live in eternal victory with our Savior and King. *Oh! blessed day*, for all who are found worthy in Jesus. He is calling, *"Hear, turn, and live."*

"Follow Me," saith the Lord.

Amen (Truly, so be it).

www.ingramcontent.com/pod-product-compliance
Lightning Source LLC
Chambersburg PA
CBHW071154300426
44113CB00009B/1206